essentials of
latin
cooking

WILLIAMS-SONOMA

essentials of
latin
cooking

GENERAL EDITOR   CHUCK WILLIAMS

PHOTOGRAPHY   SHERI GIBLIN

RECIPES   PATRICIA McCAUSLAND-GALLO
AND DEBORAH SCHNEIDER

TEXT   BEVERLY COX

Oxmoor House®

Contents

Inside these pages is the taste of the sun: hot chiles and tart limes, juicy tomatoes and sweet corn, and the perfume of fruit and flowers. Latin food is deceptively simple, yet boldly flavored. Its roots go back thousands of years to the great civilizations of the Americas. Woven into this history are the flavors of Africa and the traditions of peasant Europe. For someone like me, raised in an austere country of ice and snow and trained in classic European cuisine, the big, fresh tastes of Latin cooking were, from my first bite of *pico de gallo*, utterly irresistible.

The delicious melting pot called Latin cooking originated during the global explorations that began in the fifteenth century and is still evolving today. In a tangible way, the cuisines of Latin America are history on a plate—a rich reflection of what the New World and the Old World have exchanged over centuries.

The Europeans who first came ashore in the Americas found themselves in Eden. They encountered the ancient and highly evolved cultures of the Aztec, Maya, and Inca with their spectacular cities and teeming markets full of exotic foods. The fierce conquest that ensued ended one world and forever changed the menus of Europe and Asia. The conquerors took away the edible prizes of the Americas: corn, chiles, tomatoes, chocolate, potatoes, beans, turkey, and squash, and returned with beef, pork, and chicken, grapes and olives, wheat and rice, spices from the Indies, and African greens and coffee, along with new cooking techniques and trades such as cheesemaking and the distilling of alcohol. From this merging grew one of the world's great cuisines.

Latin cuisine is as varied as the region's cultures and landscapes: the piquant seafood ceviche of Mexico, the hearty pork *pupusas* of El Salvador, the sprightly *chimichurri* sauce of Argentina, the fish *escabeche* of Peru, and the savory red rice and beans of Cuba. A single book can never encompass the sprawl of Latin foodways, but you can taste the story that this food tells of people, and time, and memory. Here, then, is a new world for you to explore.

Deborah Schneider

The World of Latin Food

In 1492, when Christopher Columbus, a Genoese sea captain sailing under the flag of Spain, stepped ashore in San Salvador, the Bahamian island now called Watling Island, he set in motion a series of events that dramatically altered history—and changed forever the way the world eats.

THE COLUMBIAN EXCHANGE

The interchange of animals and agricultural products that took place after Columbus's arrival on new shores, termed the "Columbian Exchange," enlivened the inventories of time-honored traditional cuisines and brought Old World foods such as olives, grapes, bananas, peaches, pears, citrus fruits, radishes, garlic, onions, wheat, sugar, coffee, nutmeg, cinnamon, cloves, and domestic livestock and dairy products to the Americas.

The "new" world Columbus found was relatively unspoiled, but by no means primitive. The native people of the Caribbean islands, where the Spanish first landed, lived simply, but in Central and South America, rich, sophisticated agricultural societies had been flourishing for many centuries. The dominant powers at the time of the Spanish Conquest, in the sixteenth century, were the Aztecs of Central Mexico, the Maya of the Yucatan Peninsula and Central America, and the Inca, who controlled much of South America from Cuzco, their magnificent capital in the Andes.

It was the glitter of Aztec, Mayan, and Incan gold that first lured Spanish invaders to American shores, and they found it; but the greatest and most enduring treasure that filled the holds of Spanish galleons returning to Seville was food. The New World was a cornucopia of culinary wonders previously unknown in Europe, Africa, and Asia, including corn, tomatoes, chiles, chocolate and vanilla, peanuts, and potatoes.

A LAND OF GREAT CONTRASTS

Latin America is a land of dramatic landscapes and varied climates, ranging from steaming tropical rain forests to rolling grasslands and mild mountain valleys to snow-capped volcanic mountains, vast deserts, and frozen tundra. A rich indigenous Latin American culture and cuisine existed before any European contact; post conquest, the arrival of settlers from Spain and Portugal, African slaves, and Chinese indentured servants brought even more diversity to Latin America's cooking.

COMIDAS

In Spanish, the verb *comer* means "to eat." *La comida*, or the main meal, consists of 4 or 5 courses and is traditionally served mid-afternoon—followed, famously, by a siesta, if possible. Of course, there are many other opportunities to nibble, starting with *desayuno*, or breakfast, which in Cuba might be a steaming cup of *café con leche* and toast spread with guava jelly; in Mexico and Central America, *atole* (a corn-based drink) or hot chocolate served with a tamale is traditional; and in South America, the morning repast may be *pan dulce*, a sweet roll served with coffee, *maté*, or perhaps a mug of *api de quinoa*, a nourishing hot breakfast drink flavored with cinnamon and vanilla. Mid-morning, throughout Latin America people pause to snack on *pastelitos* (sweet pastries) or *empanadas* (savory meat turnovers). Mid-afternoon is a good time for a *refresco* (a fruit- or almond-based drink), and around six o'clock is the hour of *la merienda*, a well-loved tradition of enjoying savory and sweet *bocaditos*, "little bites" that satisfy the appetite until *la cena*, or dinner. Unless it's a special occasion, the last meal of the day is a light one.

Cactus paddles at the market; Crisp, cooling radishes from the Old World complement Latin cuisine.

Plentiful baskets of colorful chiles on display at the bustling outdoor markets of Mexico.

THE OUTDOOR MARKETS

Since pre-Columbian times, the outdoor markets of Latin America have been vibrant centers of commerce and social activity. A soldier named Bernal Díaz, who accompanied Hernán Cortés on his first expedition to Mexico in 1519, describes in his journal the amazement of the Spanish when visiting the great market at Tlateloco, sister city of the Aztec capital, Tenochitlán: "We were astounded at the number of people, and the quantity of merchandise it contained, and the good order and control that was maintained, for we had never seen such a thing before." In his account, Diaz mentions cacao beans and honey, both articles of trade that were used as currency. He goes on to talk about the amazing variety of spices and fresh produce, and stands that sold beverages, fresh tamales, and other prepared foods.

Today, despite the inroads being made by extra-large, import-heavy *super-mercados*, many Latin American cooks still prefer the hustle and bustle of the outdoor market, and enjoy having the opportunity to buy fresh food directly from the people who grow it. Markets range in size and can be held daily, weekly, or monthly. Mexico City's Mercado de Jamaica is huge, while in the Andean villages in Peru and Bolivia, the markets are often small weekly gatherings of farmers and artisans. In Cuba, the colorful monthly market fills Havana's Plaza de la Revolution with the beats of salsa music and truckloads of locally grown vegetables and ripe tropical fruits. The foods sold at Latin America's outdoor markets depend on geography, climate, and the season, but the markets are always lively places, popular for casual dining, shopping, and mingling with neighbors and visitors.

ESTADOS UNIDOS

OCEANO ATLÁNTICO

GOLFO
DE MÉXICO

MÉXICO

CUBA

HAITI

LA REPÚBLICA DOMINICANA

BELIZE

HONDURAS

GUATEMALA

MAR CARIBE

EL SALVADOR

NICARAGUA

COSTA RICA

PANAMÁ

COLOMBIA

VENEZUELA

GUYANA

SURINAM

GUAYANA FRANCESA

ECUADOR

BRAZIL

PERÚ

BOLIVIA

OCEANO PACÍFICO

PARAGUAY

CHILE

URUGUAY

ARGENTINA

OCEANO ATLÁNTICO

0KM 500 1000 2000
0MI 500 1000 2000

The Regions

From the vast country of Mexico to the Caribbean islands, and from Central to South America, there are noticeable differences in the cuisines of these Latin American regions. However, they also share many common foods and dietary customs, as you will see in the following pages.

MEXICO

The cornerstones of Mexican cooking are the great pre-Columbian staples: corn, beans, squash, and chiles; but that doesn't mean every Mexican plate looks the same. In this vast country, there is great diversity of climate, geography, and ethnicity among the indigenous inhabitants. To really understand Mexican cooking, it is necessary to explore it region by region.

NORTHERN MEXICO

Land of Ranchos and Vaqueros

Northern Mexico is made up of the states of Sonora, Chihuahua, Coahuila, Nuevo León, Durango, and Zacatecas. The North is famous for its high-desert cattle ranches and *vaquero* (cowboy) traditions. *Norteño* dishes are hearty and straightforward, like the men and women who live in this arid land. On big cattle drives from Texas up to Montana in the mid-1800s, cooks and *vaqueros* prepared *caldillo*, a dish also know as *chile con carne*. Today, *caldillo* competitions are famous in Mexico.

Culinary Signature: Beef

Beef is the signature ingredient of *Norteño* cooking. *Machaca*, a *vaquero* invention of beef dried with chiles and spices and then rehydrated and pounded until tender, is typical of the state of Nuevo León. It is commonly shredded and scrambled with eggs for breakfast or used in fillings for tacos, burritos, and *flautas*.

Regional Specialties

Flour tortillas Usually homemade, flour tortillas are served with virtually every meal in *Norteño* households.

Pinto beans There are many *Norteño* recipes for pinto and *bayo* beans, such as *frijoles borrachos*, or "drunken beans," cooked with beer from the famous breweries of Monterrey.

Anaheim chiles These mild green chiles are preferred in salsas and cooked tomato sauces in the north.

BAJA CALIFORNIA

From Desert to Oasis

Baja California lies between the rough swells of the Pacific and the more tranquil waters of the Gulf of California. A paradise for whale watchers, the peninsula is also famous for its fish and shellfish. Although the southern region of Baja is harsh desert, there are temperate areas in the north where citrus groves thrive. There have been vineyards in Baja since colonial times, and some of them are producing excellent wines today, including delicious whites that are a perfect complement to seafood. While Baja's reputation for wine-making is widespread, nonalcoholic fruit drinks like strawberry *agua fresca* are popular in the region too, as are festive fruit cocktails, such as mango daiquiris.

Culinary Signature: Fresh Fish

The Gulf of California, also called the Sea of Cortez, is one of the world's great fisheries. It is home to nine hundred different species of fish, including corbina, snapper, tuna, and several species of bass.

Regional Specialties

Fish tacos A favorite street food in Baja, strips of sea bass or red snapper are dipped in beer batter and fried until crisp and golden, then wrapped in warm corn tortillas, topped with shredded cabbage, and drizzled with guacamole and assorted salsas.

Caracol marino Sea conch, butterflied, pounded, breaded, and sautéed in butter, is a specialty of Cabo San Lucas, the resort town located at the southern tip of the peninsula.

THE NORTH PACIFIC

Mexico's Rice Bowl

The North Pacific states—Sinaloa, Nayarit, Jalisco, and Colima—provide much of the rice, sugar, wheat, and fresh vegetables produced in Mexico. Coconut is a very important ingredient in Colima. *Horchata de coco* (a coconut-rice beverage) and coconut ice cream are local favorites. Jalisco is known for beautiful beaches, deep-sea fishing, and tequila. Specialties of its famous resort, Puerto Vallarta, include margaritas and freshly caught red snapper grilled on the beach. Inland, in Guadalajara, a colonial city that has grown into a sprawling metropolis, the signature dish is *pozole*, a robust hominy- and pork-based stew seasoned with lime juice and oregano and topped with shredded radishes, onions, and cabbage.

Culinary Signature: Tequila

Tequila is distilled from the sap of the blue agave plant, a large succulent. To be labeled "tequila," the spirit must be distilled in Jalisco (or limited regions in several other states).

Regional Specialties

Birria A spicy tomato and mutton (or goat) soup typical of Guadalajara, it is both delicious and a reported hangover cure.

Tamales de camaron Shrimp tamales wrapped in corn husks are a specialty of Sinaloa.

THE SOUTH PACIFIC

The Heart of Mexican Cooking

The South Pacific states of Guerrero, Oaxaca, and Chiapas have a vast variety of cultures and culinary traditions. In the highlands, fertile mountain valleys are separated by the craggy peaks of the Sierra Madres. Living in relative isolation, the people in these valleys developed different dialects and customs. One thing they do share is reliance on the sacred trinity of Mesoamerican foods: corn, beans, and squash.

Oaxaca City, the capital of the state of Oaxaca, is the culinary heart of the highlands. Over the centuries, the cooking traditions of indigenous Zapotec and Mixtec people have melded with colonial Spanish influences to create a sophisticated cuisine. *Flores de calabaza rellenas*, delicate golden squash blossoms stuffed with *queso fresco*, is an elegant *antojito* (appetizer) you might enjoy at one of the city's finer restaurants. Known as the "Land of the Seven Moles," Oaxaca has become a Mecca for gourmets from all over the World.

The tropical coastal regions of Guerrero, Oaxaca, and Chiapas have an almost Caribbean atmosphere. Acapulco, Guerrero's largest city, is a world-class resort as famous for its *ceviche* as its bikini-clad beauties. In early colonial times, Acapulco was a port of call for Spanish galleons bringing spices and

Carnitas, little bits of crispy pork (above), are served with corn tortillas, earthy, rich chipotle salsa, and freshly made guacamole.

silks back from Manila, and these East Asian influences are still evident in typical dishes such as *arroz con pulpo al curry* (rice with octopus in curry sauce).

Culinary Signature: Mole

Moles are ground mixtures of chiles, nuts, seeds, herbs, and spices. The spice mixtures are a cornerstone of Oaxacan cuisine and form the basis for many wonderful sauces and stews.

Regional Specialties

Avocados The Mixeca region of Oaxaca is famous for its avocados and the chunky style of guacamole made there. The leaves of avocado trees have a nice anise flavor when dried and are often used for seasoning.

Chilapitas These small, crisp masa (cornflour dough) shells are typical of Guerrero, and usually filled with refried beans, guacamole, or chicken and served as an appetizer.

THE BAJIO

Spanish Tradition in the New World

The Bajio, made up of the states of Michoacán, Querétaro, Guanajuato, and San Luis Potosí, is most influenced by Spanish colonialism. Even the landscape reminds visitors of Spain's high central plateau. *Puchero*, a boiled dinner in which the meat and vegetables are served separately from the broth, is a traditional dish in this region.

Culinary Signature: Sweet Desserts

Michoacán, is known for sweet desserts, such as *cajeta*, a rich caramel made with goat's milk and used as a topping for ice cream and a filling in cakes, and *arroz con leche* (rice pudding). Rich and studded with raisins, the rice puddings of the Bajio are sometimes formed into patties, dipped into beaten egg and bread crumbs, and fried like fritters.

Shrimp, fresh from the sea, is sautéed with classic Mexican flavorings: tequila, orange, and cilantro.

Regional Specialties

Sopa de frijoles estilo Patzcuaro This spicy but soothing bean soup is from the area around Lake Patzcuaro, Michoacán.

Pan de muerto A rich, orange-flavored egg bread, this is made for the observance of *Todos Santos*, All Saints Day.

CENTRAL MEXICO

Convent Gastronomy

Central Mexico is made up of the states of Puebla, Tlaxcala, and Hidalgo. Puebla is the birthplace of two of Mexico's most famous dishes: *mole poblano* (a complex sauce, usually served over turkey, that includes many spices and chocolate), and *chiles poblanos en nogada* (poblano chiles stuffed with mincemeat, battered and fried, covered with a sauce of cream and crushed walnuts, and garnished with fresh pomegranate seeds). In Tlaxcala and Hidalgo, the main crop is maguey, a fleshy-leaved variety of agave. Maguey sap is used to make *pulque*, a mildly alcoholic drink that was enjoyed by the Aztecs. *Pulque* is often used as a marinade for meat.

Culinary Signature: Pipián

Pipiánes are elegant red or green chile sauces thickened and enriched with ground pumpkin or squash seeds. They have been a mainstay of Mexican cuisine since pre-Hispanic times.

Regional Specialties

Nopalitos Paddle-shaped stems of prickly pear cactus plants are eaten as a vegetable and used in soups and salads, especially in the states of Tlaxcala and Hidalgo.

Leche quemada This rich and luxurious pudding, a creamy sweet made with caramel and walnuts, is a favorite dessert made in the state of Puebla.

MEXICO CITY

Cutting-Edge Cuisine

Mexico City is a culinary world unto itself. It's a place where people and food from all parts of Mexico, and other nations, come together. In its closely-watched restaurants, innovative chefs reinterpret Mexico's pre-Columbian cuisine.

Culinary Signature: *Huitlacoche*

Huitlacoche is a strange-looking but delicious fungus that grows on ears of corn. It was a delicacy for the Aztec and is still an expensive treat today—almost like buying truffles.

Regional Specialties

Crepas de huitlacoche Popular in Mexico City, these delicate crepes are stuffed with *huitlacoche* or squash blossoms and served with béchamel sauce and a sprinkling of cheese.

Alegrias This ceremonial Aztec sweet was once made with puffed amaranth and honey or blood and formed into the shape of gods. Modern *alegrias*, bound with sugar syrup and made in geometric shapes, are sold by street vendors in Mexico City.

THE GULF COAST

Land of Chocolate and Vanilla

Some of the best seafood in all of Mexico is found along the Gulf Coast in the states of Veracruz and Tabasco. Two of the most costly ingredients in the world, vanilla and chocolate, are also grown in Veracruz. Vanilla, the fruit of a climbing orchid, was first discovered by the Totonac people of Veracruz who learned to cultivate the orchids and developed the method of fermenting and processing the beans to release their flavor and fragrance. Cacao is also an ancient crop of the Gulf Coast, thought to have first been cultivated by the Olmec and Maya around 1000 BC.

Culinary Signature: *Huachinango a la Veracruzana*

Huachinango a la Veracruzana, a dish of red snapper baked in tomato sauce with capers, pimento-stuffed green olives, herbs, and jalapeños, reflects the fusion of Spanish and Mexican influences in Veracruz.

Regional Specialties

Salpicon de jaiba This popular appetizer from Tabasco is made with fresh lump crabmeat that is sautéed with seasonings, then returned to its shell, sprinkled with bread crumbs and butter, and baked.

THE YUCATÁN PENINSULA

Recados: The Curries of Mexico

In the states of Yucatán, Campeche, and Quintana Roo, Mayan culture has blended with influences from the Caribbean, Europe, and Asia. Yucatecan cooking is built on *recados*, seasoning mixtures that are often compared to the curries of India. *Recado colorado*, a red paste colored with *achiote* (tropical annatto seeds, which have a mild anise flavor), is the most widely used of these seasonings.

Culinary Signature: *Cochinita Pibil*

Cochinita pibil, pork marinated with *recado colorado* and traditionally roasted in an underground pit called a *pib*, is the Yucatán's foremost signature dish. When sliced, wrapped in fresh, warm tortillas, and served with *xnipec*, a fiery habanero salsa, the moist, tender pork is a feast for the senses.

Regional Specialties

Habanero chiles Small, extremely hot, lantern-shaped orange chiles.

Sweet potatoes (camotes) Candied sweet potatoes wrapped in brown paper cones are a popular street food in the Yucatán.

The classic cubano sandwich is made with slow-cooked pork, ham, cheese, yellow mustard, and pickles.

CUBA, PUERTO RICO, AND THE DOMINICAN REPUBLIC

Islands of Opportunity

Sailors and soldiers returning to Spain with Columbus raved about the beauty of the Caribbean islands, and also touted the opportunity they offered enterprising settlers: the land was richly suited to raising sugarcane, and therefore to making men rich. The first fifteen hundred Spanish settlers, all men and mostly hailing from the southern region of Andalucia, traveled to Hispaniola, the island now shared by the Dominican Republic and Haiti, on Columbus's second voyage in 1493. Across the Dominican Republic, and later in Cuba and Puerto Rico, the Spanish established sprawling sugar plantations. When, tragically, many of the native Taino and Arawak people died as a result of invasive diseases and mistreatment, African slaves were imported as field hands and cooks for the plantation owners. In the rich cuisines of Cuba, Puerto Rico, and The Dominican Republic, you can still see the distinct facets of this cultural convergence.

Spanish-Caribbean Creole Cooking

Spanish-Caribbean creole, or *criollo*, cooking was created by a blending of Native American, Spanish, and African influences. From the Arawak and Tainos, who were farmers, fishermen, and hunters, came yuca (also called cassava or manioc), *maiz* (corn), beans, squash, *ajíes* (peppers), annatto seed, cotton, and tobacco. The Spanish brought livestock, especially pigs and chickens, and planted Old World fruit trees, such as orange and mango, and countless numbers of crops. They introduced their favorite ingredients and spices—rice, olive oil, capers, cumin, oregano, bay leaves, and saffron—and traditional Spanish recipes like flan, rice pudding, empanadas, and paella. Africa's contribution included okra and plantains, and also taro root (called *malanga isleña* in Cuba and *yautia* in Puerto Rico) and peanuts, both plants that originated in South America but came to the Caribbean via Nigeria.

Culinary Signature: Pork

From the time Columbus released eight sleek Iberian swine on the Island of Hispaniola on his second voyage in 1493, pork has been a favorite Caribbean food. *Ibéricos*, an ancient Spanish breed, adapted well to living in free-range conditions and soon became abundant on the islands. In the south of Spain, *Ibéricos* traditionally graze on (or have their diet restricted to) acorns, lending an earthy richness to their flesh; and in Cuba, the best-quality pork comes from pigs that eat *palmiche*, the fruit of a palm tree. A typical Cuban preparation is to marinate a pork roast in *mojo*, a seasoning made with *naranja agria* (sour orange juice), vinegar, garlic, cumin, black pepper, salt, and oregano, then roast it slowly until tender and succulent.

Regional Specialties

Congrí This Caribbean staple dish of red beans and rice is called *Moros y Cristianos* (Moors and Christians) when made with black beans.

Plantains A tougher-skinned relative of the banana, plantains always require cooking and are eaten as a vegetable when green (unripe) or yellow (fully or partially ripe), and used for desserts when they reach their very sweet ripe or overripe stage, signaled by yellow skins that have brown spots or are turning black overall.

CENTRAL AMERICA

A Land of Volcanoes and Rain Forests

The Isthmus of Central America, the land bridge that connects Mexico to Colombia, is home to seven countries: Belize, Guatemala, Honduras, El Salvador, Nicaragua, Costa Rica, and Panama. Central America has an amazing variety of geography and climates. There are more active volcanoes along its mountainous spine than in any other place on Earth, and its tropical rain forests are home to many exotic creatures. Rich volcanic soil makes this region's temperate highlands and mountain valleys ideal places to grow coffee and cacao, major export crops, as well as fruits and vegetables. In the tropical areas nearer the coasts, plantains and other tropical fruits, and yuca (also called cassava or manioc) are cultivated.

When discussing Central American food, most people think of black or red beans, rice, plantains, and fried yuca. While these are indeed important regional foods, one does not need to look far for each country to reveal its own culinary personality.

The Maya Heartland

Guatamala, Belize, Honduras, and El Salvador have a strong Mayan influence in their cooking. Corn, in the form of *atole* (a corn drink), tamales, and tortillas, is the most important staple. In Belize, a former British possession, English and Garifuna (Afro-Caribbean) cooking traditions are seen in dishes like meat pies. In Guatemala, El Salvador, and Honduras, Spanish influence is reflected in dishes like empanadas (meat turnovers) and *flan de leche* (caramel custard).

Regional Specialties

Guatemala: Tamales Guatemala boasts many kinds of tamales, including unfilled *pochitos*, typical of the Guatemalan city of Cobán, and *ooben*, black bean–filled "jelly-roll" tamales from the highlands.

Belize: Red beans and coconut rice The Belizean version of beans and rice is made with red kidney beans and rice cooked with coconut milk, onion, garlic, and spices, and garnished with grated fresh coconut.

Honduras and El Salvador: Pupusas Thicker than tortillas and stuffed with meat, cheese, or beans, *pupusas* are typically served with *curtido* (shredded cabbage salad) and *salsa casera* (tomato and chile salsa).

Where Many Cultures Meet

In Nicaragua and Panama, the main influences are Native American, Spanish, Afro-Caribbean, and Chinese. Costa Rica meshes European and Native American culinary traditions.

In Nicaragua, *mondongo* (tripe soup) is often served with a side of *rosquillas*, baked cornmeal and cheese biscuits shaped like doughnuts. In Panama, fresh seafood comes from both the Caribbean and Pacific oceans, and fresh ceviche is a popular snack. Costa Rican food is generally less spicy, with Spanish-style seasonings and delicious empanadas and tamales.

Culinary Signature: Gallo Pinto

Nicaragua, Panama, and Costa Rica all consider a dish of beans and rice—*gallo pinto* (literally, "spotted rooster")—to be their national dish, but the recipes differ: In Nicaragua, red beans, rice, *chiloma* (chile sauce), and garlic are stir-fried together. Panamanian recipes call for black beans, cilantro, and a dollop of sour cream; and in Costa Rica, the dish is served with lizano sauce, a semi-sweet condiment with some spice.

Here, the favorite "fast food" of El Salvador, *pupusas*, are stuffed with pork and served with coleslaw and salsa.

From the top: Grilled Chicken with Chimichurri; Grilled Lamb Chops with Spicy Mint Salsa; and Lima Beans with Citrus-Herb Sauce

SOUTH AMERICA

Before the Europeans settled on the continent in the early 1500s, the Inca, who were skilled agriculturalists, inhabited most of the land. The varied climatic conditions combined with the skill of the farmers produced a tremendous variety of crops. The most important Inca foods were corn, potatoes, sweet potatoes, beans, squash, avocados, yuca, quinoa (the "Mother Grain"), and *ajíes* (chiles). These foods still form the base of South American cooking today.

THE NORTH

The Lands Along the Equator

Columbia, Venezuela, Guyana, Suriname, and French Guiana are the countries that make up the northern region of South America.

All of these countries are known for their fish and seafood dishes. In Colombia, *pargo*, a fish similar to red snapper, is baked in a sauce of olive oil, onions, garlic, hot chiles, and tomatoes. Pickled fish is popular in Venezuela.

Regional Specialties

Arepas These cornmeal griddle cakes of indigenous origin, are made with *arepa* flour (see page 21), and served all day in Colombia and Venezuela.

Ajiaco bogotano This thick potato soup is a Colombian specialty made with different varieties of potato, corn, cumin, and capers.

Arroz con leche de coco Rice cooked with coconut milk, sometimes with raisins added, is popular in coastal areas throughout this region.

BRAZIL

An Exotic *Feijoada*

Brazil covers almost half of South America and borders every mainland country except Chile

and Ecuador. The rain forests of central and southern Brazil are the source of precious tropical foods like Brazil nuts and *açaí* berries. It is the world's largest producer of coffee, oranges, papayas, and sugar, and a major exporter of rice, bananas, and cacao. Brazil is also a big beef producer; thousands of cattle graze on the southern grasslands along its borders with Argentina and Uruguay.

Brazilian food is an exotic mixture, combining indigenous cooking traditions with those of Portugal, Africa, Germany, Italy, and Japan. In that respect, Brazil is a bit like *feijoada*, its national dish: a black bean stew containing a variety of meats and flavored with Old World herbs and New World seasonings.

Culinary Signature: *Caipirinha*

This delicious, potent drink, made with *cachaça* (page 32), fresh lime juice, and sugar is Brazil's signature alcoholic beverage.

Regional Specialty

Pudim de pão com coco This rich bread pudding is made with shredded coconut, coconut milk, eggs, and rum, and baked in a caramel-coated mold.

THE SOUTHERN CONE

European South America

Most of the people of Argentina, Chile, and Uruguay are of European decent. The broad boulevards of Buenos Aires, Santiago, and Montevideo remind visitors of Paris or Rome. In Paraguay, there is a larger indigenous population with enclaves of Europeans.

Spanish and Italian influences combine in the cooking of Argentina and Uruguay. In Argentina, the beef, raised on vast grasslands, is world famous and a common saying is, "beef is king." For many Argentinians, the most satisfying meal is grilled *bife* (steak) topped

Grilled skirt steak with *chimichurri* sauce is a favorite of the Argentinian *parilla*, or grill.

with *chimichurri* sauce (parsley-garlic salsa). Chile is famous for *porotos granados*, a bean, squash, and corn stew. Paraguayan cooking relies on indigenous staple ingredients, primarily corn and yuca (cassava). *Bori Bori*, beef soup with cornmeal dumplings, is a specialty of Paraguay's capital, Asunción.

Regional Specialties

Dulce de leche This thick caramel sauce made from sweetened condensed milk is used as a topping for fruit or ice cream.
Yerba maté This favorite drink of *gauchos* (South American cowboys) is a caffeine-rich beverage made from the dried leaves of a shrub belonging to the holly family.

THE ANDEAN REGION

Heart of South American Cuisine

The Humboldt Current, a cold sea current, provides the region with some of the most

magnificent seafood in the world. Following the coastline, the Andes rise from rocky beaches to temperate, terraced plateaus to towering icy peaks.

Traditional cooking marries with Spanish influence in the cuisine of this region. In Bolivia, dishes like *pastel de quinoa*, a savory pudding made with cooked quinoa, eggs, and cheese blends. In Ecuador, a regional specialty is *biche de pescado*, a hearty fish chowder.

Peru is known for its sophisticated food. Here, Andean staples like potatoes, corn, and quinoa rise under the hands of innovative cooks.

Regional Specialties

Salteñas These Bolivian-style empanadas are filled with a spicy beef filling and raisins.
Ceviche In Ecuador, shrimp is marinated in sour orange juice and garnished with *cancha* (corn nuts).
Pisco sour A potent drink made with Pisco, a South American grape brandy (see page 43).

SOUTH AMERICAN WINE

Although grapes have been cultivated in South America for over 400 years, the wine industry in the region is fairly young compared to its European counterparts. Today, South American wines are highly esteemed and are often more of a bargain than wines from Europe.

The two most prolific wine-producing countries in South America are Chile and Argentina, whose temperate climates create the perfect conditions for raising grapes. These neighbors produce both the highest quality and the largest quantities of wine on the continent. Other South American countries such as Brazil and Bolivia produce wine, but in smaller quantities and with mixed results.

Signature grapes

Malbec A mild, black grape with low acidity, this varietal is used to make the celebrity reds of Argentina. Its juice fashions full-bodied, moderately tannic wines with dried fruit and overtones of plum. It is great paired with grilled beef.

Torrontés A medium-size, round, golden grape considered to be a wholly Argentine variety. This varietal makes fresh, light white wines with big bouquets. These wines have floral aromas and raisin and tropical fruit flavors. They are best enjoyed young, and are a good pairing with spicy foods.

Carménère A French grape imported from Bordeaux in the mid-1800s, this varietal is the key to Chile's big, bold, complex Cabernet blends. It is excellent with lamb or poultry.

Tannat Brought to Uruguay by Basque settlers in the 1800s, this varietal makes the base wine for blended Beaujolais and Port-style wines. It is best paired with strongly flavored dishes.

The Latin Diet: Old World Meets New World

Over half of the foods eaten in the world today originated in Latin America. Farmers in America's pre-Columbian civilizations enjoyed a more varied diet than Europeans merchants, and Maya, Aztec, and Inca nobles nibbled on delicacies beyond the imaginations of Old World monarchs.

THE PRE-COLUMBIAN DIET

The pre-Columbian diet was a modern nutritionist's dream—low in animal fat and high in monounsaturated fats from avocados, nuts, and squash seeds. Small amounts of meat, fish, and seafood were supplemented by protein-rich legumes and seeds and vitamin-rich fruits and vegetables, such as squash and corn.

OLD WORLD FOODS

The modern Latin American diet is built on the sturdy base of pre-Columbian staples combined with the dietary influences from Europe, Africa, and Asia. Among the foods and seasonings incorporated into the Latin diet from Old World cuisines are: olive oil, onions, garlic, rice, wheat, grapes, bananas, plantains, citrus fruits, grapes, mangoes, peaches, apricots, pears, apples, sugar, coffee, wine, beer, raisins, olives, capers, cinnamon, cloves, and domestic livestock and dairy products. Cooking techniques first introduced by Old World cooks include sautéing and deep-frying in fat.

LATIN AMERICA'S CREOLE DIET

The result of the meeting of Old and New World foods is a Creole (or *Criollo*) cuisine that has evolved to combine the best of both worlds. Olive oil, now produced in Latin America, combines with onions, garlic, and chiles to give Latin American dishes their distinctive flavor. Plantains, originally from Africa, grew easily in the tropical regions of the Caribbean and Central and South America, and soon became a staple. Citrus seedlings, originally sent from Spain, thrived in temperate regions of Latin America; their fruits are used to make marmalades, while the acidic juices are key for meat and poultry marinades, and for "cooking" seafood for ceviches. Rice, an Old World staple, soon joined forces with New World beans to provide protein and become an invaluable part of the Latin American diet.

ANCIENT FOODS REDISCOVERED

Some ancient foods were forgotten with the introduction of Old World foods. Agave nectar, the preferred sweetener of the Aztecs, was largely replaced by sugar. Now, as concern about diabetes grows in Latin America, honey-like agave is enjoying newfound popularity. The same is true of quinoa and amaranth, two health-packed, versatile seeds.

Tortillas being cooked on a *comal* (left); fresh water trout stuffed with aromatics and tied before cooking (center); fresh salsa being made in a *molcajete (right)*.

Grinding corn the traditional way—on a large, rectangular *metate*—is still a daily ritual in parts of Mexico.

CORN, LATIN AMERICA'S SACRED STAPLE

For the pre-Columbian peoples of Latin America, *maíz* (corn) was not only their most important crop, it was central to their creation stories, ceremonial rites, and religious life. Corn remains a staple in Latin American cooking. Following is a short glossary of corn in all of its forms.

Masa Simply "dough" in Spanish, the term is generally understood to mean the fresh dough made from ground pozole that is used to make tortillas and tamales.

Masa harina This fresh corn masa dough has been dried and ground into flour. It is sold in Latin and Mexican markets and in most well-stocked supermarkets. Reconstituted with water or other liquids, it can be substituted for fresh masa in most recipes.

Masarepa (arepa flour) This precooked corn flour is used to make *arepas* and tamales in Columbia and Venezuela. This commercial product saves cooks the labor-intensive process of soaking and pounding corn to remove the seed germ and outer lining and yield the desired corn flour for traditional *arepas*. Masarepa should not be confused with masa harina.

Nixtamalization This process was discovered by the Maya to loosen the hulls from corn by soaking, then boiling the kernels in a solution of water and slaked lime. The kernels are then rinsed in fresh water to remove the hulls. The process makes corn easier to grind, but it also enhances the protein value of the corn.

Pozole (hominy) This term is used for whole kernels of nixtamalized corn and for the traditional drinks, soups, and stews made from that corn.

Chiles

Chiles, whether fresh or dried, have distinctive flavors and degrees of heat, so they typically cannot be used interchangeably. Here is a visual guide to the chiles used in this book. For more information on South American ají peppers, see page 278.

Jalapeño

The most popular and widely available of fresh chiles, this tapered chile, 2–3 inches (5–7½ cm) in length, has thick flesh and varies in degree of hotness. It is found in green and sweeter ripened red forms.

Habanero

Renowned as the hottest of all chiles, this 2-inch (5-cm) lantern-shaped variety from Yucatán combines its intense heat with flavors of tomatoes and tropical fruits. Available in unripe green and ripened yellow, orange, and red forms.

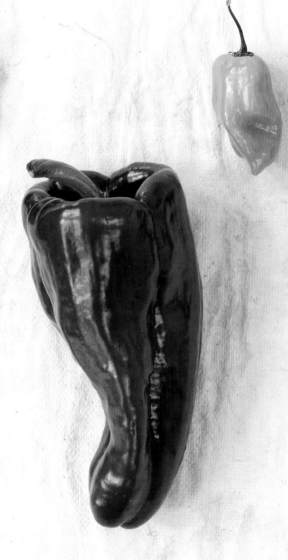

Anaheim

This long, green, and mild to moderately spicy chile is found in most markets; it is similar to the New Mexican variety of chile.

Serrano

These slender chiles measure 1–2 inches (2½–5 cm) long and are very hot, with a brightly acidic flavor; available in both green and ripened red forms.

Poblano

Named for the state of Puebla in Mexico, this broad-shouldered, tapered, moderately hot chile is 5 inches (13 cm) long and a polished deep green.

Ancho

The ancho is a dried poblano. It measures 4½ inches (11.5 cm) long, and has wide shoulders, wrinkled, deep reddish brown skin, and a mild, bittersweet flavor reminiscent of chocolate.

Chipotle

The smoke-dried form of the ripened jalapeño, this chile is rich in flavor and very hot. Sold in its dried form, it is typically a leathery brown, although some varieties are a deep burgundy.

Árbol

This smooth-skinned, bright reddish-orange chile measures about 3 inches (7½ cm) long, narrow in shape, and fiery hot.

Pequín

Oval-shaped, light orange-red, and small (about 1½ inches/ 2½ cm long), this chile is fiery, but the heat is short-lived.

Guajillo

Moderately hot, this burgundy chile is about 5 inches (13 cm) long, tapered, and with rather brittle smooth skin and a sharp, uncomplicated flavor.

Pasilla

This skinny, wrinkled, raisin-black chile is about 6 inches (15 cm) long, with a sharp, fairly hot flavor.

Latin Produce and Pantry

Latin American cooking draws on a bounty of fresh, seasonal produce and fruits; hearty, nutritious grains and legumes; fresh cheeses; corn in all of its forms; and a pantry of flours, spices, seasonings, and sweeteners. Here is a guide to some of the common ingredients used in Latin cooking.

FRESH VEGETABLES

Beets, bell peppers, cabbage, cactus paddles (*nopales;* page 105), carrots, cauliflower, celery, chard, chayote (page 278), corn, cucumbers, green beans, eggplant, jicama (page 280), kale, lettuce, malanga (page 280), okra, onions, potatoes, pumpkins, radishes, spinach, sweet potatoes, tomatillos (page 281), tomatoes, watercress, wild mushrooms, winter squash (*calabasas*), yellow squash, yuca, zucchini

FRUITS, BERRIES, AND MELONS

Açai berries (page 278), apples, avocados, bananas, blackberries, blueberries, cherimoya (page 279), coconuts, figs, grapefruit, grapes, guava (page 280), limes, mangoes (page 280), oranges, papaya (page 281), passion fruit, persimmons, pineapples, plantains (page 281), plums, pomegranates, quince, raspberries, sour oranges, star fruit, strawberries, tamarind (page 281), watermelons

HERBS AND AROMATICS

Ají peppers (page 278), chiles (pages 22–23), cilantro (fresh coriander), epazote (page 279), garlic, ginger, mint, parsley

CHEESES AND DAIRY PRODUCTS

Cotija (also called *queso blanco;* page 279), *crema* (page 279), evaporated milk, *queso añejo* (page 278), *queso fresco* (page 279), *queso menonita* (page 279), sweetened condensed milk

CORN PRODUCTS

Corn tortilla chips, corn tortillas, dried corn husks (for wrapping tamales), *huitlacoche* (page 15), masa (page 21), *masarepa* (page 21), masa harina (page 21), *pozole* (dried, frozen, or cooked hominy; page 21)

GRAINS, SEEDS, AND NUTS

Amaranth (page 190), almonds, Brazil nuts, cashews, peanuts, pine nuts (*piñones*), pumpkin seeds (*pepitas;* page 281), quinoa (page 281), walnuts

LEGUMES

Black beans, black-eyed peas, cannellini beans, chickpeas (garbanzo beans), lentils, lima beans, navy beans, pinto beans, red beans

PANTRY STAPLES

Coconut milk, corn flour, corn oil, lard, olive oil, peanut oil, rice, semolina pasta, sweetened flaked coconut, wheat flour

SUGAR AND OTHER SWEETENERS

Agave nectar, confectioner's (icing) sugar, granulated sugar, honey, molasses, *piloncillo* (page 281)

WINE, BEER, AND SPIRITS

Cachaça (page 32), light beer, light and dark rum, kahlúa, Pisco (page 32), red and white wine (page 19), tequila (page 281)

LATIN AMERICAN DRIED HERBS, SPICES, AROMATICS, AND OTHER SEASONINGS

Dried Spices and Herbs

Achiote seeds (annatto seeds)

Allspice

Aniseed

Bay leaves

Canela (also called true cinnamon bark or Mexican cinnamon)

Chile powder

Cloves, whole and ground

Coriander seeds

Cumin

Oregano, Mexican dried

Peppercorns, black

Aromatics and Other Seasonings

Chocolate

Currants, dried

Piloncillo sugar (Mexican brown sugar)

Raisins, golden and brown

Sesame seeds

Vanilla, beans and extract

Spice Mixtures and Pastes

Achiote paste

Ají chile pastes, *amarillo*, *panca*, and *verde* (yellow, red, and green)

Moles (Mexican ground-spice mixtures)

Recados (Maya ground-spice mixtures)

Latin Holidays and Celebrations

Latin Americans are serious when it comes to having fun. Holidays and celebrations, whether religious, secular, or family, hold a special place in Latin American culture. They are usually celebrated with food, drink, and either somber respect or lots of gaiety, color, and costumes.

El Dia de los Reyes Magos (Three Kings' Day)

On this Mexican holiday (January 6), children receive a gift and a decorative wreath-shaped, cakelike bread called *rosca de reyes* is served. A figurine of the baby Jesus is hidden inside the bread, and whoever finds it must take it to church for a blessing on the *Día de la Candelaria* on February 2, a celebration of Jesus' first trip to the temple, then host a party where tamales are served.

Carnaval

Carnaval (January or February) is the last chance to celebrate before the beginning of the 40-day Lenten season of fasting and prayer. It is a time of dancing and fun. The most famous *Carnival* is in Rio de Janeiro where scantily but elaborately clad dancers parade to pounding samba rhythms. Occasional stops for food are needed to keep the dancers going, but their main fuel seems to be caipirinhas.

Semana Santa (Holy Week)

Easter Week (March or April) is the most important religious festival in Latin America. The most famous week-long celebrations are in Peru, Chile, and Colombia. Special foods for this festival include *aguas frescas*, ice cream and other frozen treats, fried plantains, and dishes made with *bacalao* (salt cod).

Dia de Todos Santos (All Saints' Day)

Also known as *Dia de los Muertos*, this holiday (November 1 and 2) is celebrated throughout Latin America to honor the dead; it is a joyous occasion. Traditional Mexican and Central American dishes include tamales, candied pumpkin, and *pan de muerto* (a sweet bread), usually served with hot chocolate. In the Andes, specialties include *t'antawawas* (bread figurines), *chicha* (a fermented beverage), candies, and decorated pastries.

Navidad (Christmas)

Navidad (December 25) is the most joyous Christian celebration of the year. On Christmas Eve, families throughout Latin America attend midnight mass, then return home for *la cena de Navidad* (Christmas dinner). Traditional dishes include *pavo relleno* (turkey stuffed with sweet and savory force meat) and roast suckling pig. Tamales, *buñuelos* and *pristiños* (fritters), *pan de Pasqua* (Christmas fruit bread), hot chocolate, and fruit punches are also traditionally served.

Quinceañeras

Besides her wedding day, a young Latinas most important right of passage is the celebration of her fifteenth birthday—an occasion that requires a special mass, a fiesta with dancing, and an elegant formal gown. The fiesta menu might include *mole poblano* in Mexico; a roast pig in Cuba; or roast beef in Argentina. The centerpiece of the dessert table is a cake—a *tres leches* cake in Cuba. Surrounding the cake are other desserts, such as pudding, Mexican wedding cookies, and, in Argentina and Uruguay, *alfajores* (cookies filled with *dulce de leche*).

Favorite Latin spirits: tequila, cachaça, and Pisco (top); Mexican wedding cookies (middle); and Pork Tamales with Red Chile Salsa (above)

ANDEAN LUNCH

Pisco Sour (page 43)

•

Black Bean, Corn, and
Quinoa Salad (page 85)

•

Shrimp, Pumpkin, and
Corn Chowder (page 102)

•

Blackberry Ice Cream
(page 244)

MEXICAN FIESTA

Margarita (page 35)

•

Guacamole with Mango and
Pomegranate (page 51)

•

Grilled Fish with Adobo Rub
(page 132)

•

Chocolate–Ancho Chile Cake
(page 256)

LATIN-STYLE BRUNCH

Hibiscus Agua Fresca
(page 40)

•

Vegetables with Pepita Dip
(page 63)

•

Huevos Rancheros (page 223)

•

Mexican Wedding Cookies
(page 267)

ARGENTINIAN STEAK DINNER

Malbec

•

Grilled Steak with Parsley-Garlic
Chimichurri (page 145)

•

Grilled Tomatoes with
Chimichurri (page 193)

•

Orange–Passion Fruit Cake
(page 264)

CUBAN FEAST

Cuba Libre or Mojito
(page 39)

•

Chicken and Cheese
Empanadas (page 64)

•

Cuban-Style Paella (page 119)

•

Tres Leches Cake (page 240)

SUMMER BBQ

Michelada (page 35)

•

Carnitas Tacos (page 150)

•

Grilled Corn with Crema
and Chile (page 194)

•

Coconut Meringue Cookies
(page 247)

SPRING DINNER PARTY

Margarita (page 35)

•

Stuffed Squash Blossoms (page 59)

•

Tortilla Soup (page 86)

•

Trout with Avocado Sauce
(page 127)

•

Creamy Coconut Tart (page 259)

LATIN SMALL PLATES

Caipirinha (page 43)

•

Halibut Ceviche
with Avocado (page 67)

•

Potato and Ham Croquetas
(page 76)

•

Grilled Lamb Chops with Spicy
Mint Salsa (page 182)

SPICED-UP WEEKNIGHT

Lime-Cucumber Cooler
(page 36)

•

Caesar Salad with Chipotle
Chile Dressing (page 89)

•

Chicken Enchiladas with Salsa
Roja (page 177)

•

Mexican Red Rice (page 214)

Drinks

About Drinks

Beverages, both hot and cold, are served throughout the day in Latin America. Some drinks provide a wake-up call and a jolt of caffeine, some are pure refreshment on a hot summer's day, and, of course, there are plenty of heady libations for festive occasions.

Wherever you travel in Latin America, there are delicious drinks for any time of day. From beer to wine to margaritas and Pisco sours, the drinks complement the food and weather, and reflect the importance Latin Americans place on hospitality and enjoying life.

BREAKFAST DRINKS

In Cuba, the choice of eye-openers includes the mighty, thimble-sized *café Cubano* for the tired but time-challenged; *café con leche* (three parts scalded milk to one part very strong coffee, or sometimes espresso) for those who want to ease into the day; the super-charged *cortadito* (three parts coffee to one part milk); and the basic *cafecito* (strong, sweet coffee) for those that want to hit the road running. Coffee is grown and consumed in many countries in Latin America, but nowhere is it brewed as strong as in Cuba—although Brazil's beloved *cafezinho* runs a close second.

In Mexico, Central America, and the Andean Region of South America, morning beverages are more soothing. Chocolate was first domesticated in Central America some two thousand years ago, and hot chocolate (made with water or milk) remains a favorite drink. *Atole*, a typical morning beverage in Mexico and Central America, is made with fresh corn and sweetened with honey or spiced with chiles. In Bolivia, where mornings can be frigid, mothers serve their children mugs of sweetened *api de quinoa* (a milk-based, quinoa-thickened drink flavored with cinnamon and vanilla) before sending them off to school.

In tropical regions throughout Latin America, sometimes it's just too hot for coffee. *Batidos*, blended beverages made with milk, fresh fruit, and ice, and *horchatas* or *chichas*, cool, nourishing drinks made with milk or coconut milk and thickened with rice or almonds, are light, but rich and fortifying in the morning.

ANYTIME DRINKS

Street venders and *refresco* stands do a lively business in Latin American countries. In Mexico and Central America, *aguas frescas*—similar to the fruit smoothies in the United States, but made with water, not dairy—are daily refreshments for many. In Uruguay, Argentina, and Chile, milk- or juice-based *liquados,* very similar to fruit smoothies but with more ice added, are a favorite pick-me up.

FIESTA DRINKS

When it comes to a party drink, in the Caribbean, fiesta equals rum. No visitor to Havana should leave Cuba without sampling a *mojito* (pronounced *moh-HEE-toh*) and visiting Papa Hemingway's favorite bar, El Floridita, to try his signature daiquiri made with grapefruit juice instead of lime.

In Mexico, sitting around the *zócalo* (plaza) waiting to meet friends for brunch, you might order a *michelada* (pronounced *me-chel-LA-da)*, an unusual iced beer drink made with lime juice and hot sauce, served in a tall salt-rimmed glass. It may sound strange, but like a similar drink from Cuba called *bul* (beer with ice, lime juice, and sugar), this beer cooler is

tasty and refreshing. Mexico brews great beer and, in Baja, produces good wines, but the country is most famous for tequila, the "white lightning" made from the fermented, distilled heart of the blue agave plant. The margarita is of course Mexico's favorite tequila cocktail. To be authentic, the lime juice must always be fresh, and many purists prefer their margaritas shaken in a cocktail shaker and served on the rocks (over ice), rather than blended with ice.

In Central America and on the Caribbean coast of South America, local rum is cheap and popular. The preferred mixed drink is the *Cuba libre* (pronounced *KOO-buh Lee-bray*), which can even be purchased pre-mixed in a can.

Brazil's signature cocktail is the *caipirinha* (pronounced *kai-pur-EEN-ya)*, a refreshing, day-at-the-beach drink made with fresh lime, sugar syrup, crushed ice, and *cachaça* (pronounced *kah-SHAH-sah)*, a Brazilian spirit distilled from fermented sugarcane juice.

Argentina and Chile are wine-making countries that produce esteemed full-bodied, fruity wines, such as Cabernet Sauvignon and Malbec, among others (see page 19). Using their wine as a base, these countries are also known for several versions of sangria using oranges, lemons, and other fruits—in Chile, *borgoña*, chilled red wine mixed with chopped fresh strawberries, is a favorite.

Conversations between Chileans and Peruvians can sometimes become heated when discussing the Pisco sour, since both countries claim this frothy, intoxicating beverage as their own. Pisco (pronounced *pee-sco*) is made from Peruvian pink grapes, and the city of Pisco is located in Peru, so the Peruvians have a strong argument; but, no matter who invented it, the Pisco sour is a popular newcomer to shores beyond its Latin homeland, where it is a favorite choice on cocktail menus.

Margarita

Tequila or mescal has been paired with citrus juice for centuries, with a lick of salt as the traditional accompaniment. It took only a few slight modifications to transform these ingredients into one of today's favorite cocktails. You can experiment with different tequilas and orange liqueurs, and puréeing the ingredients in a blender versus shaking them with ice.

Spread the salt on a small, flat plate. Working with one glass at a time, run the lime wedge around the rim of the glass to moisten it and then dip the rim into the salt to coat it evenly. Put the glass in the freezer to chill for at least 15 minutes. Repeat with the other glass, using the same lime wedge to moisten the rim.

When ready to serve, in a cocktail shaker or a jar with a lid, combine the tequila, orange liqueur, lime juice, and ice. Shake 12–15 times; the more you shake, the more the ice will diffuse into the drink. Strain the margarita mixture into the glasses, garnish each glass with a lime slice, and serve right away.

Coarse sea salt

1 lime wedge, plus 2 lime slices for garnish

3 fl oz (90 ml) silver tequila

1 fl oz (30 ml) orange liqueur, such as Cointreau, triple sec, or Grand Marnier

1 fl oz (30 ml) fresh lime juice

1 cup (8 oz/125 g) coarsely cracked ice

MAKES 2 DRINKS

Michelada

This popular drink is served all over Mexico in different iterations. The name, *Michelada*, is shortened from *mi chela helada*, or "my ice-cold beer." The drink is a refreshing combination of beer, lime juice, and seasonings, and is usually served over ice. One variation of the drink, closer to a Bloody Mary, includes 6 fl oz (188 ml) tomato juice or Clamato.

Spread the salt on a small, flat plate. Working with one glass at a time, run the lime wedge around the rim of a tall glass to moisten it and then dip the rim into the salt to coat it evenly. Put the glass in the freezer to chill for at least 15 minutes. Repeat with the other glass, using the same lime wedge to moisten the rim.

When ready to serve, fill each glass with several ice cubes. Add half of the lime juice and a dash of the Worcestershire and chile sauces to each glass.

Pour 1 beer into each glass, garnish with a lime slice, and serve right away.

Coarse sea salt

1 lime wedge, plus 2 lime slices for garnish

Ice cubes

½ cup (4 fl oz/120 ml) fresh lime juice

Worcestershire sauce

Habanero chile sauce or other hot pepper sauce

2 bottles (24 fl oz/750 ml) Mexican beer such as Superior or Bohemia

MAKES 2 DRINKS

Strawberry Agua Fresca

5 cups (1¼ lb/625 g) hulled strawberries, plus strawberry slices for garnish

½ cup (4 oz/125 g) sugar

⅓ cup (2½ oz/75 ml) lime juice

Coarse sea salt

Ice cubes

Mint sprigs

MAKES 4 DRINKS

Combine 2½ cups (1⅛ lb/313 g) of the strawberries and 1½ cups (12 fl oz/ 375 ml) water in a blender. Purée until smooth. Place a fine mesh sieve over a bowl. Pour the purée into the sieve, using a silicone spatula to press the mixture through the sieve. Discard the strawberry seeds left in the sieve. Repeat with the remaining strawberries and 1½ cups (12 fl oz/375 ml) more water.

Pour the strawberry purée into a pitcher. Stir in the sugar, lime juice, and ¼ teaspoon salt. Add an additional 1–2 cups (8–16 fl oz/250–500 ml) of water to reach the desired consistency.

To serve, fill the glasses with ice cubes. Pour the *agua fresca* into the glasses, dividing evenly, and garnish with strawberry slices and a mint sprig, if desired.

Refreshing fruit waters, or *agua frescas,* such as this one add a colorful accent to any meal and are appreciated as thirst quenchers on a warm day. Other popular flavors include mango, melon, tamarind, and watermelon. To make watermelon *agua fresca,* replace the strawberries with 1 small watermelon, peeled, seeded, and cut into 2-inch (5-cm) chunks.

Lime-Cucumber Cooler

1 cup (8 fl oz/250 ml) fresh lime juice, from 4–5 large limes

6 tablespoons (3 oz/85 g) superfine (caster) sugar

Ice cubes

1 bottle (24 fl oz/750 ml) sparkling water, chilled

Thin cucumber slices

Thin lime slices

MAKES 4 DRINKS

Divide the lime juice and the sugar evenly among 4 tall glasses and stir well to dissolve the sugar.

Fill the glasses with ice and then top each glass with sparkling water. Add several cucumber and lime slices to each glass and serve right away.

Two of the most refreshing ingredients, cucumber and lime, combine in this non-alcoholic drink to make the ultimate thirst quencher. If possible, use a mandoline to slice the cucumber and lime to get very thin, uniform slices.

Mojito

Originating in Cuba, the Mojito has a fresh, sweet-crisp taste that comes from the perfect marriage of lime, sugar, and mint. Muddling the ingredients together is a key step in achieving this balance. Be gentle when muddling, though. The goal is to bruise, not crush, the mint to release its essential oils and flavor.

Divide the mint, sugar, and lime juice evenly among 4 glasses. Using a muddler (page 280) or the end of a spoon, stir vigorously, or muddle, to bruise, but not pulverize, the mint.

Add several ice cubes and ¼ cup (2 fl oz/63 ml) of the rum to each glass.

Top each glass with sparkling water, stir well, and serve right away.

32 fresh mint sprigs

4 tablespoons (1¾ oz/50 g) superfine (caster) sugar

Juice of 4 limes

Ice cubes

1 cup (8 fl oz/250 ml) light rum

1 bottle (24 fl oz/750 ml) sparkling water

MAKES 4 DRINKS

Cuba Libre

Fresh lime juice is what makes the difference between a true Cuba Libre and a mere rum and coke. To cut down on the amount of sugar or caffeine in this drink, make a Cuba Pintana by replacing 1 part cola with 1 part club soda.

Fill a shaker two-thirds full of ice cubes and pour in the rum and lime juice. Shake well. Fill 2 glasses with ice cubes and divide the rum-lime mixture between them.

Add half of the cola to each glass and stir briefly. Add a lime wedge to each glass and serve right away.

Ice cubes

⅔ cup (5 fl oz) light rum

4 tablespoons fresh lime juice

1½ cups (12 fl oz/ 355 ml) cola

2 lime wedges

MAKES 2 DRINKS

Sangria

1 bottle (24 fl oz/750 ml) full-bodied red wine

½ cup (4 fl oz/120 ml) brandy

½ cup (4 fl oz/120 ml) Simple Syrup (page 277)

½ cup (4 fl oz/120 ml) *each* fresh orange and lemon juice, strained

¼ cup (2 fl oz/60 ml) orange liqueur (page 35)

1 cup (8 fl oz/240 ml) sparkling water

Ice cubes

MAKES 4–6 DRINKS

Pour the wine, brandy, simple syrup, orange and lemon juices, and orange liqueur into a large pitcher. Stir to mix well. Cover and refrigerate until well chilled, at least 4 hours or up to 8 hours.

About 2 hours before serving, add the desired fruit accompaniments (see below) to the pitcher and return to the refrigerator.

Just before serving, stir in the sparkling water. To serve, place a few ice cubes in each glass. Pour some of the sangria into each glass and then use a slotted spoon to add several pieces of fruit to each glass. Serve right away.

FRUIT ACCOMPANIMENTS A wide variety of fruits are delicious when mixed into this sweetened wine-brandy sangria base. In Argentina, the most common additions are thinly sliced lemons and oranges and mixed sliced or chopped fruits, such as peaches, strawberries, apples, plums, and pears.

Though perhaps best known as an accompaniment to *tapas* in Spain, this fruity wine drink is also quite popular in South America, especially in the wine-making countries of Argentina and Chile. For the most authentic version, choose a full-bodied South American red wine (see page 19).

Hibiscus Agua Fresca

2 cups (6 oz/185 g) dried *jamaica* (hibiscus) flowers (see Note)

Zest of 1 orange

½ cup (4 oz/125 g) sugar or (6 oz/185 g) honey, or as needed

2 tablespoons fresh lime juice

Still water, sparkling water, or fresh orange juice

Ice cubes

Lime slices

MAKES 10–12 DRINKS

In a saucepan over medium-high heat, combine 6 cups (48 fl oz/15 l) water, the *jamaica* flowers, and orange zest. Bring to a simmer and cook for 5 minutes. Pour into a heatproof glass bowl, stir in the sugar, and let cool for 10 minutes.

Strain the mixture through a fine-mesh sieve into a glass or plastic container and add the lime juice. Taste for sweetness, adding more sugar if necessary. Cover and refrigerate until cold, at least 1 hour or up to 3 days.

To serve, dilute the *agua fresca* to taste with the still water, sparkling water, or orange juice. Place a few ice cubes in tall glasses and pour some of the *agua fresca* into each glass. Garnish with the lime slices and serve right away.

This vivid wine-colored drink, called *Agua de Jamaica* in Spanish, is made from the dried red calyxes that surround the yellow petals of the *Hibiscus sabdariffa*, a smaller version of the showier ornamental. It is one of Mexico's most beloved thirst quenchers. The *jamaica* flowers are sold packaged as a tea or as a diuretic in health food stores, well-stocked markets, and in Latin American grocery stores.

Pisco Sour

There is no substitute for Pisco brandy, a clear South American spirit distilled from Muscat grapes. If you can't find it easily, most liquor stores can order it for you. Some bartenders sprinkle the bitters on top instead of mixing them in.

Fill a shaker two-thirds full of ice cubes. Pour the brandy, lemon juice, egg whites, bitters, and simple syrup into the shaker and shake very well.

Strain the cold mixture into chilled cocktail glasses and serve right away.

Ice cubes

½ cup (4 fl oz/120 ml) Pisco brandy

3 tablespoons fresh lemon juice

2 egg whites (see note, page 279)

4 dashes Angostura bitters

2 tablespoons Simple Syrup (page 277)

MAKES 2 DRINKS

Caipirinha

This national drink of Brazil is made with a rum known as *cachaça*, which is distilled from fresh sugarcane juice. If you can't find *cachaça*, use light rum instead.

Divide the lime wedges and simple syrup among 2 low cocktail glasses and, using a muddler or the end of a spoon, stir vigorously, or muddle, to release all of the juice from the limes.

Fill each glass with some crushed ice, and pour in the *cachaça*, dividing it evenly among the glasses. Stir thoroughly and serve right away.

1 lime, cut into 8 wedges

2 tablespoons Simple Syrup (page 277)

Crushed ice

½ cup (4 fl oz/120 ml) *cachaça*

MAKES 2 DRINKS

Coconut Horchata

2¾ cups (19 oz/590 g) uncooked rice

2 teaspoons ground cinnamon, plus more for garnishing

15 blanched almonds, lightly toasted and finely ground (page 268)

1 can (14 fl oz/420 ml) unsweetened coconut milk

1 cup (8 oz/250 g) sugar

Zest of 1 lime, cut into strips

Ice cubes

Cinnamon sticks for garnish

MAKES 6–8 DRINKS

One day in advance, add the rice to a spice grinder and pulse to pulverize it into a fine powder. In a bowl, combine the rice powder, ground cinnamon, and 4 cups (32 fl oz/1 l) hot water. Cool, cover, and set aside. Refrigerate if the weather is hot.

When ready to serve, stir the nuts and coconut milk into the rice mixture. Working in batches, add the rice mixture to a blender and process until smooth, about 5 minutes. Strain through a medium-mesh sieve and pour into a pitcher.

In a saucepan over low heat, combine the sugar, 1 cup (8 fl oz/ 250 ml) cold water, and the lime zest. Cook, stirring, until the sugar dissolves into the water to make a syrup. Let the syrup cool, then remove the lime zest. Pour the syrup into the pitcher and stir to mix well. If the drink is too thick for your taste, add more water. Cover and refrigerate until chilled, about 1 hour. Mix well before serving.

When ready to serve, place a few ice cubes in tall glasses and pour the *horchata* into the glasses. Garnish with more ground cinnamon and a cinnamon stick and serve right away.

Horchata de Coco is one of Mexico's most cooling, refreshing *agua frescas*. It is made with a base of ground rice or melon seeds and is often flavored with cinnamon and almonds. This recipe calls for canned coconut milk for ease of use, but to extract milk from the meat of a fresh coconut yourself, see page 269.

Mexican Hot Chocolate

3 cups (24 fl oz/750 ml) milk or water

3 wedges (3 oz/90 g each) Mexican chocolate, crumbled

MAKES 6 DRINKS

In a saucepan over medium heat, warm the milk until small bubbles form along the edge of the pan. Add the chocolate and stir until it melts, then simmer gently to blend the flavors, about 5 minutes.

Beat with a *molinillo* (see Note), an electric mixer set on low speed, or a flexible wire whisk until very frothy. Pour into small cups or mugs and serve right away.

In Mexico, hot chocolate is traditionally made only with water, but the milk in this version makes it more luxurious. The signature frothy finish is achieved by beating the hot chocolate with a wooden *molinillo,* a wooden stick with carved grooves, but an electric mixer or a whisk will also do the trick.

Starters and Snacks

About Starters and Snacks

In Latin America, small bites kick off celebratory meals with family and friends, and are eaten almost any time of the day as a snacks. Snack stands and street carts have emerged from this tradition, offering prepared treats to take home or eat right away.

All over Latin America, outdoor markets in bustling areas of towns and cities are host to snack stands selling a wide array of prepared foods. Even in post-revolutionary Cuba, where small children were forbidden to open lemonade stands, so strong is the tradition of street food that now, some fifty years later, the streets of Havana are filled with kiosks and pushcarts where enterprising Cubans sell all kinds of foods from snow cones to *croquetas*.

APPETIZERS

Appetizers, also called *aperitivos* or *antojitos*, in Latin America can be as simple as a bowl of guacamole with tortilla chips served at a restaurant in Mexico City, or as elegant as an artistically arranged plate of hearts of palm with pink mayonnaise sauce *(palmitos con salsa golf)* served at a dinner party in Buenos Aires. Sometimes they are simply bowls of olives and almonds to nibble when meeting friends for drinks at a bar in Santo Domingo, and sometimes they replace the salad course with dishes like stuffed avocado halves or vegetables and fruits with pumpkin seed dip.

SNACKS

For Latin Americans, snacks are often foods you buy from street vendors and at roadside stands. In the Caribbean, these may be crispy treats like fried green plantain chips *(mariquitas)* and fried yuca sticks *(palitos de yuca)*; but there are also more filling *comidas ambulantes* ("meals to go") like the famous

Cubano sandwich—half a loaf of Cuban bread split and spread with mustard and mayo, filled with ham, cheese, roast pork, and pickles, and toasted in a giant sandwich press—now that's a *comida*!

A popular Mexican street snack is boiled or grilled whole ears of corn threaded onto sticks and sprinkled with chile, lime, and cheese. In Honduras, kids at bus stations offer travelers pickled watermelon rinds *(acetiones)*, and in the Yucatan and Guatemala, you often see people on market day stroll by nibbling on candied sweet potatoes wrapped in brown paper cones.

South Americans have their own distinctive *bocaditos*, or snacks. *Arepas*, cornmeal cakes, filled with beans, cheese, meat or any combination thereof, are so popular in Columbia and Venzuela that snack bars in these countries are often called *areparias*. Street vendors in Lima, Peru prepare skewers of marinated, grilled beef heart *(anticuchos)* on portable charcoal grills and serve them with an incendiary *ají* pepper sauce. Many vendors also prepare *anticuchos* with chicken and fish.

POPULAR VARIETY

Certain starters and snacks, such as empanadas, tamales, fritters, croquettes, and ceviche, are popular throughout Latin America, but the recipes vary considerably from country to country.

Empanadas in Cuba are often wrapped with yuca (cassava) dough. In Mexico, shrimp empanadas from Veracruz have wafer-thin crusts of corn masa tinted gold with achiote (annatto seeds). Bolivia's spicy beef *salteñas* are enclosed in a flaky crust made with lard and wheat flour, and in Brazil, where *empadinhas* are small, round tartlets instead of turnovers, the crust is made with cream cheese. A favorite filling there includes crab meat, chopped hard-boiled eggs, and hearts of palm.

Beloved and in many places ubiquitous, tamales come in many sizes and shapes; they may be filled or unfilled, sweet or savory. In Mexico, tamales are usually made with corn masa and wrapped in corn husks. In Nicaragua, you'll find delicious pork *nacatamales* made with mashed potatoes and wrapped in banana leaves. Throughout South America tamales are wrapped in banana or plantain leaves instead of corn husks. In the Andes of South America, tamale dough may be made with quinoa.

Fritters and *croquetas* are both inexpensive and tasty fried treats. In Puerto Rico, taro and green banana fritters stuffed with beef or seafood *(alcapurrias)* are a local specialty, and in the Dominican Republic, a day at the beach wouldn't be complete without buying a bag of shrimp, mashed potato, and cheese fritters *(bombas de camarones y papas)* from a vendor. Brazilians munch on salt cod and potato fritters *(bolinhos de bacalhau)*.

Ceviche *(cebiche)*, a simple dish of fresh, raw seafood marinated in citrus juice, probably originated in Peru, but is popular all along the Pacific coast from Mexico to Chile. Depending on the region, it may be made with fish, shrimp, octopus, or a mixture of fish and shellfish.

While the dishes in this chapter are often bought prepared in Latin America, the following recipes make these favorite starters and snacks easy to make at home.

Guacamole with Mango and Pomegranate

Creamy, rich, and unctuous, guacamole complements everything from tortilla chips to tacos. An essential part of Mexican cuisine since ancient times, it is generally kept simple—avocado with just a splash of lime juice and a little salt is traditional—and used as an accompaniment. However, sparked with crunchy onion, spicy chile, and a sprinkling of fresh herbs and studded with bright, tart fruit, always popular guacamole can leap to the center of attention.

Cut the avocados in half and remove the pits. Scoop the flesh into a bowl. Using a fork or a potato masher, mash the avocado with the lime juice and ½ teaspoon salt until the guacamole is smooth but still has a little texture and some chunks.

Stir in the onion, chile, and cilantro. Taste and adjust the seasoning.

Spoon the guacamole into a serving bowl or a *molcajete* (shown). Scatter the mango, pomegranate seeds, and tomatoes on top. Serve right away with the jicama sticks and tortilla chips for dipping.

VARIATIONS Pretty red pomegranate seeds and mango are used here, but any tart-sweet fruit, such as pineapple and strawberries, will work just as well. Or, try crumbling 1 tablespoon salty cotija cheese or goat cheese, or 1 tablespoon toasted pumpkin seeds over the top with the fruit and tomatoes.

3 ripe avocados

2 teaspoons fresh lime juice

Salt

¼ small white onion, finely diced

1 small serrano chile, seeded and minced

3 fresh cilantro (fresh coriander) sprigs, stemmed and chopped

2 tablespoons diced mango

2 tablespoons pomegranate seeds

½ small plum (Roma) tomato, cored, seeded, and finely diced, about 2 tablespoons

FOR SERVING

1 small jicama, peeled, cut into sticks

Tortilla chips, homemade (page 277) or purchased

MAKES 4 SERVINGS

Mixed Seafood Ceviche

Salt and freshly ground white pepper

1 lb (500 g) cleaned octopus

1 lb (500 g) medium shrimp (prawns), peeled and deveined

1 lb (500 g) cleaned small squid bodies, cut into rings ¹/₄ inch (6 mm) thick

3 stalks celery, chopped

1 teaspoon peeled and grated fresh ginger

1 red bell pepper (capsicum), roasted, peeled, and seeded (page 268)

1 tablespoon *ají verde* paste (page 278)

1 teaspoon hot *ají panca* paste (page 278)

4 cloves garlic, minced

Juice of 5 limes

3–4 tablespoons chopped fresh cilantro (fresh coriander) leaves

1 small red onion, thinly sliced

¹/₄ teaspoon minced seeded habanero chile

MAKES 4 SERVINGS

Bring a saucepan three-fourths full of salted water to a boil over high heat. Have ready a large bowl of ice water. Add the octopus to the boiling water and blanch for 20 seconds. Using tongs or a slotted spoon, transfer the octopus to the ice water and let cool; return the water in the saucepan to a boil. When the octopus has cooled and the water has returned to a boil, again add the octopus to the boiling water and blanch for 20 seconds, then transfer to the ice water. Repeat to blanch a third time, refreshing the ice water if necessary. Return the octopus to the boiling water and cook for 25 minutes.

While the octopus is cooking for the final time, bring another saucepan three-fourths full of salted water to a boil over high heat. Have ready another bowl of ice water. Cut the shrimp in half lengthwise. Set aside one shrimp half. Add the remaining shrimp and the squid to the boiling water and blanch for 30 seconds, then quickly transfer to the ice water. When cooled, drain thoroughly and set aside.

In a blender or food processor, combine the celery, the reserved shrimp half, ginger, and ½ cup (4 fl oz/125 ml) water and process to a smooth purée. Transfer to a bowl and set aside. Add the roasted pepper and *ají* pastes to the blender or food processor and process to a smooth purée. Set aside.

When the octopus is done cooking, drain it in a colander and place under cold running water to cool.

Cut the octopus tentacles into ½-inch (12-mm) pieces and discard the head. In a large, nonreactive bowl, combine the shrimp, octopus, squid, celery purée, red pepper purée, garlic, ¼ teaspoon salt, and ½ teaspoon white pepper and stir to mix well. Stir in the lime juice and cilantro. Taste and adjust the seasoning. Add the red onion and minced chile and toss to distribute. Cover and refrigerate until well chilled, at least 30 minutes and up to 2 hours.

When ready to serve, if serving family-style, toss the ceviche to coat it with the juices in the bottom of the bowl, and garnish with some chopped cilantro. If serving in individual serving glasses, divide the ceviche evenly among each glass, spoon some of the remaining juices over each serving, and serve right away.

Peruvian ceviche uses less lime juice than other styles, with the acidity further softened by two purées, one of celery, water, and a little fish and one of roasted red peppers and chile pastes. Blanching the octopus 3 times is time-consuming, but it ensures that the octopus will be tender and flavorful. Be sure to serve the ceviche very cold.

Cheese and Poblano Chile Quesadillas

Masa, the dough used for making many *antojitos* (little bites), such as these quesadillas, is the foundation of much of Mexican cooking. Using homemade masa dough, as in this recipe, makes a flavorful difference. You can also assemble quick quesadillas using thin, purchased white corn tortillas, but they will not seal quite as well as homemade tortillas.

To make the dough, in a bowl, and using your hands, mix the masa harina with the warm water until smooth and pliable. Cover the bowl with a damp kitchen towel and let stand 5–10 minutes. Add ¼ teaspoon salt and knead gently in the bowl for 1 minute. Divide the dough into 12 equal portions and form each portion into a ball. Cover with the damp towel.

To make the filling, in a frying pan over medium heat, warm the oil. Add the onion and sauté until golden brown, about 5 minutes. Stir in the garlic and oregano and continue cooking for 1 minute. Add the chiles and ½ teaspoon salt and stir until everything is thoroughly heated, about 1 minute longer. Taste and adjust the seasoning with more salt, if necessary. Set aside.

To make the quesadillas, put 2 sheets of plastic wrap or a plastic storage bag cut into 2 sheets inside a tortilla press (page 269). Put a dough ball between the sheets and gently press down the top plate of the press. Remove the top piece of plastic and place a generous tablespoon of the shredded cheese on half of the tortilla, keeping the edges free. Top with 1 epazote leaf, if using, and a spoonful of the chile-onion mixture. Lift the lower piece of plastic to fold the uncovered side of the tortilla over the filling. Press the edges together with your fingers, remove from the press, and set aside, covered with a barely damp towel. Repeat until all the quesadillas are made.

Preheat the oven to 200°F (95°C). Pour oil to a depth of 1 inch (2.5 cm) into a deep, heavy frying pan and place over medium-high heat until the oil shimmers. Working in batches to avoid overcrowding, fry the quesadillas until golden, 1–2 minutes. Using a slotted spatula, transfer the quesadillas to paper towels. Let drain briefly, then transfer to a heatproof platter and keep warm in the oven. Serve right away with the guacamole and salsa.

FOR THE MASA DOUGH

2 cups (11 oz/340 g) masa harina

1¼ cups (10 fl oz/310 ml) plus 2 tablespoons warm water

Sea salt

FOR THE FILLING

1 tablespoon canola or safflower oil

1 white onion, thinly sliced

2 cloves garlic, finely chopped

½ teaspoon dried oregano, preferably Mexican

2 poblano chiles, roasted and seeded (page 268), cut lengthwise into 12 strips each ¼ inch (6 mm) wide

Sea salt

½ lb (250 g) Muenster or Monterey jack cheese, shredded (about 2 cups/ 8 oz/250 g)

12 fresh epazote (page 279) or fresh cilantro (fresh coriander) leaves (optional)

Canola oil for frying

FOR SERVING

Basic Guacamole (page 272)

Salsa Fresca (page 273) or Avocado-Tomatillo Salsa (page 273)

MAKES 6 SERVINGS

Beef Empanadas

FOR THE FILLING

¼ lb (125 g) unsalted butter

1 large yellow onion, diced

1 bunch green (spring) onions, white and tender green parts, thinly sliced

1 lb (500 g) beef round, freshly ground (minced) by the butcher

¼ cup (1½ oz/40 g) dried currants

Salt

1 teaspoon paprika

1 teaspoon red pepper flakes

¼ teaspoon ground cumin

FOR THE DOUGH

½ cup (4 oz/125 g) cold unsalted butter

2½ cups (12½ oz/390 g) all-purpose (plain) flour, plus flour for dusting

1 teaspoon baking powder

Salt

1 large egg

2 hard-boiled eggs, each cut into 6 slices

12 green olives, pitted and chopped

¼ cup (1½ oz/45 g) almonds, toasted (page 268) and chopped

MAKES 4–6 SERVINGS

To make the filling, in a frying pan over medium heat, warm the butter. Add the yellow and green onions, and cook, stirring often, until translucent, 5–7 minutes. Add the ground beef and cook, breaking up any large chunks, until the meat is no longer pink, 2–3 minutes. Add the currants and cook, stirring, for 1 minute. Remove from the heat and stir in 1½ teaspoons salt, the paprika, red pepper flakes, and cumin. Let cool. Transfer the filling to a nonreactive container, cover, and refrigerate until ready to assemble the empanadas.

To make the dough, cut the butter into tablespoon-sized pieces and set aside in the refrigerator. In a food processor, combine the 2½ cups (12½ oz/390 g) flour, the baking powder, and ½ teaspoon salt and pulse to blend. Add the butter to the food processor 1 piece at a time, pulsing to blend after each addition. When all of the butter has been added, if necessary, continue processing just until the mixture is the consistency of coarse crumbs, 15–20 seconds. Do not over mix. Add ¼ cup (2 fl oz/60 ml) water in a slow stream, pulsing 2–3 times until a soft dough forms and pulls away from the sides of the bowl, about 20 seconds total. Remove the dough from the work bowl, pat into a disk, and wrap tightly in plastic wrap. Refrigerate for 1 hour.

Preheat the oven to 350°F (180°C). Lightly grease a large baking sheet or line with aluminum foil or parchment (baking) paper.

Unwrap the dough. On a lightly floured work surface, roll the dough out about ⅛ inch (3 mm) thick. Using a 3-inch (7.5-cm) round cookie cutter, cut out 12 rounds of dough. Quickly and briefly knead the dough scraps together just until smooth, pat out the dough, and cut out additional circles. Transfer the dough rounds to the prepared baking sheet.

Beat the egg with 2 tablespoons water to make an egg wash. To assemble the empanadas, brush one side of the dough rounds with the egg wash and mound 2 heaping tablespoons of the beef filling in the center. Top with 1 slice of hard-boiled egg and about 1 teaspoon each of the olives and almonds. Fold the dough in half over the filling to form a half-moon and pinch to seal, fluting the edges, if you like, or crimp the edges with a fork to seal. Transfer to the prepared baking sheet. Repeat to assemble the remaining empanadas.

Brush the tops of the empanadas with the remaining egg wash. Bake until lightly golden, about 35–45 minutes. Serve warm or at room temperature.

The secret to good Argentinean empanadas is plenty of meat juices. Traditionally, Argentinean cooks achieve this by using an ample dose of beef or veal suet called *grasa de pella* in the filling. You can substitute other suet or beef fat from your butcher, or use unsalted butter, as called for in this recipe.

Stuffed Squash Blossoms

Beautiful yellow squash blossoms (*flor de calabasa*) are delicious with a traditional filling of corn, fresh hot chile, and *queso fresco* (a mildly salty fresh cheese). Epazote, a wild herb with an unusual taste somewhere between mint and marjoram, is a distinctive addition to many Mexican recipes. These little *rellenos* are especially good with a spoonful of Roasted Tomato Salsa (page 273).

Remove the husk and silk from the ear of corn. Hold the ear upright on a cutting board or in a small bowl and, using a sharp knife, cut off the kernels, keeping the blade angled so you get the whole kernel but none of the tough cob. You should have about ¾ cup (4½ oz/140 g) kernels. Set aside.

In a frying pan, warm 1 tablespoon of the olive oil over medium-high heat. Add the onion, garlic, and chile, if using, and cook, stirring constantly, until fragrant, about 1 minute. Add the corn, zucchini, and tomato and cook, stirring constantly, until the vegetables are tender-crisp, 2–3 minutes longer. Season with ½ teaspoon salt and ¼ teaspoon pepper. Remove from the heat and stir in the epazote. Taste and adjust for seasoning. Set the filling aside.

To clean the squash blossoms, have ready a bowl of cold, lightly salted water. Remove the small green leaves beneath the flower. If there is a stem, leave it on; the pistils and stamens may be left in or removed. Swish the blossoms quickly in the salt water and hold upside down to drain briefly, then place on paper towels to drain further. Pat gently with paper towels to dry completely before stuffing.

Carefully tear a slit down 1 side of each zucchini blossom. Tuck 2 or 3 cubes of the *queso fresco* into the bottom of each blossom. Using a small spoon, stuff each blossom with about 1 tablespoon of the vegetable filling, or as much as it can hold without tearing or spilling out. Overlap the petals to close the opening and press gently to compact the filling.

In a large frying pan, over medium heat, warm the remaining 1 tablespoon olive oil. Working in batches, add the stuffed zucchini blossoms and cook gently until light golden brown and heated through, turning once, about 4 minutes. The *queso* will soften but not melt. Transfer to individual plates or a platter, sprinkle with the *cotija* cheese, if using, and serve right away.

VARIATIONS You can vary this recipe in many ways, according to your tastes. Try adding 1 roasted poblano chile (page 268), peeled, seeded, and finely diced, to the filling. Or, substitute chopped squash blossoms for the diced zucchini, or a mild goat cheese or Monterey jack cheese for the *queso fresco*.

1 ear sweet white corn

2 tablespoons olive oil

½ white or red onion, finely diced

1 large clove garlic, minced

½ serrano chile, seeded and minced (optional)

1 cup (5 oz/155 g) finely diced zucchini (courgette)

1 plum (Roma) tomato, seeded and finely diced

Salt and freshly ground pepper

1 tablespoon minced fresh epazote (page 279) or fresh cilantro (fresh coriander)

12 large squash blossoms

4 oz (125 g) *queso fresco*, cut into ½-inch (12-mm) cubes

2 tablespoons crumbled *cotija* cheese (optional)

MAKES 4–6 SERVINGS

Chicken and Chorizo Arepas with Chimichurri

FOR THE CHICKEN FILLING

1 tablespoon olive oil

1 large yellow onion, finely diced

1 clove garlic, minced

¾ lb (375 g) skinless, boneless chicken breasts, cut into 2-inch (5-cm) chunks

1 tablespoon minced fresh flat-leaf (Italian) parsley

Salt and freshly ground pepper

1 large ripe avocado, pitted, peeled, and diced

¼ cup (2 fl oz/60 ml) good-quality mayonnaise

1 tablespoon Dijon mustard

FOR THE *AREPAS*

2 cups (10 oz/315 g) precooked white cornmeal such as Harina P.A.N. or ArepArina (page 21)

Sea salt

1 tablespoon olive oil

½ lb (4 oz/125 g) pork chorizo sausages, preferably South American or Mexican

Red Chile–Cilantro Chimichurri Sauce (page 275)

MAKES 4 SERVINGS

To make the chicken filling, in a saucepan over medium heat, warm the olive oil. Add the onion and cook, stirring often, until translucent, 5–7 minutes. Add the garlic and cook for 1 minute. Transfer the onion mixture to a bowl. Add the chicken to the pan and stir in the parsley, 1 teaspoon salt, and ¼ teaspoon pepper. Reduce the heat to medium-low, cover, and cook, stirring occasionally, until the chicken is opaque throughout, about 10 minutes. Transfer the chicken to a plate and let cool slightly. When cool enough to handle, finely shred the chicken and add to the bowl with the onion mixture, along with any remaining juices. Toss to mix, then set aside and let cool. Add the avocado, mayonnaise, and mustard and stir gently to mix well. Cover and refrigerate until ready to serve.

Preheat the oven to 200°F (95°C).

To make the *arepas*, in a bowl, stir together the cornmeal and 2 teaspoons salt. Add 2 cups (16 fl oz/500 ml) water and stir until all of the cornmeal is moistened, adding up to 4 tablespoons (2 fl oz/60 ml) more water, 1–2 tablespoons at a time, as needed. Cover and let stand, about 2 minutes. Using your hands, knead the dough in the bowl until smooth and no longer sticky, 2–3 minutes. Turn the dough out onto a work surface. Dampen your hands and roll the dough into a log about 8 inches (20 cm) long. Cut into 8 equal pieces, then form each piece into a ball. Working with 1 ball of dough at a time, flatten into a disk about 3 inches (8 cm) in diameter and ½ inch (13 mm) thick.

In a large frying pan over medium-low heat, warm the olive oil. Add half of the *arepas* and cook until a light crust forms on both sides, 3–4 minutes per side. Transfer the cooked arepas to a plate and place in the oven to keep warm. Repeat to cook the remaining *arepas*.

Meanwhile, remove the chicken filling from the refrigerator to bring to room temperature. Heat a small frying pan over medium heat. Arrange the chorizo slices in the hot pan and cook, turning as needed, until lightly golden on both sides, about 3 minutes total. Transfer to paper towels to drain briefly, then transfer to a bowl, add 1 tablespoon of the *chimichurri* sauce, and toss to coat.

Cut the *arepas* in half horizontally. Fill each *arepa* with the some of the chicken filling and chorizo slices, drizzle with some of the *chimichurri* sauce, and serve. Or, arrange the cut *arepas* on a platter with the fillings alongside, and instruct diners to fill their own *arepas*. Pass the remaining *chimichurri* at the table.

Reina pepiada, a rich combination of chicken, avocado, and mayonnaise, is a popular Venezuelan filling for hearty, patty-shaped *arepas.* The filling combinations are endless, however, so have fun experimenting with your favorite meats and cheeses. If you can't find Harina P.A.N., the popular Venezuelan brand of cornmeal for *arepas,* use any brand of precooked cornmeal, but be sure to start with only 1 cup (8 fl oz/250 ml) of water for each cup of corn flour, as grinds can vary slightly.

Vegetables with Pepita Dip

This dip or spread, known as *Zicil-P'ak*, is a classic pre-Columbian dish. The name is a combination of the Mayan words for pumpkin seeds and tomato. The ground seeds are softened while marinating in the tomato-chile mixture, giving this delicious concoction a satisfying texture. Serve this dip as an appetizer before a festive Mexican dinner.

Heat a heavy frying pan over medium-low heat until hot. Add the pumpkin seeds and, as soon as they start to pop, stir constantly until they begin to puff up. Don't let them brown. Pour onto a plate to cool completely, then grind them in a spice grinder until very fine.

In a blender or food processor, combine the tomato and chile and process briefly. Pour into a small bowl and stir in the ground pumpkin seeds, cilantro, chives, and 1 teaspoon salt. Let the mixture stand for 30 minutes.

While the mixture stands, prepare the vegetables. Wash and dry the radishes and carrots. Cut the radishes in half or leave whole. Leave the carrots whole, if small, or cut in half or into matchsticks, if larger. Peel the jicama and cut into matchsticks.

Just before serving, stir the lime juice into the dip. The dip should spread easily. If it is too thick, add a little water. Spoon the dip into a serving bowl, place on a platter with the vegetables and tortilla chips, and serve right away.

1 cup (5 oz/155 g) raw hulled green pumpkin seeds (*pepitas*) (page 281)

1 large, ripe tomato or 4 plum (Roma) tomatoes

1 habanero chile, roasted and seeded

2 tablespoons finely chopped fresh cilantro (fresh coriander)

2 tablespoons finely chopped fresh chives

Sea salt

Squeeze of lime juice

FOR SERVING

Radishes, carrots, and jicama

Tortilla chips, homemade (page 277) or purchased

MAKES ABOUT 1 CUP DIP (8 OZ/250 G)

Chicken and Cheese Empanadas

FOR THE FILLING

2 tablespoons olive oil

2 skinless, boneless chicken breast halves, 4–6 oz (125–185 g) each, cut into slices 1 inch (2.5 cm) thick

1 white onion, minced

2 tablespoons tomato paste

¼ cup (2 fl oz/60 ml) dry sherry

1 tablespoon chopped fresh flat-leaf (Italian) parsley

FOR THE DOUGH

3 cups (15 oz/470 g) all-purpose (plain) flour

2 teaspoons baking powder

1 teaspoon sugar

Salt

¾ cup (6 oz/185 g) cold butter, cut into ½-inch (12-mm) cubes

⅓ cup (3 fl oz) ice water

1 large egg plus 2 large egg yolks

4 oz (125 g) low-fat cream cheese or farmer's cheese, at room temperature

8 oz (250 g) Monterey jack or Cheddar cheese, shredded

MAKES 12 EMPANADAS

To make the filling, in a large frying pan over medium heat, warm 1 tablespoon of the olive oil. Add the chicken and cook, turning once, until opaque throughout, about 5 minutes. Transfer the chicken to a cutting board and let cool, then cut into ½-inch (12-mm) dice.

In the same frying pan over medium heat, warm the remaining 1 tablespoon olive oil. Add the onion and cook, stirring, until transluscent, 1 minute. Stir in the tomato paste and cook for 1 minute. Add the sherry and cook, stirring, until all of the juices have evaporated, 5–7 minutes. Remove from the heat and stir in the diced chicken and parsley. Refrigerate until completely cooled, about 1 hour.

To make the dough, in a food processor, combine the flour, baking powder, sugar, and 1 teaspoon salt and pulse to blend. Add the butter a few pieces at a time, pulsing to blend after each addition. Continue pulsing, if necessary, just until the mixture is the consistency of fine crumbs, about 15 seconds. Do not overmix. In a bowl, beat together the ice water, the whole egg, and 1 of the egg yolks and add to the machine in a slow stream, pulsing 2 or 3 times until a soft dough forms and pulls away from the sides of the bowl, about 20 seconds. Turn the dough out onto a work surface, roll it into a log, and wrap tightly in plastic wrap. Refrigerate the dough for 30 minutes before rolling it out.

Preheat the oven to 375°F (190°C). Lightly grease a large baking sheet or line with parchment (baking) paper. Remove the filling from the refrigerator and stir in the cream cheese and jack cheese. In another small bowl, beat the remaining egg yolk with ½ teaspoon water to make an egg wash.

Unwrap the dough, divide into 12 equal pieces, and gently shape each into a ball. On a lightly floured work surface, roll out each piece of dough into a circle 5 inches (13 cm) in diameter. Brush one side with the egg wash. Place about ¼ cup (2 oz/60 g) of the filling just off center on each. Fold the empanadas in half over the filling to form a half-moon. Crimp the edges with a fork to seal. Transfer to the prepared baking sheet.

Brush the tops of the empanadas with the remaining egg wash. Bake until golden brown around the edges, about 30 minutes. Serve warm or at room temperature.

Empanadas are amazingly versatile; they can be large or small, and stuffed with almost any combination of meat, vegetables, cheese, and herbs. These empanadas have an egg-rich dough with a tender crumb enfolding a sumptuous filling of chicken and cheese, and spiked with sherry. The empanadas taste even better after a short time out of the oven, so they're the perfect treat for parties, picnics, and portable meals.

Halibut Ceviche with Avocado

All along Mexico's Pacific coast are *palapas* that serve satisfying beach snacks, both fresh and fried. In this fresh fish ceviche, the acidity of lime juice "cooks" the raw seafood, while the olives add a kick of salt and brininess to highlight the flavors of the fish. Use any firm, white-fleshed fish such as sea bream, sea bass, cod, sole, halibut, or flounder.

Cut the fish fillets into small pieces and put them into a large nonreactive bowl, such as glass or ceramic. Pour the lime juice over the fish, making sure all the pieces are covered. Let the fish stand in the lime juice for 3–4 hours.

Drain the fish and pat dry on paper towels. Put the fish cubes back into the bowl and add the tomatoes, chiles, cilantro, and salt and pepper to taste. Stir to mix well and refrigerate for at least 2 hours.

When ready to serve, pit, peel, and dice the avocado and stir it into the fish mixture, along with the olives and oregano. Drizzle the ceviche with the olive oil and spoon into 6 individual serving glasses. Serve right away with tortilla chips, if desired, or store in the refrigerator for up to 12 hours.

1¼ lb (600 g) halibut fillets, or other white fish fillets

½ cup (4 fl oz/125 ml) fresh lime juice

2 firm but ripe tomatoes, peeled, seeded, and cut into small dice

2–3 serrano chiles, seeded and minced

⅓ cup chopped fresh cilantro (fresh coriander)

Salt and freshly ground pepper

1 avocado

10 green olives, preferably *manzanillos*, pitted and coarsely chopped

1 teaspoon dried Mexican oregano

2 tablespoons extra-virgin olive oil

Tortilla chips, homemade (page 277) or purchased (optional)

MAKES 6 SERVINGS

Red Pepper, Black Bean, and Cheese Arepas

FOR THE FILLING

1 tablespoon olive oil, plus 2 teaspoons

½ large yellow onion, thinly sliced

1½ teaspoons minced garlic

¾ teaspoon ground cumin

Salt and freshly ground pepper

1 can (15 oz/470 g) black beans, rinsed and drained

2 red bell peppers (capsicums), seeded and cut into thin slices

FOR THE *AREPAS*

2 cups (10 oz/315 g) precooked white cornmeal such as Harina P.A.N. or ArepArina

Salt

2 tablespoons unsalted butter, at room temperature

1 tablespoon olive oil

FOR SERVING

1 cup (4 oz/125 g) shredded *queso blanco* or farmer's cheese

1–2 jalapeño chiles, seeded and thinly sliced

MAKES 4 SERVINGS

To make the filling, in a frying pan over medium heat, warm the 1 tablespoon olive oil. Add the onion and cook, stirring often, until translucent, about 5 minutes. Add 1 teaspoon of the garlic, ½ teaspoon of the cumin, ½ teaspoon salt, and ½ teaspoon pepper and sauté for 1 minute. Add the beans and cook until warmed throughout and the flavors blend, about 10 minutes. Remove from the heat and cover to keep warm until ready to serve.

In another frying pan over medium heat, warm the 2 teaspoons olive oil. Add the bell peppers and the remaining ½ teaspoon garlic, the remaining ¼ teaspoon cumin, and ¼ teaspoon salt. Season with pepper to taste. Cook until the bell peppers are tender, 7–8 minutes. Remove from the heat and cover to keep warm until ready to serve.

Preheat the oven to 200°F (95°C).

To make the *arepas*, in a bowl, stir together the cornmeal and 2 teaspoons salt. Add 2 cups (16 fl oz/500 ml) water and stir until all of the cornmeal is moistened, adding up to 4 tablespoons (2 fl oz/60 ml) more water, 1–2 tablespoons at a time, as needed. Cover and let stand, about 2 minutes. Add the butter to the bowl and, using your hands, mix well. Still using your hands, knead the dough in the bowl until smooth and no longer sticky, 2–3 minutes. Turn the dough out onto a work surface. Dampen your hands and roll the dough into a log about 8 inches (20 cm) long. Cut into 8 equal pieces, then form each piece into a ball. Working with 1 ball of dough at a time, flatten into a disk about 3 inches (7 cm) in diameter and ½ inch (12 mm) thick.

In a large frying pan over medium-low heat, warm the oil. Add half of the *arepas* and cook until a crust forms on both sides, 3–4 minutes per side. Transfer to a plate and place in the oven to keep warm. Repeat to cook the remaining *arepas*.

Cut the *arepas* in half horizontally and arrange on a platter or place on individual plates. Transfer the black beans and bell peppers to serving bowls. Put the cheese and jalapeño in small serving bowls as well and serve, instructing diners to fill their *arepas* as they like.

Guests will enjoy piling the fillings of their preference on these soft, crusty corn cakes. Use creamy, shredded mozzarella cheese in place of the *queso blanco*, if you like. Instead of serving the cheese alongside the *arepas*, you can mix it into the dough or tuck into the middle of the dough rounds before flattening and frying, so the cheese melts as you bite into each hot *arepa*.

Shrimp-Stuffed Avocados

Throughout South America, this simple shrimp "cocktail" is prepared with fresh local shrimp, creamy indigenous avocados, green herbs, and one ubiquitous import: American ketchup. Serving as the tomato ingredient common to many classic dishes in South American cuisine, ketchup supplies a ready-made sweet-and-savory blend that is brightened by lime juice, deepened with fresh cilantro, and spiced up with chile.

To prepare the avocados for stuffing, using a large chef's knife, cut each avocado in half lengthwise, cutting down and around the pit. Hold the avocado so that one of the halves rests in each hand. Gently rotate in opposite directions to separate the halves. Holding the avocado half with the pit in one hand, strike the pit with the heel of the blade of the knife, lodging it into the pit. Twist the knife carefully to lift out the pit.

To make the shrimp stuffing, in a nonreactive bowl, combine the ketchup, onion, cilantro, olive oil, lime juice, Worcestershire sauce, and habanero and stir with a fork to mix well. Add the shrimp and stir to coat thoroughly with the sauce. Cover and refrigerate until well chilled.

Spoon the shrimp into the hollows of the avocado halves and serve right away.

2 avocados

¾ cup (6 fl oz/180 ml) ketchup

3 tablespoons finely chopped white onion

2 tablespoons minced fresh cilantro (fresh coriander)

2 tablespoons extra-virgin olive oil

2 tablespoons fresh lime juice

1½ tablespoons Worcestershire sauce

¼ teaspoon seeded and minced habanero chile

¼ lb (125 g) pre-cooked bay shrimp

MAKES 4 SERVINGS

Corn and Pea Empanaditas

FOR THE DOUGH

2 cups (10 oz/315 g) all-purpose (plain) flour

1 teaspoon baking soda (bicarbonate of soda)

Salt and freshly ground pepper

FOR THE FILLING

2 ears white sweet corn, husks and silk removed

1½ tablespoons olive oil

1 medium white onion, minced (about ¾ cup/ 4 oz/125 g)

1 small green bell pepper (capsicum), seeded and minced (about ¾ cup/ 4 oz/125 g)

1 tablespoon seeded and minced jalapeño chile

2 cloves garlic, minced

½ cup (2½ oz/75 g) fresh or frozen green peas

½ cup (4 fl oz/125 ml) tomato sauce

¼ cup (⅓ oz/10 g) chopped fresh cilantro (fresh coriander)

Vegetable oil for frying

MAKES 16 EMPANADITAS

To make the dough, in a food processor, combine the flour, baking soda, 1 teaspoon salt, and ½ teaspoon pepper and pulse to blend. Add ½ cup (4 fl oz/ 125 ml) water to the machine in a slow stream, pulsing 2 or 3 times until a soft dough forms that sticks together when pinched. If the mixture is still crumbly, drizzle about 2 tablespoons water over the dough and pulse again several times. Remove the dough, roll into a log, and wrap tightly in plastic wrap. Refrigerate for 30 minutes.

To make the filling, working with 1 ear of corn at a time, hold the ear upright on a cutting board or in a small bowl and, using a sharp knife, cut off the kernels, keeping the blade angled so you get the whole kernel but none of the tough cob.

In a frying pan over medium heat, warm the olive oil. Add the onion, bell pepper, chile, and garlic and cook, stirring, until softened, about 2 minutes. Add the corn and peas and cook, stirring, until tender, about 5 minutes. Add the tomato sauce and cook, stirring often, until the mixture thickens, about 5 minutes longer. Remove from the heat and let cool. Stir in the cilantro.

Unwrap the dough, divide into 16 equal pieces, and gently shape each into a ball. On a lightly floured work surface, roll out each ball into a circle about 4 inches (10 cm) in diameter. Brush the edges of the dough with water. Place about 1 tablespoon of filling in the center of each. Fold the dough in half over the filling to form a half-moon and pinch to seal, fluting the edges, if you like, or crimp the edges with a fork.

Meanwhile, pour oil to a depth of 1 inch (2.5 cm) into a heavy frying pan over medium-high heat and heat to 350°F (180°C) on a deep-frying thermometer. Place a few *empananditas* in the hot oil, being careful not to crowd the pan, and fry, using tongs to turn as needed, until crisp and well browned on all sides, 3–5 minutes total. Transfer to paper towels to drain. Repeat to fry the remaining *empananditas*. Serve warm or at room temperature.

From the black pepper–spiked dough to the spicy corn and pea filling, these bite-sized fried empanaditas are influenced by cultures around the world—from Europe and Africa to Central America. Any seasonal vegetables can be substituted, and the sturdy crust holds up to a variety of fillings.

Shredded Chicken Flautas

The secret to making these long rolled tacos is the *raspadas*, tortillas that have had the top layer literally rasped off and discarded, before they are wrapped around a tasty filling and fried until crisp. If time is a concern, omit this step and simply use regular corn tortillas. The flautas can be filled up to 45 minutes before frying, if wrapped in plastic wrap and kept at room temperature.

To make the filling, place the chicken in a large saucepan and add 4 cups (32 fl oz/1 l) water and the ¼ onion. Bring to a boil, reduce the heat to medium, cover, and simmer until the chicken is cooked through, 15–20 minutes. Remove the chicken and set aside to cool, reserving the broth for another use. Shred the meat, discarding the skin and bones.

In a frying pan over medium heat, warm the oil. Add the chopped onion, chiles, and garlic and sauté just until softened, about 3 minutes. Raise the heat to medium-high, add the tomato, and cook, stirring occasionally, until the color of the tomato deepens and the excess moisture is absorbed, 10–15 minutes longer. Remove from the heat and stir in the shredded chicken and salt to taste. Set aside.

If making the *raspadas* (see Note), heat a hot, dry *comal*, griddle, or heavy frying pan over low heat. Place a tortilla on it and allow it to just dry out, 3–5 minutes; do not allow it to brown. Remove from the pan and immediately use a table knife to scrape and then pull off the top layer of the tortilla, which should puff up, making it easier to scrape. Repeat to rasp off the tops of the remaining tortillas.

To fry the tortillas, pour about 3 tablespoons oil into a deep, heavy frying pan over medium-high heat. When the oil is hot but not smoking, pass each tortilla briefly through it, turning once. Transfer to absorbent paper to drain.

To form each *flauta*, put a large spoonful of the filling along the center of a tortilla, roll it up tightly, and secure with a wooden toothpick placed almost horizontally.

Add oil to a depth of 1 inch (2 cm) into the same frying pan and place over medium-high heat until hot. Working in batches, add the *flautas* to the oil and fry, turning several times to cook evenly, until lightly browned and crisp, about 2 minutes. Using tongs, lift the *flautas* out of the oil, allowing any excess oil to run off, and lean them against a pan on absorbent paper so they can completely drain. Keep warm in a low oven while frying the rest of the flautas.

Line a serving platter with the cabbage, if using, then top with the *flautas*. Drizzle with the avocado salsa and *crema*. Garnish with the radishes, if using, and serve the chile salsa on the side. Serve right away.

FOR THE FILLING

2 bone-in chicken breasts

¼ white onion plus ½ cup (2 oz/60 g) chopped white onion

1 tablespoon safflower or canola oil

3 serrano chiles, seeded and chopped

1 clove garlic, minced

1 large, ripe tomato, finely chopped, or 1 can (7 oz/220 g) diced tomatoes, drained

Sea salt

FOR THE TORTILLAS

12 purchased thin corn tortillas, 6–7 inches (15–18 cm) in diameter

Canola oil for frying

FOR SERVING

2 cups (6 oz/185 g) thinly shredded cabbage, seasoned with the juice of 1 lime (optional)

Avocado-Tomatillo Salsa (page 273)

1 cup (8 fl oz/250 ml) Crema (page 277) or sour cream

12 radishes, sliced (optional)

Pasilla and Árbol Chile Salsa (page 274)

MAKES 6 SERVINGS

Potato and Ham Croquetas

Salt and freshly ground black pepper

2 lb (1 kg) russet potatoes, peeled and cut into 2-inch (5-cm) chunks

2 large eggs, beaten

2 tablespoons minced fresh flat-leaf (Italian) parsley

½ teaspoon cayenne pepper

⅓ cup (2 oz/60 g) all-purpose (plain) flour

⅓ cup (2 oz/60 g) minced cooked ham

2 green (spring) onions, white and tender green parts, thinly sliced

¼ cup (1 oz/30 g) finely diced provolone or Swiss cheese

2 cups (8 oz/250 g) unseasoned dried bread crumbs

Vegetable oil for frying

MAKES ABOUT 20 *CROQUETAS*

Bring a saucepan three-fourths full of water to a boil over high heat. Add 1 teaspoon salt to the boiling water and stir to dissolve. Reduce the heat to medium, add the potatoes, and cook until tender when pierced with the tip of a sharp knife, 25–30 minutes.

Drain the potatoes in a colander and return to the warm pan. Place over medium-low heat and stir to steam-dry the potatoes, about 2 minutes. Pass through a ricer or use a fork or potato masher to mash the potatoes in the saucepan until smooth. Add the eggs, parsley, ½ teaspoon black pepper, and the cayenne and stir to mix well. Beat in the flour. Taste and adjust the seasoning.

In a bowl, toss together the ham, green onions, and cheese. Place the bread crumbs in a deep bowl. To make the *croquetas*, dampen your hands with water. Scoop up about ⅓ cup (2½ oz/75 g) of the potato mixture with your hand and pat with your palms to flatten it into a patty about 3 inches (7.5 cm) in diameter. Cup your hand slightly, then place about ½ tablespoon of the ham mixture in the center of the patty. Gently fold up the edges of the patty to enclose the filling, and roll the *croqueta* between your palms to give it a round shape. Roll the *croqueta* in the bread crumbs to coat thoroughly on all sides and place on a plate. Repeat to make the remaining *croquetas*. (If you prefer, gently flatten the *croquetas* into thick patties before frying.)

Pour oil to a depth of 1 inch (2.5 cm) into a heavy saucepan over medium-high heat and heat to 350°F (180°C) on a deep-frying thermometer. Place a few *croquetas* in the hot oil, being careful not to crowd the pan, and fry, using tongs to turn as needed, until crisp and well browned on all sides, 5 minutes total. Transfer to paper towels to drain. Repeat to fry the remaining *croquetas*. Serve hot, or let cool for 5–10 minutes and serve warm.

Fat, golden *croquetas* are like Cuban fritters, typically made with a pepper-laced potato dough. They are delicious when stuffed with a savory combination of meat and cheese, although myriad versions exist. In these classic *croquetas*, tiny bits of ham swim in melted cheese, a mixture that is brightened by the herbal notes of parsley and green onion. The bread crumbs and potato keep the filling moist and the crust extra crisp.

Shredded Beef Sopes

All over Mexico, these *sopes* are made on large wood-fired griddles and handed out to market-goers while still steaming hot. You'll know a *sope* from a tortilla or *arepa* by its rim, which is traditionally formed with bare hands while the dough is cooking. Experienced cooks let the masa cook on one side, then, quickly pinching up the sides and rotating the dough, they form the rim that holds in the filling. In this version, the lightly cooked dough is removed from the pan before the rim is created; be careful not to cook the dough too much at first, or it will be difficult to shape.

To make the *sopes*, place the masa harina in a bowl and add ½ teaspoon salt, the ⅓ cup (3 fl oz/80 ml) oil, and 1¾ cup (14 fl oz/430 ml) lukewarm water. Using your fingers, mix to form a soft dough that is not sticky. Divide into 12 equal balls. Cover the lower surface of an opened tortilla press with a sheet of plastic wrap that extends beyond its edges and place the dough ball in the center. Cover the dough with another sheet of plastic wrap. (Alternatively, use a plastic storage bag, cut down the sides, with the bottom left intact.) Lower the top and push down gently. The *sope* should form a circle about 4 inches (10 cm) in diameter.

Warm a heavy frying pan or griddle over medium-high heat. Open the tortilla press and peel off the top sheet of plastic wrap. Using the bottom sheet, lift the *sope* from the press and turn it over onto your hand. Peel off the bottom sheet. Gently place the *sope* on the preheated surface. Cook until the edges begin to dry out, about 45 seconds. Turn and cook the second side until lightly browned, about 45 seconds. Remove from the heat and, while still warm, pinch up the sides to form a ¼-inch (6-cm) rim. Repeat to form 12 *sopes*.

Pour about 2 tablespoons oil into the pan, just to coat the bottom. Working with 2–3 *sopes* at a time, return them to the pan, flat side down, and continue to fry until golden brown, 1–2 minutes. Flip the *sopes* and fry on the rim side for another minute to brown. Transfer the cooked *sopes* to a plate and cover with a kitchen towel until all the *sopes* are ready.

Just before serving, preheat the pan or griddle over medium-high heat. Working in batches, place the *sopes* on the hot surface and drizzle lightly with some of the oil. They are warmed through when the oil begins to sizzle. Transfer to individual plates and top with the meat, cheese, and one or more of the salsas, and serve right away.

FOR THE SOPES

3 cups (15 oz/470 g) masa harina (page 21)

Salt

⅓ cup (3 fl oz/80 ml) canola oil, plus oil for drizzling and frying

FOR SERVING

Shredded Beef (page 275)

1 cup (5 oz/155 g) crumbled *queso fresco*

Avocado-Tomatillo Salsa (page 273)

Roasted Tomato Salsa (page 273)

MAKES 12 *SOPES*

Soups and Salads

About Soups and Salads

The bounty of fruits and vegetables that grow in the Caribbean, Mexico, and Central and South America have generated a rich tradition of delicious soups and fresh salads that range from simple weekday fare to elegant dishes perfect for holiday occasions and get-togethers.

Soup is an indispensable first course for the substantial midday meal, when Latin Americans sit down together at the family table. The soups for these meals tend to be light, broth-based dishes, as there are always more courses to come. On other occasions, rich and hearty stewlike soups can serve as meals by themselves, accompanied by tortillas or bread.

Although a variety of fruits and vegetables are grown throughout Latin America, ample tossed green salads are something that seldom graces Latin American tables. Salads are usually thought of as an accompaniment to the main course, and are typically composed of citrus fruits; vegetables such as cactus and jicama; crumbled or shaved cheese; and seeds, such as pumpkin. However, because green salads have grown in popularity, they have begun to appear on modern Latin menus with ingredients such as hearts of palm, avocado, chiles, and pumpkin seeds. The salads in this chapter draw on this contemporary trend.

LIGHT AND HEARTY SOUPS

First-course soups in the Caribbean run a range of styles from earthy Cuban black bean soup sprinkled with chopped red onion, cilantro, and a dash of rum, to more delicate soups lightened with cream, like creamy pumpkin soup *(puré de calabaza)*. Perennial favorites also include broth-based soups such as Puerto Rico's *caldo de pollo*, a flavorful chicken broth with bite-sized plantain dumplings. On hot days, Caribbean cooks prepare refreshing chilled soups made with avocado or mango. Renowned main-course soups include a hearty white bean, potato, ham, chorizo, and collard green soup *(caldo gallego)* with roots going back to early Spanish settlers. *Ajiaco*, Cuba's national dish is a stewlike soup that combines a whole history's worth of different meats and vegetables.

In Mexico, Yucatecan-style chicken soup with lime *(sopa de lima)* is light and delicious, but unless you like a lot of spice, be careful not to eat the sliver of habanero chile that is often used as a garnish. Along the Pacific coast, chilled fresh coconut soup, typical of the state of Colima, is the perfect beginning to a meal of grilled fresh shrimp *al ajillo* (sautéed with garlic). Mexican entrée soups include *pozole*, from Jalisco, made with hominy, pork, garlic, onions, and red or green chiles, and Baja California's *sopa de mariscos*, a recipe that calls for fresh fish, clams, shrimp, crab, and lobster.

In Central America, *caldos*—flavorful soups based on well-seasoned broth and studded with meat or chicken and cooked rice—are popular everywhere, and puréed black or red bean soups represent timeworn and revered traditions.

South Americans are soup aficionados. Venezuelans and Brazilians each have their own version of black bean soup that is similar to the Cuban version, but with a hint of sweetness from the addition of orange juice and a kick of spice from hot red chiles. When preparing cream soups, cooks in South America add coconut milk to enrich the soup instead of cream—a substitution that produces wonderful shrimp, avocado, and plantain soups. The chowders *(chupes)* of Ecuador, Peru, and Bolivia may be made with fresh corn, peanuts, pumpkin, or shrimp and may be served as a first course or a light main course. In Argentina, Uruguay, Paraguay, and Chile, *locros*—thick, chunky soups made with *mote* (corn similar to hominy), beans, winter squash, potatoes, and sometimes meat—are often served as a main course.

SALADS, LATIN AMERICAN—STYLE

Fruit is a big part of the diet in Latin America, which also includes a variety of vegetables. However, the Latin American idea of a salad is not one that is centered around greens as it is in other cultures. In Cuba, a "fresh salad" often means sliced tomatoes and mild white onions drizzled with vinegar and olive oil.

In Mexico, fresh salads are more popular. *Xec*, a Yucatecan specialty prepared for the long, elaborate, and hugely festive Day of the Dead holiday in November, is made with crisp jicama and juicy sweet orange sections and sprinkled with lime juice, ground red chile, and chopped cilantro.

Pickled vegetables and cooked vegetable salads are also popular throughout Latin America. *Ensalada rusa*, cooked vegetables dressed in a mayonnaise sauce, is often served as an appetizer. In Argentina and Uruguay, where many people are of Italian ancestry, salads made with semolina pasta are often served as a side dish, and in Peru, where such a great variety of potatoes grow, a wonderfully spicy mashed potato salad, called *causa,* is usually presented as a separate course.

Black Bean, Corn, and Quinoa Salad

This delicious salad, very similar to Mediterranean tabbouleh, is a staple throughout the Andean region. Quinoa, one of the ancestral Inca and Chibcha Indian crops, and is harvested from Colombia to Argentina in the higher Andean plains. Quinoa is prized for its earthy yet delicate flavor, as well as its nutritional value. The medley of the Peruvian corn with glossy black beans, pale gold quinoa, and red tomatoes and bell pepper make this an eye-catching and colorful salad.

To make the dressing, in a bowl, whisk together the lime juice, vinegar, cilantro, *ají* paste, oregano, ½ teaspoon salt, and ½ teaspoon pepper. Add the oil in a thin stream, whisking constantly until smooth and emulsified. Set aside.

In a saucepan over medium-high heat, combine the quinoa and 1½ cups (12 fl oz/ 375 ml) water. Stir in ¼ teaspoon salt. Cover and bring to a boil, then reduce the heat to low and simmer until the quinoa is tender and all the water has been absorbed, about 10 minutes. Transfer the quinoa to a colander and rinse under running cold water. Drain thoroughly, then transfer to a large, nonreactive bowl.

Add the black beans to the bowl with the quinoa. Pat the corn dry with paper towels and add to the bowl, along with the tomato and bell pepper. Pour in the dressing and toss to coat all the ingredients well. Transfer the salad to a large serving bowl or individual plates and serve right away.

FOR THE DRESSING

2 tablespoons fresh lime juice

3 tablespoons white vinegar

2 tablespoons minced fresh cilantro (fresh coriander)

¼ teaspoon *ají amarillo* paste (page 278)

¼ teaspoon dried oregano

Salt and freshly ground pepper

½ cup (4 fl oz/125 ml) olive oil

½ cup (4 oz/125 g) quinoa

Salt

1 cup (7 oz/220 g) drained cooked black beans (page 276), or purchased

⅔ cup (4 oz/125 g) thawed frozen corn kernels, preferably Peruvian

1 medium tomato, seeded and finely diced

1 small red bell pepper (capsicum), seeded and finely diced

MAKES 6 SERVINGS

Tortilla Soup

6 purchased thin corn tortillas

4 ancho chiles, seeded

½ cup (4 fl oz/125 ml) canola oil, or as needed

½ white onion, chopped

2 cloves garlic, peeled but left whole

1 ripe tomato, roughly chopped, or 1⅓ cups (8 oz/250 g) drained, canned chopped tomatoes

6 cups (48 fl oz/1.5 l) Chicken Stock (page 270) or low-sodium broth

4–5 fresh epazote leaves (page 279) (optional)

¼ teaspoon dried oregano, preferably Mexican

Sea salt

½ lb (250 g) *queso fresco* or Monterey jack cheese, cubed

1 avocado, pitted, peeled, and cubed

MAKES 6 SERVINGS

Set 1 tortilla aside. Cut the other tortillas in half and then cut crosswise into strips ½ inch (12 mm) wide. Let them dry for 5–10 minutes. In a bowl, soak 1 chile in hot water for 10–15 minutes. Cut the other chiles lengthwise into narrow strips about 1 inch (2.5 cm) long.

In a frying pan over medium-high heat, warm 6 tablespoons (3 fl oz/90 ml) of the oil. When hot, add the tortilla strips and fry, tossing, until crisp and golden on both sides, just a few seconds. Using a slotted spoon, transfer to paper towels to drain. Fry the chile strips very quickly in the same oil—again for just seconds—then remove and drain on paper towels.

Discard all but 1 tablespoon of the oil in the frying pan. Warm the oil over medium-low heat, add the onion and garlic, and sauté until a rich golden brown, about 10 minutes. Transfer to a blender or food processor. Drain the soaking chile, discarding the liquid. Tear up the chile and the remaining tortilla and add to the blender or food processor with the tomato. Purée until smooth, adding up to ¼ cup (2 fl oz/60 ml) water if needed to achieve a smooth consistency.

In a Dutch oven or other large, heavy pot over medium-high heat, warm 1 tablespoon of the oil. Add the purée and fry, stirring continuously, until the sauce has deepened in color, about 5 minutes. Stir in the broth and the epazote, if using, and simmer to blend the flavors, about 15 minutes. Add the oregano and season to taste with salt at the end of the cooking.

When ready to serve, divide half of the tortilla strips among warmed bowls, then ladle the hot soup into the bowls. Top with the remaining tortilla strips, the cheese, chile strips, and the avocado. Serve right away.

This soup, with its layers of flavors and textures, is the ultimate one-dish meal. The earthy tomato-chile broth thickened with a corn tortilla is a hearty, satisfying base for a variety of toppings, such as cheese, avocado, and toasted chile. If you can't find fresh epazote, many Mexican markets sell dried epazote or you can omit it. If using the dried herb, enclose about 1 teaspoon in a tea ball so that it's easy to remove after cooking.

Caesar Salad with Chipotle Chile Dressing

Although there are many stories explaining the origins of this salad, it is widely believed that the classic Caesar salad, consisting of romaine leaves and croutons tossed in a dressing of Parmesan cheese, lemon juice, olive oil, egg, Worcestershire sauce, and black pepper, was first created by an Italian-born cook, Césare Cardini, who lived in Tijuana, Mexico. This modern version accentuates the salad's Mexican heritage with the addition of chipotle chiles in the dressing, chile-dusted croutons, and *queso añejo* cheese on top.

To make the croutons, preheat the oven to 350°F (180°C). In a large bowl, combine the oil, chile powder, ½ teaspoon salt, and ½ teaspoon pepper. Add the bread cubes to the bowl and toss to coat. Spread the bread cubes on a baking sheet and bake, turning once or twice, until golden, about 15 minutes. Remove the bread cubes from the oven and let cool on the baking sheet.

To make the dressing, in a blender, combine the egg, if using, the garlic, lime juice, chipotle chile and adobo sauce, ½ teaspoon salt, and ½ teaspoon pepper. Blend until mixed well, then with the motor on low speed, slowly drizzle in the oil to make a thick dressing.

To serve family style, transfer the dressing to a large salad bowl. Add the lettuce leaves and three-fourths of the croutons to the bowl with the dressing and mix to coat the leaves thoroughly with the dressing. Top with the remaining croutons. Scatter the cheese over the salad and serve right away.

For individual servings, divide the lettuce leaves among salad plates, drizzle the dressing over the leaves, and top with some of the croutons and cheese.

NOTE This dish contains raw egg. If you have health and safety concerns, omit the egg. For more information, see page 279.

FOR THE CROUTONS

3 tablespoons canola oil

½ teaspoon ancho chile powder

Salt and freshly ground pepper

2 cups (4 oz/125 g) cubed sourdough or other coarse country bread, cut into 1-inch (2.5-cm) cubes

FOR THE DRESSING

1 large egg (optional); see Note

3 cloves garlic, peeled

3 teaspoons lime juice

1 canned chipotle chile in adobo sauce, plus 2 teaspoons adobo sauce

⅓ cup (3 fl oz/80 ml) canola oil

2 hearts romaine (cos) lettuce, separated into leaves

Queso añejo (page 278) or **Parmesan cheese shavings**

MAKES 4–6 SERVINGS

Black Bean Soup

3 cups (21 oz/655 g) dried black beans

1 bay leaf

1 ham bone or ham hock

2 tablespoons olive oil

2 yellow onions, chopped

1 red bell pepper (capsicum), chopped

4 cloves garlic, minced

1 tablespoon ground cumin

1 teaspoon dried oregano

1/2 teaspoon ground cinnamon

1/8 teaspoon ground cloves

2–3 tablespoons fresh lime juice, strained

1 teaspoon hot-pepper sauce, such as Tabasco, or more to taste

Salt and freshly ground pepper

FOR SERVING

Chopped fresh cilantro (fresh coriander)

Chopped red onion

Crema (page 277) or sour cream

MAKES 8 SERVINGS

Pick over the beans and discard any misshapen beans or stones. Rinse the beans under cold running water, drain, and place in a saucepan. Add water to cover and bring to a boil over high heat. Boil for 2 minutes, then remove the beans from the heat, cover, and let stand for 1 hour.

Drain the beans and return to the saucepan. Add 8 cups (64 fl oz/2 l) water, the bay leaf, and the ham bone. Bring to a boil over high heat. Cover partially, reduce the heat to low, and simmer.

Meanwhile, in a large frying pan over medium heat, warm the oil. Add the onions and bell pepper and sauté, stirring occasionally, until the vegetables are tender and the onions are translucent, about 10 minutes. Add the garlic, cumin, oregano, cinnamon, and cloves and cook, about 2 minutes longer. Add the onion mixture to the beans and simmer until very tender, 1–1½ hours; the timing will depend upon the age of the beans.

Remove the soup from the heat. Remove the ham bone and bay leaf and discard. Working in batches, purée the soup in a blender (or pass through a food mill). Return the soup to a clean saucepan and season with the lime juice, hot pepper sauce, ½ teaspoon salt, and ¼ teaspoon pepper. Gradually reheat over medium heat, stirring often to prevent scorching. Thin with 1–2 cups (8–16 fl oz/250–500 ml) water if the soup is too thick, then taste and adjust the seasonings.

Ladle the soup into warmed individual bowls. Top each serving with the cilantro, red onion, and *crema*, and serve right away.

In this soup, black beans, a staple of Latin American cooking, are simply cooked in water and aromatics until tender, then puréed to make a creamy, warming soup that's filling enough for a meal, especially when served with warmed tortillas. The soup is also the perfect canvas for an array of toppings. Besides the garnishes at left, you can add diced avocado, shredded cheese, and pass hot pepper sauce at the table for seasoning.

Pozole

Pozole refers to both the dish itself and the large corn kernels which are softened in a lime solution to make hominy. This pork and hominy soup is made all over Mexico with slight variations. You can turn this into *pozole verde* by replacing the tomatoes with tomatillos. Traditionally made with partially cooked hominy (*nixtamal*), this modern version uses drained and rinsed canned white hominy.

In a soup pot over medium heat, warm the oil. Working in batches if necessary to avoid overcrowding, add the pork and sauté until opaque on all sides but not browned, about 3 minutes per batch. Transfer the meat to a bowl and set aside.

Add the onion to the same pot and sauté until softened, 3–5 minutes. Add the garlic, chili powder, cumin, and oregano and cook, stirring to blend the spices evenly, about 1 minute longer.

Add the stock, tomatoes, hominy, jalapeño chile, sautéed pork with any juices, and salt and pepper to taste, and bring to a boil over high heat. Reduce the heat to low, cover, and simmer until the pork is cooked through and the soup is fragrant, about 15 minutes.

Ladle the soup into warmed bowls and garnish with the avocado slices and green onions; serve right away with the lime wedges and warm tortillas alongside.

2 tablespoons corn or canola oil

1 lb (500 g) pork tenderloin or pork shoulder, cut into ¹/₂-inch (12-mm) pieces

1 yellow onion, finely chopped

3 cloves garlic, minced

1¹/₂ tablespoons chili powder

¹/₂ teaspoon ground cumin

¹/₂ teaspoon dried oregano

3 cups (24 fl oz/750 ml) Chicken Stock (page 270) or low-sodium broth

1 can (14¹/₂ oz/455 g) diced fire-roasted tomatoes, with juice

1 can (15 oz/470 g) white hominy, rinsed and drained (see Note)

1 jalapeño chile, seeded and diced

Salt and freshly ground pepper

FOR SERVING

Avocado slices

Sliced green (spring) onions

Lime wedges

Warm corn tortillas, homemade (page 276), or purchased

MAKES 4 SERVINGS

Jicama, Grapefruit, and Avocado Salad

2 small jicama (about 1 lb/500 g)

1 ruby red grapefruit

1 large avocado

FOR THE DRESSING

2 tablespoons fresh lime juice

1 tablespoon fresh orange juice

2 teaspoons honey

Pinch cayenne pepper

Salt

¼ cup (⅓ oz/10 g) fresh cilantro (fresh coriander) leaves

MAKES 4–6 SERVINGS

Cut each jicama in half and, using a peeler or a sharp knife, remove the peel. Place the jicama halves cut side down on a cutting board, and cutting lengthwise, cut ¼-inch (6-mm) slices off the jicama. Stack the slices in piles of 3 or 4 and cut each stack in half crosswise at ¼-inch (6-mm) intervals to create matchsticks. If some of the matchsticks seem too long, cut them in half. Place the matchsticks in a serving bowl.

Cut the ends off the grapefruit to expose the flesh and stand it upright on a cutting board. Following the curve of the fruit, cut away all the peel and the bitter white pith. Continue in this fashion, working your way around the fruit. Working over a bowl, make a cut on both sides of each segment to free it from the membrane, letting the segment and juice drop into the bowl below. Reserve 2 tablespoons of the grapefruit juice for the dressing.

Cut the avocado in half lengthwise and remove the pit. Using a paring knife, score each avocado half by cutting parallel lines just down to the peel, then turn 90 degrees and cut another set of parallel lines perpendicular to the first ones. Scoop the avocado squares into the bowl with the jicama and grapefruit.

To make the dressing, in a small bowl, stir together the reserved grapefruit juice, the lime juice, orange juice, honey, cayenne, and season to taste with salt. Mix well to dissolve the honey completely. Pour about half of the dressing over the salad and toss gently. Taste, then add more dressing, if necessary, and adjust the seasoning with more salt, if necessary.

Transfer the salad to a serving platter or individual bowls or plates, garnish with the cilantro leaves, and serve right away.

Jicama salads are popular throughout Mexico and South America, especially during the warm-weather months. In this salad, the jicama and grapefruit are refreshing and light, while the avocado adds a satisfying creaminess. A simple dressing of citrus juice and a pinch of cayenne completes the salad, which is the perfect accompaniment to Fish or Carnitas Tacos (pages 120 and 150).

Mixed Greens with Hearts of Palm, Red Onion, and Avocado

Hearts of palm and avocado, two popular ingredients in South America, are combined in this vibrant, fresh salad. You can use other lettuces, such as red or green butter (Boston) lettuce, endive, arugula (rocket), or baby spinach, or a combination of lettuces. Serve this salad as a starter course before *Grilled Chicken with Chimichurri* (page 149), and finish with *Orange–Passion Fruit Cake* (page 264).

To make the dressing, in a small bowl, whisk together the lime juice, ½ teaspoon salt, ¼ teaspoon pepper, the olive oil, and 1 tablespoon of the minced cilantro.

In a large bowl, toss the greens with the 1 cup (1 oz/30 g) cilantro. Drizzle the dressing over the greens and toss to coat the greens evenly with the dressing.

Cut the avocados in half lengthwise and remove the pits. Working with one half at a time, and using a paring knife, cut parallel lines in the avocado flesh, cutting just down to the peel. Use a large spoon to scoop the avocado slices into a bowl.

Rinse the hearts of palm and pat dry with paper towels. Cut each heart of palm crosswise into ½-inch (12-mm) slices.

To serve, divide the dressed greens among individual plates and top each serving with some of the sliced avocado, hearts of palm, and onion. Serve right away.

FOR THE DRESSING

2 tablespoons fresh lime juice

Salt and freshly ground pepper

2 teaspoons extra-virgin olive oil

3 tablespoons minced fresh cilantro (fresh coriander), plus 1 cup (1 oz/30 g) lightly packed whole leaves

6–8 cups mixed baby greens

2 avocados

½ red onion, thinly sliced

1 can (14 oz/440 g) hearts of palm, drained

MAKES 6 SERVINGS

Corn and Roasted Poblano Soup

8 cups (64 fl oz/2 l) whole milk

2 tablespoons cumin seeds

1–2 chipotle chiles, coarsely chopped

2 bay leaves

1 large fresh rosemary sprig or ½ teaspoon dried rosemary

2 tablespoons unsalted butter

2 tablespoons olive oil

2 large yellow onions, diced

Salt

4–6 cloves garlic, minced

2 teaspoons ground cumin

Kernels cut from 8 ears of corn (about 8 cups/ 3 lb/1½ kg) (page 206)

6–7 large poblano chiles, roasted, peeled, seeded (page 268), and diced

6 green (spring) onions, including about 2 inches (5 cm) of green, finely chopped

MAKES 6 SERVINGS

Pour the milk into a heavy saucepan. In a small, dry frying pan over high heat, toast the cumin seeds, shaking the pan constantly until they are aromatic and begin to change color, about 4 minutes. Remove from the heat and immediately add to the milk. Add the chipotle chiles, bay leaves, and rosemary and place over low heat. Cover and bring to a gentle simmer; do not allow to boil. Remove from the heat and let stand, covered, about 20 minutes.

Meanwhile, in a stockpot over medium heat, melt the butter with the olive oil. Add the onions and 2 teaspoons salt and sauté, stirring, until the onions are soft and golden brown, 15–20 minutes. Reduce the heat to medium-low, add the garlic and ground cumin, and sauté, stirring constantly, until aromatic, about 5 minutes. Stir in the corn and poblano chiles, and continue to cook until the corn is lightly browned, about 5 minutes.

Using a fine-mesh sieve, strain the milk into the corn mixture. Bring to a gentle simmer and continue to simmer until the flavors have melded, about 15 minutes. Remove from the heat and let cool, about 5 minutes.

In a food processor, purée one-third of the soup. Return the purée to the stockpot, stirring well. If necessary, place over low heat to reheat gently. Taste and adjust the seasonings. Ladle the soup into warmed soup bowls, garnish with the green onions, and serve right away.

Roasting the poblano chiles to give them a mellower, sweeter taste is one of the secrets to making this robust soup. The other secret is to steep the cumin seeds, bay leaves, rosemary, and chipotle chiles in warm milk to infuse the milk with their flavors. The result is a soup that is earthy and complex, yet light and fresh. Serve with tortilla chips for enjoying alongside or crumbling on top.

Cucumber, Cilantro, and Jalapeño Salad

This simple, light, and refreshing salad is punctuated with heat from the slivered jalapeño chiles and tanginess from soft goat cheese. Serve alongside grilled fish or chicken for a delicious and healthy meal.

Peel the cucumbers and cut them in half lengthwise. Use a teaspoon to scrape out the seeds. Cut crosswise into half moons about ¼ inch (6 mm) thick.

In a nonreactive bowl, combine the cucumbers, cilantro, and chile. Sprinkle with ½ teaspoon salt and add the lime juice and oil. Stir to mix well, then let stand to allow the flavors to blend, about 30 minutes.

When ready to serve, transfer the salad to individual serving bowls or plates. Crumble the goat cheese on top, dividing it evenly. Serve right away.

2 medium cucumbers or 1 English (hothouse) cucumber

1 cup (1½ oz/45 g) coarsely chopped fresh cilantro (fresh coriander)

1 red or green jalapeño chile, seeded and very thinly sliced

Salt

¼ cup (2 fl oz/60 ml) fresh lime juice, strained

2 tablespoons canola oil

4–6 oz (125–180 g) soft goat (goat's milk) cheese

MAKES 4 SERVINGS

Shrimp, Pumpkin, and Corn Chowder

1½ tablespoons olive oil

½ large yellow onion, diced

2 tablespoons *ají panca* paste (page 278)

1 teaspoon *ají amarillo* paste (page 278)

2 cloves garlic, minced

Salt

4 cups (32 fl oz/1 l) Fish Stock (page 271), warmed

4 cups (32 fl oz/ 1 l) Shellfish Stock (page 270), warmed

½ small pumpkin such as Sugar or Sugar Pie, peeled, seeded, and diced (about 2 cups/1 lb/500 g)

3 yellow potatoes, about 1½ lb (750 g) total weight, peeled and cut into ½-inch (12-cm) pieces

1 or 2 ears corn, husks and silk removed, cut crosswise into 6 pieces

1 cup (5 oz/155 g) fresh or thawed frozen green peas

2 lb (1 kg) medium shrimp (prawns), peeled and deveined

Cooked white rice (optional)

2 teaspoons unsalted butter

6 small chicken eggs or quail eggs

MAKES 6 SERVINGS

In a soup pot over medium heat, warm the olive oil. Add the onion and cook, stirring often, until softened, about 3 minutes. Add the *ají* pastes, the garlic, and 1½ teaspoons salt and stir to mix well. Sauté until fragrant, about 2 minutes. Pour in the warm fish and shellfish stocks, add the pumpkin, and stir to mix well. Cover, raise the heat to medium-high, and bring to a boil. Reduce the heat to medium-low and simmer, partially covered, until the pumpkin is tender, about 20 minutes.

When the pumpkin is tender, remove the soup from the heat and let cool slightly. If you like a thicker soup, using a slotted spoon, transfer half or up to all of the pumpkin to a blender or food processor and process until smooth, then return to the pot. Work in batches, if necessary, and be careful of the hot pumpkin splattering. (Alternatively, use an immersion blender to mash some or all of the pumpkin in the pot until the soup is the desired thickness.) Add the potatoes and cook for 5 minutes, then add the corn and peas and cook until the vegetables are tender, about 10 minutes longer. Using a potato masher, or immersion blender, break up some of the potatoes to thicken the soup further, if you like. Add the shrimp to the pot and cook until opaque throughout, 3–5 minutes.

While the shrimp are cooking, gently reheat the rice over medium heat in the saucepan you cooked it in, or in a microwave-safe bowl in the microwave. In a large frying pan over medium heat, melt the butter. Lift and tilt the pan to coat the bottom with the butter. Carefully crack the eggs into the pan, in batches if necessary, cover, and fry until the yolks film over and set slightly but are still soft. Remove from the heat.

To serve, place some of the rice, if using, in each of 6 warmed bowls, or serve the rice on the side. Ladle the soup into the bowls and carefully slide a fried egg on top. Serve right away.

Chupe de camarones, affectionately known as just *chupe,* is the most famous of all Peruvian chowders. Regional cooks select from the wide variety of indigenous *ajís,* or chile peppers, that grow in Peru. You can find some of these peppers fresh in your local Latin or gourmet produce market or online, or peruse those same sources for the many high-quality and authentic pastes of these spicy peppers available in jars. For more on *ají* pastes, see page 278.

Nopales Salad

Nopales, the paddles of the cactus plant, are widely used in a variety of preparations in Mexico. They are often sliced or chopped and added to soups, stews, and salads, or stirred in with rice, beans, and eggs. The cactus becomes slimy when boiled, so it is important to wash it under running water as soon as it is tender. You can also add a little baking soda or a copper coin to the cactus while it cooks to reduce the slimy effect.

To prepare the *nopales*, use a sharp paring knife or vegetable peeler to scrape off the stickers and their "bumps." Cut off the base end and trim the outer edges. Cut into strips ¼ inch (6 mm) wide, then into pieces about 1 inch (2.5 cm) long.

Bring a large saucepan three-fourths full of water to a boil. Add the *nopales,* the thick slice of onion, garlic cloves, tomatillo husks, and 1 teaspoon salt. Reduce the heat to medium and cook at a slow boil until the *nopales* are tender but still green, 5–10 minutes, depending on the age of the paddles. Drain and quickly place under running cold water to remove the slimy residue and stop the cooking. Remove the onion, garlic, and husks from the saucepan, and discard. Shake the *nopales* to remove as much moisture as possible and put in a bowl.

To make the salad, add the thinly sliced onion, oregano, lime juice, and Worcestershire sauce to the bowl holding the *nopales.* Then whisk in just enough of the olive oil to bind the ingredients. Season to taste with salt and gently mix in the toasted chiles. Allow the salad to stand for at least 10 minutes. (The salad can be prepared 3–4 hours ahead and refrigerated. Bring to room temperature before serving.)

Just before serving, add the cilantro and tomato and toss to combine. Spoon onto a serving platter or individual plates, and serve at once.

7 small fresh nopales

1 thick slice of white onion, plus 1 small onion, thinly sliced

2 cloves garlic, peeled but left whole

10 tomatillo husks or 1 teaspoon baking soda (sodium bicarbonate)

Sea salt

1 teaspoon dried oregano, preferably Mexican

Juice of 1 lime or 1 tablespoon mild vinegar, or to taste

1 teaspoon Worcestershire sauce

¼ cup (2 fl oz/60 ml) olive oil

3 árbol chiles, toasted and crushed (page 268)

1 cup (1½ oz/45 g) chopped fresh cilantro (fresh coriander)

1 large, ripe tomato or 4 plum (Roma) tomatoes, finely diced

MAKES 6 SERVINGS

Pumpkin Soup with Cilantro-Ginger Picadillo

FOR THE *PICADILLO*

1½ tablespoons minced fresh cilantro (fresh coriander)

1½ tablespoons seeded and minced red bell pepper (capsicum)

1½ tablespoons fresh lime juice

1½ tablespoons minced green (spring) onion

1 teaspoon minced pickled ginger

⅛ teaspoon seeded and minced habanero chile

½ teaspoon sugar

Salt and freshly ground black pepper

1 tablespoon olive oil

1 small pumpkin such as Sugar or Sugar Pie (about 2 lb/1 kg)

4 cups (32 fl oz/1 l) Chicken or Vegetable Stock (page 270), or low-sodium broth

1 large yellow onion, quartered

1 clove garlic, chopped

1 teaspoon peeled and grated fresh ginger

Sea salt and freshly ground white pepper

4–6 tablespoons (2–3 oz/60–90 g) Crema (page 277) or sour cream

MAKES 4–6 SERVINGS

Sweet cooking pumpkins, called *ahuyama* or *zapallo* in Colombia and in other regions, are one of the most loved and frequently used indigenous foods in all of Latin America. Pumpkin is used for soups, side dishes, breads, and sometimes tamales. This recipe is an updated version of a traditional soup garnished with a signature Colombian *picadillo*, a zesty pepper-and-onion salsa.

To make the *picadillo*, in a bowl, stir together the cilantro, bell pepper, lime juice, green onion, pickled ginger, habanero, sugar, 1 teaspoon salt, ¼ teaspoon black pepper, and olive oil. Let stand at room temperature to allow the flavors to blend for at least 1 hour or until ready to serve.

Cut the pumpkin in half. Scoop out the seeds and discard. Using a sharp knife and following the contours of the squash, cut off the skin. Cut the flesh into ½-inch (1-cm) chunks. You should have about 3½ cups (20 oz/625 g).

In a soup pot over medium heat, combine the pumpkin, stock, yellow onion, garlic, grated ginger, 1 teaspoon salt, and a pinch of white pepper. Bring to a boil and cook, stirring occasionally, until the pumpkin is tender, about 15 minutes. Remove from the heat and let cool slightly. Working in batches, transfer the soup to a blender or food processor and process until smooth. Alternatively, use an immersion blender to process the soup in the pot until smooth.

Return the soup to the pot, if necessary, and reheat gently over medium heat. Taste and adjust the seasoning. Garnish each serving with about 1 tablespoon of the *picadilllo* and 1 tablespoon *crema*. Serve hot, passing the remaining *picadillo* at the table.

Watercress-Orange Salad with Toasted Pumpkin Seeds

Although leafy green salads aren't always easy to come by in Mexico, watercress is a popular addition to citrus salads. The peppery bite of watercress pairs well with the bright, sweet taste of oranges. Pepita seeds, or pumpkin seeds, often ground and used in mole sauces (see page 161), are also delicious when toasted and sprinkled over salads.

In a small bowl, toss the pumpkin seeds with the 1 teaspoon olive oil and the cumin. Spread the pumpkin seeds in a dry frying pan over medium heat and cook, stirring constantly, just until they begin to darken, about 5 minutes. Transfer the seeds to a plate to cool.

To make the dressing, in a small bowl, whisk together the lime juice, chile, 1 teaspoon salt, and ¼ teaspoon pepper. Pour in the ⅓ cup (3 fl oz/80 ml) olive oil in a thin, steady stream, whisking constantly, until thoroughly emulsified.

Working with 1 orange at a time, cut a slice off the top and the bottom to reveal the flesh. Place the orange upright on the cutting board and, using a sharp knife, cut down along the sides, removing all the white pith and membrane. Cut the orange in half vertically then cut each half crosswise into slices ¼ inch (6 mm) thick. Repeat with the remaining 2 oranges. Place the orange slices in a bowl, add the watercress, and toss to mix.

Just before serving, drizzle the dressing over the watercress mixture. Taste and adjust the seasoning with salt. Divide the salad among serving plates, sprinkle each serving with the toasted pumpkin seeds, and serve right away.

¼ cup (2 oz/57 g) pumpkin seeds

1 teaspoon extra-virgin olive oil

1 teaspoon ground cumin

FOR THE DRESSING

¼ cup (2 fl oz/60 ml) fresh lime juice, strained (from about 2 limes)

1 jalapeño chile, thinly sliced and seeded

Sea salt and freshly ground pepper

⅓ cup (3 fl oz/80 ml) extra-virgin olive oil

3 navel oranges

2 bunches watercress, about ½ lb (250 g) total weight, large stems removed

MAKES 6 SERVINGS

Fish and Shellfish

About Fish and Shellfish

With coastline in the Caribbean, along the Gulf of Mexico and the Gulf of California (also known as the Sea of Cortez), and both the Pacific and Atlantic Oceans, Latin America is rich in ocean fish and shellfish. Inland, lakes and rivers also provide a wide variety of freshwater seafood.

CARIBBEAN FISH SPECIALTIES

In the Caribbean, fish and seafood play a central role in the region's cooking. Regional dishes showcase the catch of local waters and include Mexico's grilled sea bass with adobo rub, chiles, lime, and avocado; Cuba's paella, made with Caribbean spiny lobster, scallops, shrimp, chicken and chorizo; Dominican fish in coconut sauce *(pescado con coco)*; shrimp sautéed in olive oil with garlic, fresh lime juice, and cilantro *(camarones al ajillo)* in Puerto Rico; and any catch of the day served with a bright mango salsa.

BOLD FLAVORS IN MEXICO

In Mexico, many regional specialties draw on the bounty of the seas and streams. Baja California is renowned for crispy fish tacos and spicy shellfish dishes like mussels steamed in beer and tequila with jalapeños. Further down the Pacific coast, in the state of Jalisco, a simple but elegant local specialty is shrimp sautéed with onions, garlic, chiles, and orange zest, then flamed with tequila and sprinkled with fresh cilantro. Veracruz, the beautiful colonial port city on the Gulf coast, is world famous for its preparation of red snapper with a spicy Creole-style tomato, olive, and caper sauce. Mexico also has loads of prized freshwater fish. Trout from the mountain streams of Oaxaca are delicious served simply or stuffed with onion, garlic, lime, and herbs and sautéed; classic accompaniments are a piquant sauce made with tomatillos, Oaxacan avocados, onions, and cilantro.

ABUNDANCE IN CENTRAL AMERICA

Along the isthmus of Central America's coasts, there is an abundance of saltwater fish and seafood, but visitors are often surprised to find that there also volcanic mountains with lakes and streams that supply freshwater fish. Ceviche, made with fish and shellfish, is a specialty in Panama, at the narrowest point on the isthmus; and in the mountains of Guatemala, Mayan cooks rub bass or catfish with pumpkin-seed *recado* (seasoning), stuff them with tomatoes, cilantro, and chiles, and bake them wrapped in banana leaves.

VARIETY IN SOUTH AMERICA

From Venezuela to the tip of Chile, there is wonderful seafood in South America. Fish dishes in Venezuela reflect the cooking traditions of early Catalan settlers, including the country's national dish, *el corbullón mantuano,* which is fish simmered in a sweet pepper sauce with capers, olives, and cornmeal dumplings. In Colombia and Ecuador and along the northern coast of Brazil, an African influence is seen in fish and shellfish dishes prepared with coconut milk and spices. Brazilians are also fond of salted dried cod *(bacalhau),* an ingredient that goes back to Portugal, where it is used in many dishes, from mashed potatoes to olive oil or tomato sauces to lobster stew.

While Argentines and Uruguayans may love their beef, when they vacation at the beach resorts of Mar del Plata and Punta del Este, seafood reigns supreme. Brochettes of tiny, tender squid scent the air when grilled over wood fires at restaurants along the beach. Served with a cooling tomato-avocado salsa and peppery black beans, this dish makes a quintessential seaside lunch.

Throughout South America, fish fillets are prepared *en escabeche*, a cooking technique with ancient Mediterranean roots in which the fish is fried or poached and then marinated for a long time in a spicy vinaigrette. In Peru, escabeche is seasoned with hot Andean hot peppers *(ajíes)* and the dish is garnished with boiled potatoes, slices of corn on the cob *(choclo),* black olives, and sliced hard-boiled eggs. Peru is also famous for ceviche *(cebiche),* another ancient fish and seafood preparation that involves a marinade. This technique for "cooking" fish and seafood in citrus juice is thought to have originated in Peru, although it is popular all along the Pacific coast.

Steaming has been used to prepare fresh seafood for thousands of years along the Pacific Coast in Peru and Chile. It is a method that remains popular today, and is not only easy to prepare, but also very healthful. In Chile, the indigenous Mapuche prepare *curanto,* a kind of clambake, roasting with steam much as their ancestors did. Lima's cutting-edge chefs, practitioners of *la nueva cocina Andina* (the New Andean Cuisine), steam fish seasoned with lime juice and hot peppers *(ajíes)* and folded up in banana leaves.

Over the last five hundred years, ingredients and cooking methods from other continents have blended with the bounty of fish and seafood from local waters to create dishes with a uniquely Latin American point of view. Whether cooked whole or filleted, wrapped in banana leaves and roasted or marinated and grilled, there are recipes in this chapter for every taste and occasion.

Shrimp with Orange and Tequila

This coastal dish from Mexico pairs plump sweet shrimp with a bright orange-chile sauce. It's so simple and quick—perfect for weeknight meals. A squeeze of lime juice adds another level of flavor to the seasoned rice.

With a zester or vegetable peeler, cut the zest from the orange in very narrow strips, being careful to avoid any of the bitter white pith. If the strips are too wide, cut them lengthwise into ¼-inch (6-mm) strips.

Bring a saucepan of water to a boil over high heat. Place the orange strips in a small sieve, and plunge them into the boiling water. Remove immediately and rinse under running cold water. Repeat three times to remove the bitter taste. Pat the orange strips dry with paper towels.

In a frying pan over medium heat, melt the butter. Add the onion and sauté until translucent, 3–4 minutes. Add the garlic and shrimp and cook, stirring frequently, until the shrimp turn pink and begin to curl, 4–5 minutes. Add the chipotle chile and orange strips to the pan, stirring briefly to mix. Pour the tequila over the shrimp, carefully ignite with a long match, and let the flames burn out.

Remove from the heat, stir in the cilantro, and season to taste with salt. Spoon the rice onto a warmed platter or individual plates and top with the shrimp and some of the remaining sauce from the pan. Serve right away.

1 navel orange

6 tablespoons (3 oz/90 g) unsalted butter

2 tablespoons finely chopped white onion

2 cloves garlic

16 large shrimp (prawns), peeled and deveined, with tail segment intact

1 chipotle chile in adobo or 2 serrano chiles, finely chopped

¼ cup (2 fl oz/60 ml) *tequila reposado*

3 tablespoons coarsely chopped fresh cilantro (fresh coriander)

Sea salt

Seasoned White Rice (page 271) for serving

MAKES 4 SERVINGS

Chile-Marinated Sea Bass

4 skinless sea bass fillets, each about 6 oz (185 g) and 1½ inches (4 cm) thick

2 large yellow onions, thinly sliced

2 large ripe tomatoes, thinly sliced

½ cup (2½ oz/75 g) seeded and thinly sliced *ají dulce* peppers (page 278) or sweet Italian peppers

¼ cup (2 fl oz/60 ml) fresh lime juice

2 tablespoons olive oil, plus more for brushing

2 tablespoons Worcestershire sauce

2 tablespoons minced green (spring) onions

2 cloves garlic, thinly sliced

2 bay leaves

Salt and freshly ground black pepper

5–10 large banana leaves, prepared (see page 269)

2 habanero or scotch bonnet chiles, cut into thin strips (optional)

Coconut Rice (page 272) for serving

MAKES 4 SERVINGS

Preheat the oven to 450°F (230°C). Rinse the fish fillets and pat them dry.

In a shallow baking pan or dish, combine the onions, tomatoes, *ají dulce* peppers, lime juice, the 2 tablespoons olive oil, Worcestershire sauce, green onions, garlic, bay leaves, 1 teaspoon salt, and ½ teaspoon black pepper and stir to mix well. Place the fish fillets in the pan and spread the onion mixture all over the fish. Set aside to marinate at room temperature for 30 minutes, or cover and refrigerate for up to 2 hours.

With scissors, and using 2–3 of the plantain leaves, cut out 4 rectangles that are slightly larger than the dimensions of the fish fillets.

Place a whole plantain leaf on a work surface. Place the cut leaf rectangle over the whole leaf, centering it crosswise. If the whole leaf is not wide enough to accommodate the length of the cut rectangle, place a second (whole) leaf alongside and overlapping it. Brush the leaves with olive oil.

Center a fish fillet on the rectangle of plantain leaf. Spoon some of the vegetable mixture from the pan on and around the fish, discarding the bay leaves. Tuck the chile strips on top, if using. Lift the 2 ends of the whole plantain leaf (leaves) and line up the edges in the center, over the fish. Beginning where the leaves meet, begin to fold the joined leaves down in the same direction. Fold them together once or twice, working downward toward the fish, then tuck the ends under the fish. Tie the bundle securely with kitchen twine. Repeat to wrap the remaining fish in the banana leaves.

Place the bundles on a baking sheet and bake for 10–15 minutes. Remove the bundle from the oven and open a corner gently to test for doneness with the tip of a knife. The fish should flake easily and be opaque throughout. Serve right away with the coconut rice.

South Americans have been cooking food in plantain leaves for centuries. Sometimes the bundle is placed over a wood fire and sometimes it is simmered in buried clay pots, a technique employed by the early Andean Indians who fished and farmed in the region. A wrapper of plantain leaves helps hold in moisture and imparts a delicate, grassy flavor. You can find fresh or frozen banana leaves in Latin and Asian markets.

Cuban-Style Paella

The keys to making a perfect paella are the right rice and the right pan. Use a good-quality domestic long-grain white rice or imported Spanish short-grain rice (don't use short-grain Asian rice as it tends to be far too sticky and glutinous). The pan should be wide and shallow, with sloping sides, so the rice cooks correctly. *Paelleras* are often sold at Latin markets and are available online. A large, shallow, ovenproof frying pan may be used instead.

In a small saucepan, gently warm the wine; do not let boil. Add the saffron and remove from the heat. Set aside and let steep for 1 hour.

Position a rack in the lower third of the oven and preheat to 350°F (180°C). In a *paellera* or large, ovenproof pan, warm 1 tablespoon of the olive oil over medium-high heat. Add the chicken and cook, turning as needed, until golden brown on all sides, about 10 minutes. Sprinkle with ¼ teaspoon salt and transfer to a plate. Reduce the heat to medium.

Add the onion and bell pepper to the pan and cook, stirring often, until softened, about 2 minutes. Crumble the oregano over the onion mixture, then stir in the cumin, tomatoes, red pepper flakes, paprika, and bay leaf. Sauté until the spices are fragrant and most of the liquid has evaporated, about 5 minutes. Transfer the mixture to a bowl and set aside.

Add 1 tablespoon of the remaining olive oil to the pan and set over medium heat. When the oil is hot, add the rice and sauté until golden, 3–5 minutes. Stir in the 1 cup (8 oz/250 g) of the onion mixture and sauté for 30 seconds. Add the reserved wine and the chicken stock and stir to mix well. Arrange the chicken on top of the rice. Place in the oven and bake, uncovered, for 15 minutes.

Remove the paella from the oven. In a large sauté pan over medium-high heat, warm the remaining 1 tablespoon olive oil. Add the chorizo and garlic and sauté until the oil turns reddish in color. Add the shrimp, lobster, and scallops and cook, stirring, until the seafood is almost opaque throughout, 3–4 minutes. Stir in the remaining onion mixture.

Remove the chicken from the paella and set aside on a plate. Stir the seafood mixture gently into the rice. Discard the bay leaf. Arrange the chicken drumettes on top in a circle pattern, like the spokes of a wheel, and fit the lobster pieces in between. Lay a pimiento slice over each drumette.

Return the paella to the oven and bake until all the liquid has been absorbed, about 5 minutes longer. Remove from the oven and cover with a clean kitchen towel. Let rest at room temperature for at least 10 minutes or up to 30 minutes before serving. Serve warm or at room temperature with the lemon wedges.

½ cup (4 fl oz/125 ml) dry white wine

1 teaspoon saffron threads

3 tablespoons olive oil

8 chicken wing drumettes

Salt

1 white onion, diced

½ green bell pepper (capsicum), seeded and diced

1 teaspoon *each* dried oregano and ground cumin

2 plum (Roma) tomatoes, diced

½ teaspoon *each* red pepper flakes and Spanish paprika

1 bay leaf

1½ cups (10½ oz/330 g) long-grain white rice

2½ cups (20 fl oz/625 ml) Chicken Stock (page 270) or low-sodium broth

¾ cup (3 oz/90 g) thinly sliced dry chorizo

4 large cloves garlic, minced

8 medium shrimp (prawns), peeled and deveined, with tails intact

1 large lobster tail (about 1 lb/500 g), shells removed, cut into 1-inch (2.5-cm) chunks

4 large sea scallops, halved crosswise

8 jarred red pimiento slices, drained

1 lemon, cut into 8 wedges

MAKES 4–6 SERVINGS

Fish Tacos

FOR THE BEER BATTER

1 cup (5 oz/155 g) all-purpose (plain) flour

1 teaspoon garlic salt

¹/₂ teaspoon ground _árbol_ chile (page 268) or cayenne pepper

1 cup (8 fl oz/250 ml) beer, preferably dark

FOR THE CREAMY SAUCE

¹/₃ cup (3 fl oz/80 ml) mayonnaise

¹/₃ cup (3 oz/90 g) ketchup

¹/₃ cup (3 oz/90 g) plain yogurt

FOR THE TACOS

¾ lb (375 g) red snapper or sea bass fillet

1 teaspoon fresh lime juice

¹/₂ teaspoon garlic salt

¹/₄ teaspoon ground _árbol_ chile or cayenne pepper

Canola oil for frying

8 white corn tortillas, about 6 inches (15 cm) in diameter

FOR SERVING

Salsa Fresca (page 273)

Finely shredded cabbage

8 lime quarters

Bottled hot pepper sauce for serving

MAKES 8 TACOS

To make the beer batter, in a bowl, stir together the flour, garlic salt, and ground chile. Pour in the beer, whisking until smooth. Cover and let stand for at least 10 minutes and up to 1 hour.

Meanwhile, make the creamy sauce. In a small bowl, stir together the mayonnaise, ketchup, and yogurt until blended. Set aside.

To make the tacos, remove the skin from the fish fillet if it is still intact and run your fingers over the fillet to check for and remove any embedded bones, using tweezers or needle-nose pliers if necessary. Cut the fish into 8 strips, each 3–4 inches (7.5–10 cm) long and ¾ inch (2 cm) wide, and place in a nonreactive bowl. Sprinkle with the lime juice, garlic salt, and ground chile and toss to mix. Let marinate at room temperature for 10 minutes. Pour the oil to a depth of 1 inch (2.5 cm) into a heavy pan with tall sides and heat to 375°F (190°C) on a deep-frying thermometer.

Meanwhile, heat a _comal,_ griddle, or heavy frying pan over medium heat. When it is hot, stack 2–3 tortillas on the heated surface and leave for a few seconds. Flip the tortillas, rotating them every second or so until all are hot. Wrap in a dry kitchen towel and repeat with the remaining tortillas. They should keep warm for about 10 minutes. If they are to be held longer, wrap a damp towel around the dry towel and place in a 200°F (95°C) oven.

Pat the fish dry with paper towels. One at a time, dip a strip into the batter, allowing the excess to drip off, and slip into the hot oil. Do not allow the pieces to touch. Fry until the strips are crisp and golden, about 7 minutes. Using a slotted spatula, transfer to paper towels to drain. When all are fried, transfer to a warmed serving plate. Put the _salsa fresca_, cabbage, and lime quarters in separate small bowls and set on the table along with the fish, creamy sauce, tortillas, and hot pepper sauce. Let the diners make their own tacos, wrapping the fish in a tortilla and adding the other ingredients.

Fish tacos are eaten up and down the coast of Mexico, often accompanied by a margarita or cold beer. They are prepared differently depending on where you are. In Veracruz, corn tortillas are stuffed with fresh shredded fish and served with cabbage and _salsa fresca_. This recipe is inspired by Baja-style fish tacos. The fish is cut into strips and then fried in a light beer batter and served in corn tortillas with a creamy sauce, _salsa fresca_, shredded cabbage, and lime wedges.

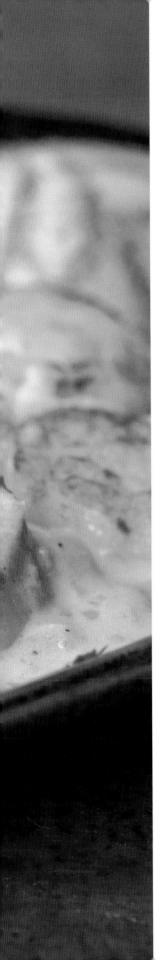

Scallops with Coconut, Chile, and Lime

Scallops are eaten throughout South American countries in a variety of preparations that reflect the continent's heritage, from Europe to Asia. This recipe is a mélange of staple ingredients from the coastal and *criollo* regions of Latin America—scallops, *ají* pepper, small green *criollo* limes, and achiote paste; lemongrass from Asia; and a sauce of wine and *beurre manié* adopted from the kitchens of French immigrants.

In a large frying pan over medium-low heat, warm 1 tablespoon of the olive oil. Add the onion, lemongrass, 1 teaspoon salt, ½ teaspoon black pepper, the chile, and the achiote and cook until the onion is translucent, about 5 minutes.

Meanwhile, in a small bowl, beat together the flour and butter to make a paste.

Add the garlic to the pan and sauté until fragrant, about 2 minutes. Push the contents of the frying pan to the sides and raise the heat to medium. Add the remaining 1 tablespoon olive oil to the center of the pan and warm, then place the scallops in the hot oil and sear, turning once, just until lightly golden on both sides, about 1 minute per side. Transfer the scallops to a plate.

Add the butter-flour paste to the pan and melt, then pull the ingredients in from the sides of the pan and cook, stirring to coat and mix well, for 2 minutes. Pour in the stock and coconut milk, raise the heat to medium-high, and bring to a simmer. Cook, stirring occasionally, to allow the flavors to blend and the mixture to thicken slightly, about 10 minutes. Stir in the lime juice and wine, then return the scallops to the pan. Cover and cook until the scallops are opaque throughout, 5–7 minutes. Ladle the scallops and broth into a warmed shallow serving dish or individual bowls, garnish with the cilantro, and serve right away.

2 tablespoons olive oil

1 small yellow onion, diced

6 lemongrass stalks, tender midsection only, smashed with the side of a chef's knife and minced (about 3 tablespoons)

Salt and freshly ground black pepper

¼ Scotch bonnet or habanero chile, seeded and minced

½ teaspoon achiote paste (page 278) or annatto oil

1 tablespoon all-purpose (plain) flour

1 tablespoon unsalted butter, at room temperature

1 clove garlic, minced

2 lb (1 kg) sea scallops

1½ cups (12 fl oz/375 ml) Shellfish Stock (page 270)

1 cup (8 fl oz/250 ml) unsweetened coconut milk

¼ cup (2 fl oz/60 ml) fresh lime juice, preferably *criollo*

¼ cup (2 fl oz/60 ml) dry white wine

3 tablespoons coarsely chopped fresh cilantro (fresh coriander)

MAKES 4 SERVINGS

Veracruz-Style Red Snapper

8 large cloves garlic

2 teaspoons fresh lime juice

Sea salt

6 skinless red snapper fillets, about 5–6 oz (155–185 g) each

FOR THE SAUCE

¼ cup (2 fl oz/60 ml) olive oil, plus oil for greasing

1 large white onion, thinly sliced

4 large cloves garlic, minced

3 lb (1.5 kg) ripe tomatoes, roasted and peeled (page 268), and finely chopped

20 small green pimiento-stuffed (sweet pepper–stuffed) olives, quartered

½ cup (¾ oz/20 g) coarsely chopped fresh flat-leaf (Italian) parsley leaves

3 bay leaves

3 pickled jalapeño chiles, cut lengthwise into strips, with 1 tablespoon pickling liquid

1 tablespoon capers

½ teaspoon *each* dried oregano, marjoram, and thyme, or 4 fresh sprigs *each*

Sea salt and freshly ground pepper

MAKES 6 SERVINGS

Using a mortar and pestle, mash the garlic to a paste and transfer it to a small bowl, or squeeze it through a garlic press. Add the lime juice and ½ teaspoon salt and mix well.

Place the fish fillets on a large plate or in a baking dish. Rub the garlic mixture over both sides of each fillet. Rub the inside and outside of the fish with the garlic mixture. Wrap the fish in plastic wrap and let it marinate in the refrigerator for at least 30 minutes or up to 2 hours, turning occasionally for even coating.

Preheat the oven to 350°F (180°C). To make the sauce, in a large, heavy frying pan over medium heat, warm the olive oil. Add the onion and sauté until soft, about 4 minutes. Add the garlic and continue cooking until golden, 1–2 minutes. Raise the heat to medium-high, add the tomatoes, and continue cooking, stirring frequently, until the sauce thickens, 5–7 minutes. Reduce the heat to low and stir in the olives, parsley, bay leaves, chiles and pickling liquid, and capers. Add the oregano, marjoram, and thyme and season to taste with pepper. Simmer, stirring occasionally, until the flavors are well blended, 8–10 minutes.

Lightly oil a large glass or ceramic baking dish. Unwrap the fish, place it in the dish, and spoon the sauce evenly over the top, discarding the bay leaves. Bake, basting occasionally with the sauce, just until the flesh is opaque throughout when tested in the thickest part, about 8–10 minutes. Serve directly from the baking dish or, using 2 spatulas, carefully transfer to a warmed platter.

Veracruz is a raucous port city on the Gulf of Mexico where seafood of all sorts is eaten morning, noon, and long into the night. The most famous of all of the city's dishes combines the silver-tinged, red-skinned snapper caught in local waters with an equally colorful sauce. When a dish is described as "a la Veracruzana," it refers to this thick, herbaceous tomato sauce studded with olives and capers that originated in Spain.

Trout with Avocado Sauce

Wild trout thrive in the mountain streams of Mexico, where they are often stuffed with herbs before cooking. The flavor of trout is delicate, but it stands up well to the bold flavors from the aromatics and can be pan-fried or wrapped in corn husks and roasted or grilled. A uniquely Mexican ingredient is dried avocado leaf, which has been used there as a flavoring for millennia. It has a mild licorice scent and flavor. If you can't find the dried leaves, fresh tarragon is a good substitute.

Rinse the trout and pat dry, inside and out. Season inside and out with salt and pepper. Stuff the cavities with the red onion, sliced garlic, sliced lime, and half of the cilantro sprigs, dividing all the ingredients evenly.

To toast the avocado leaves, using tongs, hold a leaf 2 inches (5 cm) above the flame of a gas burner on the stove top, passing each side quickly over the flame a few times until it turns a uniform brighter green. (If using an electric range, hold the leaf 4–6 inches/10–15 cm above the heat source.) Repeat to toast the second leaf. Crumble the toasted leaves into the cavities of the fish, dividing them evenly (or add 1 tarragon sprig to each). Close the trout. Cut 12 pieces of kitchen twine and tie each trout 3–4 times around the belly, gently but securely.

To make the avocado sauce, remove the papery husks from the tomatillos and rinse under running warm water to remove the sticky residue on the skins. Chop the tomatillos coarsely. In a blender or food processor, combine the tomatillos, avocado, onion, garlic, cilantro, and 1 teaspoon salt and process to a smooth purée, stopping to scrape down the sides of the blender jar or work bowl as needed. Add ¼ cup (2 fl oz/60 ml) water and pulse to combine. Add more water if you like a thinner sauce. Taste and adjust the seasoning.

In a large frying pan over medium heat, warm the oil. Spread the flour out on a large plate. When the oil is hot, lightly dredge each trout in the flour and lay it in the pan. Cook until golden brown on the first side, about 7 minutes. Using tongs or 2 spatulas, carefully turn the fish and cook until the skins are golden on the second side and the flesh is opaque throughout, about 7 minutes longer. Serve the trout on individual plates and pass the avocado sauce, rice, and lime wedges.

VARIATION Wrap the stuffed trout in soaked corn husks. Tie with strips of the corn husk and grill the fish directly over a hot fire for 7 minutes per side.

4 whole boned trout, about 6 oz (185 g) each, cleaned, with heads intact or removed

Salt and freshly ground pepper

¼ cup (1 oz/30 g) thinly sliced red onion

2 cloves garlic, thinly sliced

2 limes, thinly sliced

½ bunch fresh cilantro (fresh coriander), tough stems removed

2 dried avocado leaves (page 278) or 4 long sprigs fresh tarragon

3 tomatillos

1 large ripe avocado, pitted, peeled, and cut into chunks

1 tablespoon minced white onion

1 clove garlic, chopped

¼ cup (⅓ oz/10 g) chopped fresh cilantro (fresh coriander)

2 tablespoons vegetable oil

¼ cup (1½ oz/45 g) all-purpose (plain) flour

FOR SERVING

Cooked white rice

Lime wedges

MAKES 4 SERVINGS

Grilled Squid
with Spicy Black Beans

2 tablespoons olive oil, plus more for brushing

1 small clove garlic, minced

½ teaspoon dried Mexican oregano

Coarse sea salt and freshly ground black pepper

1 lb (16 oz/500 g) cleaned small squid, preferably extra-small *chipirones*

FOR THE BEANS

1 tablespoon olive oil

½ large yellow onion, thinly sliced

1 dry-cured chorizo sausage, about 5 inches (13 cm) long, thinly sliced

½ tomato, peeled, seeded, and diced (about ½ cup/ 3½ oz/105 g)

1 clove garlic, minced

¼ teaspoon seeded and minced habanero chile

½ teaspoon ground cumin

Salt and freshly ground black pepper

1¼ cups (10 oz/315 g) cooked black beans (page 276), drained, or purchased beans, rinsed and drained

Tomato-Avocado Salsa (page 273)

MAKES 4–6 SERVINGS

Soak four 8-inch (20-cm) bamboo skewers in water to cover for 30 minutes.

In a baking dish, combine the 2 tablespoons olive oil, garlic, oregano, ½ teaspoon sea salt, and ½ teaspoon black pepper and stir to mix well. Set aside. If the squid are larger than 1½ inches (4 cm) long, make cuts on the bodies of the squid just to score the flesh; do not cut through the body of the squid. Drain the skewers. Thread the squid lengthwise onto the skewers, dividing them evenly. Place the assembled skewers in the baking dish and turn to coat with the olive-oil mixture. Set aside and let marinate at room temperature for at least 15 minutes.

To make the beans, in a sauté pan over medium heat, warm the olive oil. Add the onion and chorizo and cook, stirring often, until the onion is translucent and the chorizo is lightly browned, about 5 minutes. Add the tomato, garlic, habanero, cumin, ½ teaspoon salt, and ½ teaspoon black pepper and cook until the tomato is tender and begins to break down, about 10 minutes. Add the beans and cook, stirring occasionally, until almost all of the liquid is absorbed and the mixture is the consistency of a thick sauce, about 10 minutes longer. Cover to keep warm until ready to serve.

Build a fire in a charcoal grill for direct grilling over high heat, or preheat a gas grill to high (see page 269). Generously oil the grill rack and position it 2–4 inches (5–10 cm) above the coals.

When the coals are very hot, arrange the skewers on the grill rack directly over the coals and, working quickly, grill just until the squid turns opaque and is nicely grill marked, up to 2 minutes per side.

To serve, spoon the beans onto a platter and arrange the squid and onions on top. Serve right away with the salsa.

Squid comes in many sizes, but the preferred type for this recipe is the diminutive *chipirone*, perhaps the smallest squid in the sea. Cooked quickly over very hot coals, they become meltingly tender. The versatile salsa can be made without the avocado, if you like, and is delicious with beef and other grilled meats like those that sizzle on a typical Argentinean *asadero*, or grill.

Stuffed Snapper in Coconut Curry

Stuffed fish is very popular along the Caribbean coast of South America. The technique and its repertoire has evolved from a cultural mix that includes the ancestry of Spanish elegance and style; a bounty of native seafood; and a fusion of Latin and African flavors and seasonings, as with the coconut and sweet *aji* peppers here. A buried treasure of succulent lobster tail and shrimp within each tender whole fish makes this dish an impressive centerpiece for entertaining.

Preheat the oven to 400°F (200°C). Line a roasting pan with aluminum foil and lightly grease the foil.

In a large saucepan over medium-low heat, melt the butter with the 1 tablespoon olive oil. Add the *aji dulce* peppers, green onions, curry powder, 1 teaspoon salt, and ½ teaspoon black pepper and sauté until the onions are softened, about 5 minutes. Add the garlic and cook for 1 minute. Sprinkle in the flour and cook for 1 minute longer, stirring with a wooden spoon to blend well and scraping up any browned bits from the bottom of the pan.

Raise the heat to medium-high and add the coconut milk, stock, bay leaves, and lobster tail in its shell. Bring to a boil, reduce the heat to medium, and simmer for 5 minutes. Add the shrimp and cook for 2 minutes longer. Remove from the heat. Take the lobster tail out of the mixture and set aside until cool enough to handle. Cut the meat into ½-inch (12-mm) dice and return it to the shrimp mixture. Stir to mix. With a slotted spoon, remove about 1 cup (8 oz/250 g) total of the shrimp and diced lobster for filling the fish and set aside the rest of the shellfish mixture.

Rinse the fish and pat it dry. Using a sharp knife, make 3 deep, diagonal cuts across both sides of the fish, about 1½ inches (4 cm) apart. Be sure to cut all the way to the bone. Rub 1 teaspoon salt on the fish, pushing it into the cuts and inside the cavity. Place the fish in the prepared pan. Divide the reserved 1 cup shellfish mixture between the cavities of the fish, arranging it evenly along the length and filling the cavity generously but not so much that it interferes with closing the fish. Close the fish neatly over the stuffing; it does not have to be tied.

Bake the stuffed fish for 20 minutes. Reduce the oven temperature to 350°F (180°C) and pour the remaining shellfish mixture over the fish, discarding the bay leaves. Bake until the fish is almost opaque throughout, 15–25 minutes longer, depending on the size of the fish. Serve right away.

1 tablespoon unsalted butter

1 tablespoon olive oil, plus more for greasing

¼ cup (1½ oz/45 g) seeded and minced *aji dulce* peppers (page 278) or sweet Italian peppers

3 green (spring) onions, white and tender green parts, thinly sliced

1 teaspoon curry powder

Salt and freshly ground black pepper

2 cloves garlic, thinly sliced

2 tablespoons all-purpose (plain) flour

1¾ cups (14 fl oz/430 ml) coconut milk

1 cup (8 fl oz/250 ml) Shellfish Stock (page 270)

2 bay leaves

1 large lobster tail, about ¾ lb (750 g) total weight

1½ lb (750 g) medium shrimp (prawns), peeled and deveined

2 whole red snappers, 1½–2 lb (750–1 kg) each, cleaned and scaled, with head and tail intact

MAKES 6 SERVINGS

Grilled Fish with Adobo Rub

FOR THE ADOBO

2 cloves garlic, minced

Salt

¼ cup (2 fl oz/60 ml) tomato sauce

1 tablespoon achiote paste (page 278)

1 tablespoon ancho chile powder

1 teaspoon dried Mexican oregano, crumbled

2 tablespoons fresh lime juice

4 skinless firm-fleshed white fish fillets such as sea bass, halibut, or striped bass about 6 oz (185 g) each

1 jalapeño chile, seeded and cut into thin strips

¼ small red onion, thinly sliced

Vegetable oil for brushing

2 tablespoons chopped fresh cilantro (fresh coriander)

FOR SERVING

Corn tortillas

1 avocado, pitted, peeled, and thinly sliced

Cilantro sprigs

Lime wedges

MAKES 4 SERVINGS

To make the adobo, in a mortar, combine the garlic and ½ teaspoon salt. Using a pestle, and working in a circular motion, grind them together until a paste forms. Alternatively, combine the garlic with the salt on a cutting board. Using a large knife, alternately chop and, using the side of the knife, press and smear the garlic until a paste forms. Transfer the garlic paste to a bowl. Add the tomato sauce, achiote paste, chile powder, oregano, and lime juice and stir until smooth.

Place the fish fillets in a large, shallow dish and, using about 1 tablespoon of the adobo per fillet, spread the adobo on both sides of the fish to coat in a thin, even layer. (Reserve the remaining adobo for another use. Store in an airtight container in the refrigerator for up to 3 weeks, or freeze for up to 3 months.) Scatter the chile and onion evenly over one side of the fish fillets and press firmly to help them adhere to the adobo. Refrigerate the fish, uncovered, for 30 minutes.

Build a fire in a charcoal grill for direct grilling over medium-high heat, or preheat a gas grill to medium-high (see page 269). Generously oil the grill rack and position it 2–4 inches (5–10 cm) above the coals. Alternatively, lightly oil a fish basket and place the fish fillets inside. Secure the basket.

Grill the fish, chile side down, until the adobo is well cooked and nicely grill marked, 5–7 minutes. Using a long, sharp-edged spatula, carefully loosen the fish from the grill and turn. If using a grill basket, turn the basket and grill on the second side until the fish is opaque throughout, about 5 minutes longer.

Meanwhile, place the tortillas on the edges of the grill or in a low oven until just warmed through and still soft. Wrap in a kitchen towel or aluminum foil to keep warm and place in a basket.

Turn the fish again, chile side down, and grill just to rewarm the adobo, about 1 minute longer. Transfer to a warmed platter. Top each fillet with a few avocado slices and cilantro sprigs. Serve at once with the lime wedges on the side.

Pescado zarandeado is a specialty of the Mexican Pacific coast. Typically, a whole fish weighing 5–6 lb (2.5–3 kg) is butterflied, then rubbed with an adobo spice paste, studded with hot chiles and onions, and grilled over a mesquite fire. The fish is cooked in a grill basket so it can be turned easily several times during the cooking (*zarandeado* means "turned" or "spun"), then placed on a platter, strewn with cilantro sprigs and avocado slices, and served family style with warm corn tortillas and a bucket of cold beers with limes. A whole fish looks terrific, but the fillets called for here are easier to handle; a grill basket is still recommended.

Beer-Steamed Mussels with Cilantro

Mussels are prepared in a similar fashion throughout the world: quickly steamed in liquid, such as wine, and aromatics, such as herbs or garlic, until they open. This recipe uses beer and tequila as the steaming liquids and fresh cilantro and lime as bright accents to give the dish a uniquely Mexican character.

In a deep pot with a tight-fitting lid, over medium-high heat, warm the olive oil. Add the garlic and chile(s) and sauté until soft, about 3 minutes. Add the beer and tequila and bring the liquid to a boil. Add the mussels, discarding any that fail to close to the touch. Cover and return the liquid to a boil. Cook until the mussels open, 4–5 minutes. Remove the pot from the heat and, using a slotted spoon, divide the cooked mussels among warmed wide, shallow bowls, discarding any that failed to open. Spoon the broth remaining in the pot into the bowls.

Sprinkle some of the cilantro over each serving, dividing it evenly. Serve with the lime wedges, squeezing a few over the mussels, and warm tortillas, if desired, for sopping up the juices.

1 tablespoon olive oil

2 cloves garlic, minced

1–2 jalapeño chiles, seeded and minced

1 cup (8 fl oz/250 ml) light Mexican beer, such as Corona, Pacifico, or Modelo Especial

¼ cup (2 fl oz/60 ml) tequila

3 lb (1.5 kg) mussels, scrubbed and debearded

3 tablespoons chopped fresh cilantro (fresh coriander)

FOR SERVING

Lime wedges

Corn tortillas, homemade (page 277) or purchased (optional)

MAKES 4 SERVINGS

Fish Escabeche

1 tablespoon olive oil

1 large yellow onion, thinly sliced

3 cloves garlic, minced

2 tablespoons *ají panca* paste (page 278)

2 tablespoons lime juice

2 bay leaves

1 teaspoon sugar

1/8 teaspoon ground cumin

Salt and freshly ground pepper

1/2 cup (4 fl oz/125 ml) *each* red wine vinegar and Fish Stock (page 271)

Olive oil for frying

3 tablespoons all-purpose (plain) flour

6 firm-fleshed white fish fillets such as halibut, 6 oz (185 g) each

6 yams, peeled, each yam cut into 4 wedges

1 cup (8 fl oz/250 ml) fresh orange juice

4-inch (10-cm) piece cinnamon stick

FOR SERVING

1 ear corn

12 cured black olives, such as Botija or Kalamata, pitted

3 hard-boiled large eggs, peeled and sliced

MAKES 6 SERVINGS

To make the marinade, in a saucepan over medium heat, warm the olive oil. Add the onion and cook, stirring often, until translucent, about 5 minutes. Add the garlic and sauté until fragrant, about 1 minute. Add the *ají* paste, lime juice, bay leaves, sugar, cumin, 1 teaspoon salt, and 1/4 teaspoon pepper and stir to mix well. Cook for 1 minute, then stir in the vinegar and stock. Raise the heat to medium-high and cook for 2–3 minutes to allow the flavors to blend. Remove from the heat and set aside to cool.

In another saucepan over medium heat, pour olive oil to a depth of 1 inch (3 cm) and warm until the temperature reads 350°F (180°C) on a deep-frying thermometer. In a wide, shallow bowl, stir together the flour, 1/2 teaspoon salt, and 1/4 teaspoon pepper. Dredge the fish fillets in the seasoned flour to coat well. Working in batches if necessary to avoid crowding the pan, add the fillets to the hot oil and fry, turning once, until lightly golden, 2–3 minutes per side. Transfer to paper towels to drain. Place the fish in a single layer in a large, shallow dish. Pour the marinade over the fish and turn to coat. Cover with plastic wrap and refrigerate for at least 4 hours or up to 24 hours.

When ready to serve, place the yam wedges, orange juice, 1/2 teaspoon salt, and the cinnamon stick in a pot. Bring to a boil over high heat, then reduce the heat to medium and cook until fork tender, about 10 minutes.

Meanwhile, remove the husks and silk from the corn. In a small saucepan fitted with a steamer basket, bring 1 inch (2.5 cm) water to a boil. Cut the ear of corn in half and place in the basket. Cover and steam until tender-crisp, 5–8 minutes. Remove from the heat and let cool. Cut the corn crosswise into slices 3/4 inch (2 cm) thick. To serve, arrange the yams, corn, olives, and hard-boiled egg slices on one side of each plate. Place a fillet in the center of each plate and drizzle with any sauce left in the bowl, discarding the bay leaves. Serve right away.

Escabeche is a popular Latin American cooking technique in which poached or fried foods are then marinated in a tangy, vinegary sauce. Variations are distinguishable by how spicy they are: Caribbean *escabeches* are the hottest while Colombian are the mildest, with Peru somewhere in the middle. Throughout Peru, *escabeche* appears on the menu frequently in many homes and is eaten cold, and like many Peruvian foods, accompanied with hard-boiled eggs, yams, and corn on the side.

Grilled Halibut with Mango Salsa

Grilled fish with boldly flavored salsa is an ideal meal—delicious, easy to make, and healthful. You can enjoy this colorful salsa whenever mangoes are in the market, as it is flavorful even when the fruit is underripe. You can also make this recipe with 2 halibut steaks, dividing each of them in half to serve 4 people comfortably.

To make the salsa, stand the mango on one of its narrow sides, with the stem end facing you. Using a sharp knife, cut down the length of the fruit, just brushing the large, lengthwise pit. Repeat the cut on the other side of the pit. Remove the peel from each half, then finely chop the flesh. Measure out 1½ cups (9 oz/280 g).

To peel the pineapple, stand it on its base and, using a large, sharp knife, cut down the length of it, cutting deeply enough under the skin to remove all the prickly "eyes." Halve it lengthwise and cut out and discard the fibrous core from each piece. Finely chop the fruit. You should have about ¾ cup (4½ oz/140 g).

In a bowl, combine the mango, pineapple, onion, chile, and orange and lime juices. Mix in the cilantro and ¼ teaspoon salt, or more to taste. Season with pepper. Set aside for at least 20 minutes to allow the flavors to meld.

Prepare a charcoal or gas grill for direct-heat grilling over high heat (see page 269). Oil the grill rack. Season the fish on both sides with salt and pepper.

Place the fish over the hottest part of the fire or heat element and grill, turning once, until the fish is opaque in the center, 5–7 minutes per side.

Remove the skin from the fish and transfer to warmed individual plates. Spoon some of the salsa on each piece of fish and serve right away with the rice.

FOR THE MANGO SALSA

1 mango

½ small pineapple, about 1 lb (500 g)

3 tablespoons finely chopped red onion

1 serrano chile, seeded and minced

¼ cup (2 fl oz/60 ml) fresh orange juice

1 tablespoon fresh lime juice

¼ cup (⅓ oz/10 g) chopped fresh cilantro (fresh coriander) or mint

Kosher salt and freshly ground pepper

4 skin-on halibut fillets, about 6 oz (185 g) each and 1 inch (2.5 cm) thick

Cilantro Rice (page 271) for serving

MAKES 4 SERVINGS

Poultry and Meat

About Poultry and Meat

From the famed Argentinian beef served with *chimichurri* to the meat tamales of Mexico and South America to the saucy chicken stews of Guatemala and Peru, Latin America gladly adopted meats from the Old World and used them to create some of the favorite dishes of this grand cuisine.

The introduction of livestock from Europe was a major dietary change for civilizations where meat was eaten rarely. There were few domesticated animals in the New World before the arrival of the Spanish in the fifteenth century. In Mexico and Central America, turkeys were the only common farm animal, and in South America llamas, alpacas, large ducks, and guinea pigs were raised.

For most people, all of these were, at best, special-occasion foods. Llamas were used as beasts of burden and alpacas were prized for their wool. On the rare occasions that these useful animals were slaughtered, the meat was preserved for long storage by making it into jerky *(charqui)*. The jerky was carried by soldiers of the Inca armies as a high-protein food that could be eaten out of hand, boiled with water to make soups, or combined with potatoes and other tubers to make stews. *Charqui* is still used in Andean cooking today.

POULTRY IN THE NEW WORLD

The arrival of chickens from the Old World to the New World soon spurred ubiquitous dishes, and throughout Latin America chicken with rice *(arroz con pollo)* became one of the most classic. In Mexico, favorite preparations of chicken, turkey, and duck are in *moles* (complex sauces made with chiles and other seasonings) and *pipianes* (dishes served with ground pumpkin seeds sauce). In the Caribbean, chicken is often paired with tropical fruits like guava, and Guatemalans prepare chicken in a tangy tomatillo sauce enriched with fresh avocado. Peru is famous for its tasty chicken dishes; among the most delicious is *ají de gallina*, chicken simmered in a creamy cheese sauce flavored with ground walnuts and spicy golden Peruvian peppers *(ajíes)*.

THE VERSATILITY OF PORK

Since Columbus released the first pigs on the islands of the Caribbean, pork has been a favorite meat. In Cuba, people say, "It's better to have a pig in your backyard than money in the bank." If you need money, you can always sell the pig, and if there is a wedding or for a *Quinceañera* party (coming-of-age celebrations for fifteen-year-olds), you can roast it. Roast pork in Cuba is traditionally seasoned with *mojo*, a marinade made with sour orange juice, garlic, salt, and olive oil. On Mexico's Yucatan Peninsula, pork is rubbed with sour orange juice or lime juice combined with *recado colorado* (a seasoning made with annatto, the red, slightly peppery seeds of the tropical achiote tree), onion, garlic, cumin, oregano, and salt. The pork is then wrapped in banana leaves and roasted slowly in an earthen oven called a *pib*. Shredded pork is also a popular filling for tacos and tamales.

THE LOVE OF GRILLED BEEF

Cattle thrived in the great open plains and grasslands of Mexico, Venezuela, Colombia, Argentina, Uruguay, Paraguay, Chile, and Brazil, and people in these regions developed a voracious appetite for beef. In Mexico, the men who cared for the cattle were called *vaqueros*, and it was from their gear and ways of handling livestock that the American cowboy tradition evolved. When Charles Darwin visited Argentina in 1832, he was amazed to find that Argentines of all social classes ate huge amounts of red meat and very few vegetables. As people become more concerned about their health, eating habits are changing, but beef cooked *llano*-style over an open fire in Venezuela—and *asados, parilladas,* and *churrascos,* similar flame-cooking techniques and tools in other South American regions—remain part of the proud *llanero, huaso,* and *gaucho* (South American cowboy) tradition.

GOAT, SHEEP, AND LAMB

The highlands of Mexico and Central and South America are well suited to sheep and goats. In Central Mexico, kid is seasoned with salt, wrapped in agave leaves, and pit-roasted. In the highlands of Guatemala, a hearty chile- and annatto-flavored lamb soup *(caldo colorado de carnero)* is a favorite winter dish. Lamb and kid are also popular meats in South America—Venezuelans serve a popular curried goat stew, and in Colombia, lamb is braised in coconut milk and spices. Uruguayans eat grilled lamb chops with mint, and in Peru, a specialty of the mountain pueblos around Lima is a savory herb-and-chile-seasoned lamb stew *(huatía)* that is cooked underground in a tightly covered clay pot.

Old World animals have become an important part of Latin American culinary tradition, and New World animals like turkeys remain as popular as ever. You will find recipes in this chapter that reflect both heritages.

Grilled Steak with Parsley-Garlic Chimichurri

In the busy steakhouses called *parrillas* or *asaderos*, an array of grilled meats is the most popular showcase for Argentina's celebrated grass-fed beef. For the most flavorful results, buy meat with little of the fat trimmed off; most of the fat will melt away and baste the meat as it grills, leaving it remarkably juicy. You can also baste the meat as it grills with Traditional Chimichurri Sauce (page 274) and serve with Grilled Tomatoes with Chimichurri (page 193) for a memorable dinner.

Build a fire in a charcoal grill for direct grilling over high heat, or preheat a gas grill to high (see page 269). Generously oil the grill rack and place it 3–5 inches (7.5–13 cm) above the coals. Remove the steaks from the refrigerator and bring to room temperature.

Season the steaks with salt and pepper. Place the steaks on the grill rack directly over the hot coals and grill for 4–5 minutes, watching for flare-ups and moving the steaks to cooler areas of the grill as needed. Turn the steaks over and cook until nicely browned, 4–5 minutes longer for medium-rare. Transfer to a carving board, tent with aluminum foil, and let rest for 5 minutes.

While the steaks are resting, make the garlic bread: In a small bowl, stir together the garlic and the 2 tablespoons olive oil. Brush the garlic oil on one side of the bread slices. Arrange the slices on the grill rack, oiled side down, and grill until the crusts are crispy and the bread is nicely grill marked, about 1 minute. Turn and grill until toasted and marked on the second side, about 1 minute longer.

Serve the steaks drizzled with the *chimichurri*, with the garlic bread alongside.

2 tablespoons olive oil, plus oil for greasing

4 New York strip steaks, each about ¾ lb (375 g) and 1½ inches (4 cm) thick

Sea salt and freshly ground pepper

1 clove garlic, crushed in a press or smashed with the flat side of a large knife

8 slices French bread, about ¾ inch (2 cm) thick

Parsley-Garlic Chimichurri Sauce (page 275)

MAKES 4–6 SERVINGS

Roasted Pork with Spicy Pickled Onions

3 lb (1.5 kg) boneless pork butt, cut into 4 equal pieces

Sea salt

½ white onion, coarsely chopped

6 large cloves garlic

2 tablespoons achiote paste (page 268)

2 tablespoons fresh lime juice

2 tablespoons white vinegar

1 tablespoon ground cumin

1 teaspoon dried oregano, preferably Mexican

1–2 banana leaves, prepared (see page 269)

⅓ cup (½ oz/15 g) chopped fresh cilantro (fresh coriander)

FOR THE SPICY PICKLED ONIONS

1 red onion, thinly sliced

1 tablespoon fresh lime juice

1 tablespoon fresh orange juice

1 tablespoon white vinegar

¼ small habanero chile, seeded and finely minced

Sea salt

MAKES 6–8 SERVINGS

Rub the pork on all sides with 2 teaspoons salt and let stand at room temperature for 30 minutes.

In a blender or food processor, combine the onion, garlic, achiote paste, lime juice, vinegar, cumin, oregano, and 1½ teaspoons salt and process to a smooth purée, stopping to scrape down the sides of the blender jar or work bowl as needed. Rub the pork on all sides with the spice paste. Place in a large glass or stainless-steel bowl, cover, and refrigerate for at least 3 hours and up to overnight.

Preheat the oven to 325°F (165°C). Place a steamer basket or small wire rack in a Dutch oven or large, ovenproof sauté pan with a lid. Pour water into the pan up to but not touching the bottom of the steamer basket.

Cut 2 pieces of banana leaf, each 12 inches (30 cm) long and 24 inches (60 cm) wide. Place 1 piece on a work surface and arrange the pork in the center; it's okay if the pieces of pork overlap. Sprinkle with the cilantro. Fold up the long ends of the leaf to cover the meat, then fold the short ends over the meat, leaving the seam on top. Lay the second banana leaf on a work surface perpendicular to the first. Place the wrapped bundle on the second plantain leaf and wrap again in the same way so that the second leaf covers the seams of the first. Tie the bundle twice in each direction with kitchen twine to secure tightly.

Place the bundle in the steamer rack, cover the pan, and place in the oven. Roast until the meat is very tender, 2–2½ hours. Remove the packet from the oven and open a corner gently to test for doneness with a skewer; the meat is done when the skewer slips easily into the meat.

Meanwhile, to make the pickled onions, in a small bowl, combine the red onion, lime juice, orange juice, vinegar, habanero, and ½ teaspoon salt and stir to mix well. Cover and let marinate at room temperature for at least 1 hour. Or, cover and refrigerate for up to 8 hours.

To serve, transfer the pork to a serving platter, snip the strings, and unwrap. Pour any juices from the pan over the meat. Serve right away with the pickled onions.

Cochinita pibil is one of the most ancient and distinctive dishes of the Yucatan region. Made in the traditional way, the dish starts with large pieces of bone-in pork rubbed with a spice paste anchored by fragrant red annatto seed and sour orange. The meat is then wrapped in banana leaves and roasted on hot rocks in a deep pit *(pib)* until meltingly tender and infused with the earthy flavors of the spices and grassy fragrance of the banana leaf. Spicy pickled onions, called *xnipec,* are often served with the roasted pork to brighten the flavors.

Grilled Chicken with Chimichurri

Argentineans do not, in general, eat a lot of chicken, but the country's classic *chimichurri* sauces provide an irresistible accompaniment to grill-roasted chicken. The marinade in this recipe is made with lots of fresh lime juice and generous quantities of dried herbs and chile powder, a combination that brings out the best flavor and texture in poultry. For the juiciest, most flavorful results, marinate the chicken overnight.

Rinse the chicken and pat it dry. In a large, deep, nonreactive bowl, combine the ¼ cup (2 fl oz/60 ml) olive oil, lime juice, green onions, rosemary, oregano, bay leaves, chile powder, 1 teaspoon salt, and ½ teaspoon pepper and mix well. Place the chicken in the bowl and turn to coat evenly. Refrigerate for at least 4 hours and up to overnight.

Build a fire in a charcoal grill for indirect grilling over medium heat, or preheat a gas grill to medium (see page 269). If using a charcoal grill, place a drip pan half full of water in the center of the fire bed. Generously oil the grill rack and position it 4–5 inches (10–13 cm) above the coals.

Remove the chicken from the bowl and discard the marinade. Place the chicken, breast side up, on the grill rack, away from the direct heat. Cover the grill and cook, rotating the chicken occasionally so that it cooks evenly on all sides, until the juices run clear when the thigh is pierced with a knife tip and the temperature registers 165°F (74°C) on an instant-read thermometer, 1½–1¾ hours. If using a charcoal grill, add more coals about halfway through the grilling. Brush the chicken with some of the Traditional Chimichurri Sauce 2 or 3 times during grilling.

Transfer the chicken to a carving board, tent with aluminum foil, and let rest, about 10 minutes. Cut the chicken into pieces and arrange the pieces on warmed individual plates. Serve right away with one or more of the *chimichurri* sauces.

1 whole chicken, about 4 lb (2 kg), neck and giblets removed

¼ cup (2 fl oz/60 ml) olive oil, plus more for brushing

½ cup (4 fl oz/125 ml) fresh lime juice

¼ cup (1 oz/35 g) chopped green (spring) onions, white and tender green parts

2 teaspoons chopped fresh rosemary

2 teaspoons dried oregano

2 bay leaves, finely crumbled

1 teaspoon chile powder

Salt and freshly ground pepper

Traditional Chimichurri Sauce (page 274)

Red Chile–Cilantro Chimichurri Sauce (page 275), or Parsley-Garlic Chimichurri Sauce (page 275) for serving

MAKES 4 SERVINGS

Carnitas Tacos

3 lb (1.5 kg) boneless pork shoulder or country-style ribs

6 cloves garlic, halved

Zest of 1 orange, cut into strips

¾ cup (6 fl oz/180 ml) fresh orange juice

Sea salt

1 tablespoon canola or safflower oil, if needed

FOR SERVING

12 corn tortillas, homemade (page 276) or purchased, warmed

Lime wedges

Roughly torn fresh cilantro (fresh coriander) leaves

Pickled Red Onions (page 275)

Salsa Fresca (page 273)

MAKES 6 SERVINGS

Cut off any big pieces of fat from the pork and put the fat in a wide, heavy saucepan or frying pan. Cut the pork into strips about 1½ inches (4 cm) long and ¾ inch (2 cm) wide. Add the pork to the pan with the garlic, orange zest, orange juice, and 2 teaspoons salt. The meat should be in a single layer, if possible. Add water to barely cover the meat and bring to a boil over medium heat. Reduce the heat to medium low, cover partially, and cook, stirring occasionally, until all of the liquid has evaporated, about 1 hour. If the meat is not yet fork tender, add a bit more water and continue cooking.

Uncover the pan and continue cooking the pork until all the fat is rendered and the meat is browning in the melted fat, 10–15 minutes longer. There is usually enough melted fat in the pan, but, if necessary, add the 1 tablespoon oil.

When the meat is brown and crisp, using a slotted spoon, transfer it to a colander and let any excess fat drain away. Transfer the meat to a serving bowl. Place the tortillas on a plate, and place the lime wedges, cilantro, pickled onions, and salsa in individual bowls. Allow diners to assemble their own tacos as they desire.

The much-loved flavor of *carnitas*, or "little bits," is derived from pork that has been slow-cooked until meltingly tender. As the liquid evaporates during cooking, the meat browns in its own fat, creating succulent yet crispy bits of meat. Instead of tacos, you can serve the carnitas on individual plates with Refried Beans (page 276), steamed rice, and salsa.

Cuban Sandwiches

The iconic Cuban sandwich is an unexpected delight— pressed flat, it becomes crisp and golden on the outside and meltingly gooey within. The proper ingredients are essential: real Cuban bread (a long, wide, sweet baguette, not sourdough) with a crusty exterior and soft white interior; tender slices of pork loin; salty ham; and nutty Swiss cheese—all set off by the unexpected crunch of dill pickles and tart hint of mustard.

Cut the bread in half horizontally and smear the cut sides with the mustard. Arrange the pickle slices evenly on the bottom half, leaving some space in between slices. Top with half of the cheese slices.

Arrange the roast pork slices evenly along the sandwich on top of the cheese, and follow with the ham. Finish with the remaining cheese and replace the top of the baguette. Press firmly. Cut the baguette in half crosswise, then cut each half in half again to make 4 sandwiches.

Preheat a sandwich grill, or heat a griddle or large frying pan over medium heat. Place the sandwiches in the grill or on the griddle or frying pan, working in batches if necessary to avoid crowding. Close the top plate of the grill, or weight the sandwiches if using the griddle or frying pan (a cast iron frying pan works well), and cook until the bread is golden and toasted and the cheese is melted, 3–5 minutes. (If using the griddle or frying pan, turn the sandwich once.) Cut each sandwich in half on the diagonal and serve right away.

1 loaf Cuban bread or other sweet baguette, about 20 inches (50 cm) long

1/3 cup (2½ oz/75 g) prepared yellow mustard

3 large kosher dill pickles, thinly sliced lengthwise

8 oz (250 g) thinly sliced Swiss cheese

8 oz (250 g) cold roast pork loin, fat removed, thinly sliced

8 oz (250 g) thinly sliced lean cooked ham

MAKES 4 SERVINGS

Turkey Mole Poblano

FOR THE MOLE

**2 ancho chiles, seeded
and torn into pieces**

**2 pasilla chiles, seeded
and torn into pieces**

3 tablespoons canola oil

1 yellow onion, chopped

1 clove garlic, minced

**¾ cup (6 fl oz/180 ml)
Chicken Stock (page 270)
or low-sodium broth**

**2 tomatoes, seeded
and chopped**

½ cup (3 oz/90 g) almonds

½ cup (3 oz/90 g) raisins

6 peppercorns

1 teaspoon ground cinnamon

**1 tablespoon sesame seeds,
plus more sesame seeds
for serving**

2 teaspoons coriander seeds

**Salt and freshly
ground pepper**

**1 oz (30 g) unsweetened
chocolate, coarsely chopped**

**3–4 lb (1.5–2 kg) skin-on
boneless turkey breast halves**

½ white onion, sliced

2 cloves garlic

Sea salt

MAKES 4–6 SERVINGS

To make the mole, put the chiles in a small bowl and add enough boiling water to cover. Let soak for 20 minutes. Drain and set aside.

In a large frying pan over medium-high heat, warm 1 tablespoon of the oil. Add the onion and sauté until softened, about 5 minutes. Add the garlic and cook for 1 minute. Add the drained chiles, ¼ cup (2 fl oz/60 ml) of the stock, the tomatoes, almonds, and raisins and bring to a simmer. Transfer the chile mixture to a food processor or blender. Add the peppercorns, cinnamon, sesame seeds, and coriander. Blend until a thick purée forms.

Place the frying pan over medium-high heat and warm the remaining 2 tablespoons oil. Add the purée and cook until bubbling, about 2 minutes. Slowly pour in the remaining stock and season to taste with salt and pepper. Add the chocolate and stir until melted. For the best flavor, let the mole cool, then cover and refrigerate overnight. Reheat the next day.

To cook the turkey, put it in a Dutch oven with the onion, garlic, and 1½ teaspoons salt. Add just enough water to cover the turkey. Bring to a boil, then reduce the heat to very low. Cook until the juices run clear when the turkey is pierced with a fork, about 15 minutes. Remove the turkey from the pot and let stand until cool enough to handle.

When ready to serve, warm the mole over medium heat, stirring occasionally, until hot, about 10 minutes. Cut the turkey into slices ½ inch (12 mm) thick and spoon the mole over and around the turkey. Sprinkle with the reserved sesame seeds and serve right away.

Mole poblano is perhaps the best known (and involved) of all the Mexican mole sauces. It is traditionally prepared with a wide assortment of ingredients, most notably, chiles, nuts, raisins, sesame seeds, and chocolate. This recipe is a simplified version of the classic. It still offers the same rich taste, but takes a fraction of the time. This recipe uses turkey, but the sauce is delicious over roasted or poached chicken as well.

Sweet Guava Chicken

Fragrant, pink guava is the fruit most evocative of the Caribbean. The peeled and seeded fruit may be preserved in heavy syrup or cooked down into either a thick marmalade, called *mermelada,* or a gelatinous paste called *até*, which is eaten with cream cheese as a dessert. Guava *mermelada* forms the base for this sweet-tart sauce, which may be cooked with the chicken in a pan or brushed on grilled chicken as a glaze. Some pass Mojo Sauce (page 169) at the table for drizzling.

In a small saucepan over medium-low heat, whisk together the guava marmalade, mustard, orange juices, vinegar, and 1 teaspoon salt until well blended. Cook just until the marmalade is melted and the sauce is warm, about 5 minutes. Remove from the heat and set aside.

Build a fire in a charcoal grill for direct grilling over medium heat (see page 269), or preheat a gas grill to medium. Generously oil the grill rack. Grill the chicken directly over the fire until opaque throughout, about 10 minutes per side.

If grilling the green onions, after you turn the chicken over, place the onions towards the edges of the grill and cook, turning often, until marked on all sides, 5–7 minutes. Baste the chicken with the guava sauce toward the end of the cooking time and grill, about 1 minute per side. Serve right away with the rice and grilled green onions, if desired, and pass the remaining sauce at the table.

NOTE The sauce may be made with canned guavas in heavy syrup instead of the marmalade. Place 1 can (14 oz/440 g) guavas with their juice in a small saucepan. Bring to a simmer over medium heat and cook, crushing the fruit with a potato masher or a wooden spoon, until the guavas are uniformly mashed and the sauce thickens, about 15 minutes. Proceed with making the sauce, using 1 cup (10 oz/315 g) of the crushed canned guava.

1 cup (10 oz/315 g) guava marmalade

2 tablespoons Dijon mustard

2 tablespoons fresh sour orange juice (page 280) or 1 tablespoon orange juice mixed with 1 tablespoon lemon juice

2 tablespoons fresh orange juice

1 teaspoon white vinegar

Kosher salt

2 tablespoons vegetable oil

6 skinless, boneless chicken breast halves or thighs, about 6 oz (185 g) each

2 bunches green (spring) onions (optional)

Cooked white rice for serving

MAKES 6 SERVINGS

Grilled Steak Tacos with Chipotle Salsa and Avocado

FOR THE STEAK

1/2 cup (4 fl oz/125 ml) vegetable oil

1 yellow onion, thinly sliced

2 cloves garlic, chopped

1 jalapeño chile, seeded and minced

1 tablespoon chopped fresh oregano

1 teaspoon ground cumin

1 tablespoon ancho chile powder

2 tablespoons chopped fresh cilantro (fresh coriander)

1 tablespoon tequila

Salt

1 skirt steak or flank steak, 2½–3 lb (1–1.5 kg), trimmed of fat and silver skin

12 corn tortillas, homemade (page 276) or purchased

FOR SERVING

Chipotle Chile Salsa (page 274)

2 avocados, peeled, halved, and thinly sliced

MAKES 4–6 SERVINGS

In a small bowl, mix together the oil, onion, garlic, jalapeño, oregano, cumin, chile powder, cilantro, tequila, and 1½ teaspoons salt. Score the steak a few times across the grain. A long, thin skirt steak should be cut into 2–4 pieces for easy grilling. Put the steak in a baking dish or zippered plastic bag and pour the marinade over. Cover or seal and let marinate, turning occasionally, for at least 6 hours at room temperature or overnight in the refrigerator. If refrigerated, remove from the refrigerator 30 minutes before grilling.

Build a fire in a charcoal grill for direct grilling over high heat, or preheat a gas grill to high (see page 269). Generously oil the grill rack and position it 4–5 inches (10–13 cm) above the coals.

Preheat the oven to 300°F (150°C). Divide the tortillas into two equal stacks and wrap each stack tightly in aluminum foil. Place the tortillas in the preheated oven and warm until ready to serve.

Remove the steak from the marinade, pat dry, and discard the marinade. Grill the skirt steak directly over the heat, turning once, until well-browned and medium-rare, 7–8 minutes for skirt steak or 9–10 for flank steak. (Move the steak to a cooler part of the grill if flare-ups occur.) The steak should not be cooked past medium-rare, as these cuts toughen when cooked longer. Transfer the meat to a platter, cover loosely with aluminum foil, and let rest for about 15 minutes.

Remove the tortillas from the oven. Slice the steak thinly against the grain. To assemble the tacos, place the meat on one side of the tortilla, spoon a little salsa and avocado on top, and fold. Serve right away.

NOTE The marinade used in this recipe is also delicious with chicken.

Carne asada tacos are popular fare of street carts throughout Mexico. The small tacos are traditionally served with chopped white onion, a sprinkle of cilantro, and a squeeze of lime. This updated version includes a spicy marinade, smoky salsa, and fresh, creamy avocado.

Chicken in Pepita Sauce

This sauce, known as *pipian verde* in Spanish, is the opposite of its cousin, the rich chocolate-enhanced *mole* on page 154. This *pipian* is a bright, light sauce with fresh tomatillos and plenty of cilantro and lime juice. The peanut butter and pumpkin seeds thicken the sauce and add a nice nuttiness.

Place the chicken pieces in a large stockpot and cover with cold water. Add 1 onion half, 3 cloves of garlic, the thyme, bay leaves, and peppercorns. Bring to a boil, skimming off any foam that rises to the surface. Cover, reduce the heat to low, and simmer until the juices run clear when a breast (or thigh) is pierced, about 30–35 minutes. Transfer the chicken to a baking dish and cover to keep warm. Using a large spoon, skim off the fat from the stock; reserve the stock to use in the sauce.

Place the pumpkin seeds in a frying pan over medium heat and toast until one pops, stirring frequently. Continue to cook, stirring, until most of the pumpkin seeds have popped and are golden, 3–4 minutes longer. Be careful not to brown the pumpkin seeds past golden or the sauce will taste slightly bitter. Cool the pumpkin seeds and set aside ¼ cup (1 oz/30 g) for garnish.

Slice the additional onion half and place in a blender. Add the remaining 2 cloves of garlic, the pumpkin seeds, tomatillos, chopped cilantro, lettuce, jalapeño, and ½ teaspoon salt. Pour in 1 cup (8 fl oz/250 ml) of the cooled stock and purée until very smooth.

In a large saucepan over medium-high heat, warm the oil. Add the purée all at once (it will sizzle some) and stir as the mixture thickens and begins to darken, about 10 minutes. Stir in 2 cups (16 fl oz/500 ml) of the stock, reduce the heat to low, and simmer until the sauce is reduced to a creamy consistency and the flavors have combined, about 20 minutes. Stir in the lime juice and cook for a few more minutes, then whisk in the peanut butter. The final sauce should be thick and not too watery. If it is too thin, cook the sauce a few minutes longer to reduce. If it is too thick, add a small amount of stock or water to reach the desired consistency. Taste and add more salt and pepper if needed.

Remove the skin from the chicken. Place the chicken pieces in the sauce and heat over medium heat until the chicken is warmed through, about 5 minutes. Transfer the chicken and sauce to a warmed serving platter, garnish with the cilantro sprigs and reserved pumpkin seeds, and serve right away.

6 bone-in chicken breast halves (or 12 chicken thighs), ½ lb (250 g) each

1 yellow onion, halved

5 cloves garlic, divided

1 sprig fresh thyme

2 bay leaves

12 peppercorns

FOR THE PEPITA SAUCE

1½ cups (7½ oz/213 g) shelled pumpkin seeds (pepitas)

6 medium tomatillos, about ½ lb (250 g) total weight, husks removed, fruit rinsed and coarsely chopped

⅓ cup (½ oz/15 g) chopped fresh cilantro (fresh coriander), plus a few sprigs for garnish

3 romaine (cos) lettuce leaves, roughly chopped

1–2 jalapeño chiles, stemmed

Sea salt and freshly ground pepper

2 tablespoons vegetable oil

2 tablespoons fresh lime juice

2 tablespoons peanut butter

MAKES 6 SERVINGS

Shredded Beef Tamales

Seasoned Beef Filling
(page 276)

Salt

2 lb (1 kg) small white
or red potatoes, peeled and
sliced ¼ inch (6 mm) thick

9 cups (72 fl oz/2 l) Beef
Stock (page 271) or broth

6 cups (2 lb/1 kg) corn
flour, such as Harina P.A.N.
or ArepArina (page 21)

1 tablespoon canola oil

2 1-lb (16-oz/454-g)
packages banana leaves

4 large hard-boiled eggs,
each cut into 6 slices

3 tablespoons capers

3 tablespoons raisins

12 green olives, pitted
and sliced

MAKES 12 TAMALES

Prepare the beef filling as directed, reserving half of the seasoning sauce. Set the beef aside. Bring a large pot of water to a boil over high heat. Stir in ½ teaspoon salt and add the potatoes. Cook until the potatoes are tender but still firm, about 10 minutes. Drain the potatoes into a colander and place under running cold water to stop the cooking. Set the potatoes aside to drain and cool completely.

In a large saucepan over medium-low heat, warm the stock. Slowly pour the corn flour into the stock, stirring to mix well. Continue to cook the mixture until it absorbs most of the stock, 1–2 minutes. Turn off the heat and stir in the reserved beef seasoning sauce and the oil.

Rinse and warm the banana leaves as directed on page 269. To assemble the tamales, cut the banana leaves into 8-by-10-inch (20-by-25-cm) rectangles. Place one of the rectangles on a work surface with the smooth, light green side facing up. Spoon a heaping ⅓ cup (3½ oz/105 g) of the masa onto the middle of the leaf and use the back of the spoon to make a small well in the center of the masa. Top with about ¼ cup (1½ oz/45 g) of the beef, 1–2 potato slices, 2 egg slices, and a pinch *each* of the capers, raisins, and olives.

To wrap the tamales, bring together the two long sides of the leaf rectangle, overlapping the edges to enclose the filling snugly. Tuck the overhanging sides underneath to create a roughly square package. Lay out another leaf rectangle on a work surface. Place the wrapped package in the center of the rectangle so that the folded sides face up. Repeat the folding to create a double-wrapped bundle. Tie the bundle securely with kitchen twine. Repeat to assemble the remaining tamales.

Bring a pasta pot with a strainer-basket insert three-fourths full of salted water to a boil over high heat. Reduce the heat to maintain a gentle simmer. Arrange the tamales, seam side down, in the strainer basket and lower it into the pot, immersing the tamales in the simmering water. Cover and cook until the masa is firm and pulls away from the wrapper, about 1 hour. Remove the basket from the pot and let the tamales cool, about 5 minutes. Serve right away, letting diners untie their tamales at the table.

Tamales are made all across Central and South America, with an endless variety of fillings and flavors. When fresh masa is not available, yellow corn flour is a fine substitute. This version uses a classic combination of ingredients to achieve a balance of savory, sweet, salty, and tangy flavors in every bite: creamy potatoes, hard-boiled eggs, sweet raisins, and zesty capers. Try pulled pork or chicken in place of the beef in this recipe, if you like.

Chicken-Tomatillo Stew

Tomatillos, called *miltomates* in Guatemala, are the tangy and flavorful foundation of the sauce in this stew, reminiscent of the classic green sauce known as *salsa verde*. The skin-on, bone-in chicken adds richness to the sauce; as the meat sears, the fat renders, and the caramelized bits left on the bottom of the pan are stirred in. Shred any leftover chicken and use to stuff enchiladas.

Remove the papery husks from the tomatillos and rinse under warm running water to remove the sticky residue on the skins. Chop coarsely and set aside.

In a large, deep, heavy-bottomed saucepan over medium heat, warm the olive oil. Add the chicken pieces and sear, turning as needed, until crisp and golden on all sides, about 5 minutes total. Remove from the heat and transfer the chicken to a plate. Pour off and discard the fat in the pan.

Return the chicken to the pan and add the tomatillos, stock, tortillas, bell pepper, onion, tomato, green onions, garlic, 1 teaspoon salt, and ¼ teaspoon freshly ground black pepper. Bring to a boil over high heat, using a wooden spoon to scrape up any browned bits from the bottom of the pan. Reduce the heat to medium-low, cover, and simmer until the chicken is opaque throughout and very tender, about 25 minutes.

Using tongs, transfer the chicken to a deep serving platter, tent with aluminum foil, and let rest for about 10 minutes.

Meanwhile, ladle 1 cup (8 fl oz/250 ml) of the sauce into a blender or food processor and let cool to room temperature. Add the avocado and cilantro and process to a smooth purée, then return to the saucepan and stir to blend thoroughly with the rest of the sauce. Pour over the chicken and serve right away with the rice and *crema* on the side.

1 lb (500 g) tomatillos

1 tablespoon olive oil

1½ lb (750 g) skin-on, bone-in chicken thighs

1½ lb (750 g) skin-on, bone-in chicken legs

2 cups (16 fl oz/500 ml) Chicken Stock (page 270) or low-sodium broth

4 corn tortillas, 8 inches (20 cm) in diameter, chopped

1 large green bell pepper (capsicum), seeded and diced

1 yellow onion, diced

1 large ripe tomato, seeded and diced

¼ cup (1 oz/30 g) minced green (spring) onions, white and tender green parts

2 cloves garlic, minced

Salt and freshly ground pepper

1 large ripe avocado, pitted, peeled, and diced

1 tablespoon minced fresh cilantro (fresh coriander)

FOR SERVING

Cooked white rice

Crema (page 277) or sour cream

MAKES 4–6 SERVINGS

Pork Pupusas with Spicy Coleslaw

1 lb (500 g) boneless
pork butt

Salt and freshly ground
black pepper

½ white onion

3 large cloves garlic, halved

1 bay leaf

3 plum (Roma) tomatoes

½ teaspoon dried oregano

4 cups (22 oz/680 g)
masa harina (page 21)

2 tablespoons ground cumin

Salt and freshly ground
pepper

⅓ cup (3 fl oz/80 ml)
vegetable oil, plus more
for greasing

Spicy Coleslaw (see Note)

Roasted Tomato Salsa
(page 273) or your favorite
tomato salsa

MAKES ABOUT 14 *PUPUSAS*

Cut the pork into 3-inch (7.5-cm) chunks and place in a small, heavy saucepan with a lid. Add just enough cold water to barely cover the meat. Stir in ½ teaspoon salt. Cut the half onion in half again and tuck 1 onion quarter, the garlic, and the bay leaf around the meat. Set the other onion quarter aside. Bring to a simmer slowly over medium heat. Reduce the heat to low, cover partially, and cook until the meat is very tender, about 2 hours. Using a slotted spoon, transfer the meat to a carving board and let cool, reserving the liquid in the saucepan.

Raise the heat to medium-high and return the cooking liquid to a boil. Simmer briskly until the water evaporates and only the fat remains in the pan. Meanwhile, using a sharp knife, trim off the excess fat from the meat. Using your fingers or 2 forks, shred into bite-size pieces. Add the meat to the hot fat and fry, stirring often, until crisp, 3–5 minutes.

In a blender or food processor, combine the tomatoes, the reserved onion quarter, and the oregano and process to a smooth purée. Add to the pan and cook, stirring, until the sauce coats the meat and most of the liquid has evaporated, about 5 minutes. Season to taste with salt. Remove from the heat and set aside.

In a bowl, whisk together the masa harina, cumin, 2 teaspoons salt, and 1 teaspoon pepper. Add 3 cups (24 fl oz/750 ml) warm water all at once and stir to mix well. Add the oil and stir until thoroughly incorporated. The dough should be very soft, but hold its shape. If it cracks around the edges or crumbles when you pinch a small piece flat, work in more water, 1 tablespoon at a time, as needed to make a smooth, manageable dough. Cover and let rest at room temperature while you make the coleslaw.

To make the *pupusas*, heat a heavy frying pan over medium-high heat. Scoop up about ½ cup (4 oz/250 g) of the masa and pat with your palms to flatten it into a patty about 3 inches (7.5 cm) in diameter. Place about 1 tablespoon of the pork in the center of the patty. Gently fold the edges of the dough up and over the pork to enclose it completely. Using your palms, flatten the *pupusa* into a disk about 5 inches (13 cm) in diameter.

Brush the hot pan with oil. Place the *pupusa* in the pan and cook until golden-brown on the first side, about 2 minutes. Repeat to brown the second side. Make the remaining *pupusas*, brushing the pan with more oil between each. Serve hot, with the coleslaw and salsa.

To make the spicy coleslaw, in a heatproof bowl, combine ½ head green cabbage, shredded, and 1 peeled and shredded carrot and toss to mix. Add boiling water to cover and let stand for 1 minute. Drain thoroughly in a colander and transfer to a serving bowl. Stir in 4 thinly sliced green (spring) onions and 1 large seeded and minced jalapeño. In a small bowl, whisk together ⅓ cup (3 fl oz/80 ml) vinegar, ¼ cup (2 fl oz/60 ml) water, 1 teaspoon dried oregano, and ½ teaspoon salt to make a dressing. Add to the cabbage mixture and toss to mix well.

Slow-Cooked Pork with Mojo Sauce

The bright flavors of traditional Cuban cooking lighten up a simple pork roast with citrus and plenty of garlic. If you want shredded pork, roast a boneless pork butt; for slicing, choose a pork loin and leave the fat on for roasting. Marinate the meat overnight, then roast with the marinade. Leftover roast pork can be used to make Cuban Sandwiches (see page 153).

In a large nonreactive bowl, combine the garlic, orange juice, lime juice, vinegar, cumin, peppercorns, oregano, and 2 teaspoons salt. Using a skewer, pierce the meat all over, about 2 inches (5 cm) apart. Place in the bowl and turn to coat with the marinade. Refrigerate for at least 3 hours and up to overnight.

Preheat the oven to 300°F (150°C). Place the pork in a small roasting pan or baking dish just large enough to hold it. Pour any marinade left in the bowl over the meat. Cover the pan tightly with a double layer of aluminum foil or a lid. Roast until the meat is very tender, 3–3½ hours.

To make the mojo sauce, in a mortar, combine the garlic and 1½ teaspoons salt. Using a pestle, and working in a circular motion, grind them together until a paste forms. Alternatively, combine the garlic with the salt on a cutting board. Using a large knife, alternately chop and, using the side of the knife, press and smear the garlic until a paste forms. Transfer the garlic paste to a bowl. Add the orange juices, lime juice, green onions, peppercorns, and oregano and stir to mix well. Taste and adjust for seasoning with salt and pepper. (The sauce should be almost explosively strong: acidic rather than sweet, and hot from the raw garlic.)

Remove the pork from the oven and let rest, 5–10 minutes. Transfer the pork to a carving board. Carve the meat across the grain into slices about ¼ inch (6 mm) thick. Serve right away with the mojo sauce.

2 tablespoons chopped garlic

⅓ cup (3 fl oz/80 ml) fresh orange juice

2 tablespoons fresh lime juice

1 tablespoon white vinegar

2 teaspoons ground cumin

½ teaspoon black peppercorns, crushed

½ teaspoon dried oregano

Salt

2 lb (1 kg) boneless pork butt or pork loin roast

FOR THE MOJO SAUCE

4 large cloves garlic

Kosher salt

¼ cup (2 fl oz/60 ml) fresh orange juice

¼ cup (2 fl oz/60 ml) fresh sour orange juice (page 280), or 2 tablespoons *each* fresh orange juice and lemon juice

¼ cup (2 fl oz/60 ml) fresh lime juice

¼ cup (1 oz/30 g) thinly sliced green (spring) onions, white and tender green parts

1 teaspoon black peppercorns, crushed

1 teaspoon chopped fresh oregano

MAKES 4–6 SERVINGS

Arroz con Pollo

4 large cloves garlic, minced

2 teaspoons red pepper flakes

1 tablespoon white vinegar

Salt and freshly ground black pepper

1 chicken, about 3½ lb (1.75 kg), cut into 8 serving pieces

3 tablespoons olive oil

4 cups (32 fl oz/1 l) Chicken Stock (page 270) or low-sodium broth

½ teaspoon saffron threads

1 red onion, diced

1 red bell pepper (capsicum), seeded and diced

1 green bell pepper (capsicum), seeded and diced

1 large jalapeño chile, seeded and minced

4 plum (Roma) tomatoes, diced

1 teaspoon ground cumin

2 bay leaves

2 cups (14 oz/440 g) uncooked long-grain white rice

MAKES 6 SERVINGS

In a bowl, combine the garlic, red pepper flakes, vinegar, 1 teaspoon salt, and ½ teaspoon black pepper, and stir to mix well. Add the chicken pieces and toss to coat with the marinade. Refrigerate for at least 1 hour and up to overnight.

In a large sauté pan or large, shallow flameproof casserole dish with a tight-fitting lid over medium heat, warm the olive oil. Remove the chicken from the marinade, reserving the marinade, and arrange in the pan, skin side down. Cook the chicken, without turning, until golden brown on the first side, 10–15 minutes. Turn the chicken, cover the pan, and cook until golden brown on the second side, about 10 minutes longer.

Meanwhile, in a saucepan over medium-high heat, warm the stock until steaming. Remove from the heat, add the saffron, and set aside to steep.

Transfer the chicken to a plate and pour off all but 2 tablespoons fat from the pan. Add the onion, red and green bell peppers, and jalapeño and sauté until softened, about 3 minutes. Add the tomatoes and cook, stirring for 1 minute. Add the cumin, bay leaves, and the rice and cook, stirring constantly, until the rice grains are translucent and have absorbed the fats and juices in the pan, 3–5 minutes.

Pour the reserved marinade and saffron-infused stock into the pan and stir briefly. Place the chicken on top and drizzle in any juices that accumulated on the plate. Raise the heat to medium-high and bring to a boil. Reduce the heat to low, cover, and simmer until the chicken is opaque throughout, the rice is tender, and all the liquid has been absorbed, about 25 minutes. Taste and adjust the seasoning. Discard the bay leaves.

Remove from the heat, uncover partially, and let rest for 5–10 minutes. Serve right away, directly from the pan.

Whether it's called *pollo con arroz* or *arroz con pollo*, this dish is all about the flavor of the rice. Seasonings differ slightly from region to region, but it is always built on a colorful *sofrito* of peppers and onions, which imbues the rice with vibrant color and flavor. *Arroz con pollo* is traditionally cooked on the stovetop, so the pan is important; it should be wide and shallow, rather than deep, with a tight-fitting lid. A large frying pan with a lid is ideal.

Duck Manchamateles

A *mole* is more than just a sauce. Healthy, earthy, and delicious, *moles* are rich and flavorful enough to be eaten alone with only beans, rice, and tortillas. *Mole manchamateles* is traditionally made with chicken and pork in a dried chile and fruit *mole*, flavors which also complement duck. The name means "tablecloth stainer"—a rueful tribute to this saucy, colorful dish.

If the giblets and neck are in the duck cavity, remove them and reserve for another use or discard. Pull out any pockets of fat from the cavity and discard. Rinse the duck and pat dry with paper towels. Cut off and reserve or discard the wing tips. Season the duck inside and out with 2 teaspoons salt, rubbing it well into the skin. Refrigerate for 24 hours.

Preheat the oven to 300°F (150°C). Line a large roasting pan with aluminum foil. Place a V-shaped rack in the prepared pan and brush the rack with oil.

Place the duck, breast side up, in the rack. Roast until the skin is golden brown and crisp, the duck is tender, and an instant-read thermometer inserted into the thickest part of a thigh registers 170°F (77°C), about 2 hours. Remove the pan from the oven, transfer the duck to a carving board, and tent with aluminum foil. Let rest for 15 minutes. Cut the duck in half lengthwise, then cut each half in half again crosswise. Cut each quarter into 2 pieces.

While the duck is roasting, make the *mole*. In a deep, heavy saucepan over medium heat, melt 1 tablespoon of the lard. Add the chiles and sauté until slightly darkened, about 2 minutes. Transfer the chiles to a plate. Add the garlic, apple, pineapple, and onion to the pan and cook until softened, about 2 minutes. Transfer to the plate with the chiles. Melt 1 tablespoon of the remaining lard in the pan and add the almonds, raisins, cinnamon stick, cloves, peppercorns, sesame seeds, bay leaf, and oregano. Cook, stirring constantly, until the sesame seeds are golden brown, about 5 minutes. Return the chiles and apple mixture to the pan, along with the roasted tomatoes. Add 1½ cups (12 fl oz/375 ml) of the stock, the sugar, 2 teaspoons salt, and the nutmeg. Raise the heat to high and bring to a boil, then reduce the heat to low and simmer gently until the stock has evaporated, about 30 minutes. Add a little stock as needed to prevent scorching. Remove the cinnamon stick and bay leaf from the *mole* and discard. Let the sauce cool slightly. Strain the sauce through a fine-mesh sieve set over a bowl and reserve the liquid. Transfer the solids to a blender and purée until smooth.

Rinse and dry the pot, add the remaining 1 tablespoon lard, and melt over medium heat. Pour the purée into the pot and fry the sauce, stirring constantly, until fragrant and thickened, about 5 minutes. Add the reserved sauce liquid and the remaining 2½ cups (20 fl oz/625 ml) stock and stir to mix well.

Arrange the duck on a platter, spoon a generous amount of sauce over the pieces, and garnish with the diced fruit and toasted sesame seeds. Serve right away.

1 duck, about 5 lb (2.5 kg)

Kosher salt

Olive oil for brushing

3 tablespoons lard, unsalted butter, or olive oil

5 large dried ancho chiles, seeded and torn into pieces

6 cloves garlic, peeled but left whole

1 large tart apple, such as granny smith, peeled, cored, and chopped, plus diced apple for serving

1 cup (4 oz/125 g) chopped fresh pineapple, plus diced pineapple for serving

½ white onion, chopped

½ cup (3 oz/90 g) *each* whole almonds and raisins

½ cinnamon stick

3 whole cloves

½ teaspoon black peppercorns

1 tablespoon sesame seeds, plus toasted sesame seeds (page 268) for serving

1 bay leaf

2 teaspoons dried oregano

3 plum (Roma) tomatoes, roasted (page 268)

4 cups (32 fl oz/1 l) Chicken Stock (page 270) or low-sodium broth

2 teaspoons sugar

¼ teaspoon freshly grated nutmeg

MAKES 4 SERVINGS

Skirt Steak with Red Chile–Cilantro Chimichurri

Olive oil for brushing

1 skirt steak, about 3 lb (1.5 kg)

Kosher salt

Red Chile–Cilantro Chimichurri Sauce (page 275)

MAKES 4 SERVINGS

Build a fire in a charcoal grill for direct grilling over high heat, or preheat a gas grill to high (see page 269). Oil the grill rack and position it 2–4 inches (5–10 cm) above the coals. Bring the steaks to room temperature before grilling.

Brush the steak with olive oil. Place on the grill rack directly over the hot coals and grill for 1–2 minutes on each side for medium-rare. Sprinkle 1½ teaspoons salt on each side before turning. Transfer the steak to a carving board, tent with aluminum foil, and let rest for 5 minutes. Carve the steak across the grain into thin slices and serve right away with the *chimichurri* sauce.

Skirt steak is prepared throughout Latin America for countless dishes using numerous techniques, from pressure cooking to grilling. In Argentina, where the famous rich pasture land is nurtured by ample rainfall and temperate climate, recipes for skirt steak abound. For the best flavor and maximum tenderness, cook the steak only to medium-rare. The *chimichurri* sauce, bright with fresh cilantro (fresh coriander), is the perfect accompaniment for grilled and roasted meats.

Chicken Enchiladas with Salsa Roja

The secret to success with these enchiladas lies in coating the bottom of the baking dish with sauce so that the enchiladas are easier to release from the pan after baking. If you prefer a spicier sauce, replace 1 ancho chile with 1–2 chipotle chiles. You can also add cheese, such as Monterey jack or *cotija,* to the chicken filling.

Place the chicken pieces in a saucepan and add boiling water to cover. Place over medium-high heat until the water returns to a boil, skimming off any foam that forms on the surface. Reduce the heat to medium-low and add the onion, peppercorns, and garlic. Cover and simmer until the meat is opaque throughout, about 20 minutes. Add salt to taste during the last 5 minutes.

Remove from the heat and transfer the chicken to a cooling rack or plate to cool. When cool enough to handle, coarsely the shred the chicken. You should have about 2 cups (12 oz/375 g) shredded chicken.

To make the *salsa roja,* tear the chiles into large pieces. Put them in a heatproof bowl and add boiling water to cover. Weight the chiles down with a plate and let soak until soft, about 15 minutes. Drain the chiles. In batches, in a blender, process the chiles, tomatoes with juice, onion, garlic, and oregano until smooth, adding ½ cup (4 fl oz/125 ml) or more of the chicken stock as needed to achieve a very smooth consistency.

Preheat the oven to 325°F (165°C). In a frying pan over medium heat, warm 1 tablespoon of the oil until it is shimmering but not smoking. Pour in the chile sauce and cook, stirring, until thickened, about 2 minutes. Add the remaining chicken stock and cook, stirring frequently, until thick, about 5 minutes. Taste and adjust the seasoning with salt. Remove from the heat. Spoon a thin layer of the chile sauce on the bottom of a 9-by-13-inch (23-by-33-cm) baking dish. Cover the sauce to keep warm.

In a frying pan over medium heat, warm the remaining 3 tablespoons oil until sizzling hot. Using tongs and a spatula, very quickly drag the tortillas, one at a time, through the oil to soften them on both sides. Pat dry with paper towels. Working with one tortilla at a time, spread 1 heaping tablespoon of the shredded chicken near the edge of the tortilla, roll it up, and place it seam side down in the prepared baking dish. Repeat with the remaining tortillas and chicken, arranging the rolled tortillas side by side in the dish. Spoon the remaining sauce over the tortillas. Bake the enchiladas until heated through, about 5 minutes.

To serve, top the enchiladas in the pan with the *crema,* onions, and radishes. Serve right away.

2 lb (1 kg) boneless skinless chicken breasts or thighs

Slice of white onion

4 black peppercorns

1 clove garlic

Sea salt

10 ancho chiles, seeded (page 268)

1 can (14½ oz/455 g) diced tomatoes, with juice

½ white onion, coarsely chopped

6 cloves garlic

1 teaspoon dried oregano, preferably Mexican

1½ cups (12 fl oz/375 ml) Chicken Stock (page 270) or low-sodium broth

4 tablespoons (2 fl oz/60 ml) canola or safflower oil

12 white corn tortillas, about 6 inches (15 cm) in diameter

FOR SERVING

½ cup (4 fl oz/125 ml) Crema (page 277) or sour cream

1 small white onion, thinly sliced and separated into rings

6 radishes, trimmed and thinly sliced

MAKES 12 ENCHILADAS, OR 5–6 SERVINGS

Shredded Chicken in Pepper Sauce

1 whole chicken, 5–6 lb (2.5–3 kg), or 4 skin-on, bone-in chicken breast halves, about ½ lb (250 g) each

8 cups (64 fl oz/2 l) Chicken Stock (page 270) or low-sodium broth

1 tablespoon unsalted butter

1 tablespoon olive oil

1 large red onion, thinly sliced

1 clove garlic, minced

2 teaspoons *ají amarillo* paste (page 278)

¼ cup (2 oz/60 g) *ají panca* paste (page 278)

1 can (10 fl oz/310 ml) evaporated milk

1 cup (4 oz/125 g) shredded *queso blanco* or farmer's cheese

8 saltine crackers (savory biscuits)

Salt

½ cup (2 oz/60 g) ground walnuts

FOR SERVING

Cooked white rice

Walnut halves

MAKES 4–6 SERVINGS

Rinse the chicken and pat it dry. Place it in a soup pot, pour in the stock, and bring to a boil over high heat. Reduce the heat to medium-low, and simmer, partially covered, until the chicken is tender and opaque throughout, about 45 minutes. Transfer the chicken to a platter and let cool. Reserve the cooking liquid. When cool enough to handle, pull the meat off the bones. Discard the skin and bones. Shred or cut the meat into bite-size pieces and set aside.

In a saucepan over medium-low heat, melt the butter with the olive oil. Add the onion and cook, stirring often, until translucent, about 5 minutes. Add the garlic and *ají* pastes and cook until fragrant, about 1 minute.

Meanwhile, in a blender or food processor, combine 1 cup (8 fl oz/250 ml) of the reserved cooking liquid, the evaporated milk, *queso blanco*, crackers, and ¼ teaspoon salt. Process until smooth, then transfer to the pan with the onion mixture and cook until the mixture thickens slightly, about 10 minutes longer. Add the chicken and ground walnuts to the sauce and stir to mix well. Cook for 2–3 minutes to allow the flavors to blend.

To serve, place a scoop of the rice in the center of each plate. Top with the chicken mixture, garnish with the walnut halves, and serve right away.

Ají de Gallina is one of Peru's classic dishes. Indigenous *ajís*, or peppers, are important to the flavor this sauce, but since the fresh peppers are hard to find, this recipe calls for the pepper pastes, which can be found in jars in Latin markets (see page 278). The dish is often served with potatoes, white rice, black olives, and hard-boiled eggs and walnuts for garnish.

Ropa Vieja with Fried Plantains

Loosely translated as "old clothes," *ropa vieja* is among Cuba's most-loved dishes, not only because it is a simple and tasty way to feed a crowd. The cooked meat can be sliced, but it is most often shredded, giving the dish its name, before being added to a colorful *sofrito* made with tomato and red annatto oil. Annatto oil is available at some Latin markets. If you use the annatto oil, omit the achiote paste.

Place the meat in a Dutch oven or other large, heavy pot with a tight-fitting lid. Add just enough cold water to barely cover the meat. Stir in 2 teaspoons salt and tuck the onion, peppercorns, and bay leaf around the meat. Bring to a simmer slowly over medium heat. Reduce the heat to low, cover, and cook until the meat is very tender, 2½–3 hours. Using tongs or 2 large forks, transfer the meat to a carving board and let cool. Strain the cooking liquid through a fine-mesh sieve set over a bowl and reserve. Discard the solids.

While the meat is cooking, make the sauce. In another Dutch oven or a large, heavy sauté pan over medium-high heat, warm the oil. Add the onion, bell pepper, carrot, garlic, and chile and cook, stirring often, until the vegetables begin to soften, about 2 minutes.

If you used the vegetable oil (not the annatto oil), crumble the achiote paste into the pot and cook, stirring, for 2–3 minutes. Add the tomatoes and cinnamon. Cook, stirring often, until almost all the liquid has evaporated. Remove the pan from the heat and set aside.

Add 1½ cups (12 fl oz/375 ml) of the reserved beef cooking liquid to the vegetables, place over medium heat, and simmer for 10 minutes to allow the flavors to blend. Using a sharp knife, trim off all the excess fat from the meat. Carve the meat across the grain into slices about ¼ inch (6 mm) thick, or shred into bite-size pieces using your fingers or 2 forks. Add the meat to the simmering sauce and cook until heated through, about 5 minutes longer.

Spoon the stew onto individual plates and top each serving with a few pimiento slices and a sprinkling of capers. Serve at once with the fried plantains and rice.

3 lb (1.5 kg) flank steak or lean chuck

Kosher salt

½ white onion, peeled but with root end intact, stuck with 1 whole clove

10 black peppercorns

1 bay leaf

FOR THE TOMATO SAUCE

2 tablespoons annatto oil or vegetable oil (see Note)

½ white onion, diced

1 green bell pepper (capsicum), seeded and diced

1 small carrot, peeled and diced

3 cloves garlic, minced

1 tablespoon seeded and minced serrano chile

2 teaspoons achiote paste (optional; see Note)

2 cups (14 oz/440 g) seeded and diced fresh tomatoes, or canned tomatoes, drained

Pinch of ground cinnamon

FOR SERVING

⅓ cup (2½ oz/75 g) jarred sliced red pimientos, drained

2 tablespoons capers, drained

Fried Green Plantains (page 217)

Cooked white rice

MAKES 6–8 SERVINGS

Grilled Lamb Chops with Spicy Mint Salsa

FOR THE SPICY MINT SALSA

¹/₂ cup (¹/₂ oz/15 g) firmly packed fresh mint leaves, coarsely chopped

¹/₂ cup (¹/₂ oz/30 g) firmly packed fresh flat-leaf (Italian) parsley leaves, coarsely chopped

¹/₂ cup (2 oz/60 g) coarsely chopped green (spring) onions, white and tender green parts

3 tablespoons distilled white vinegar

2 tablespoons fresh lime juice

¹/₂ habanero chile, seeded and chopped

Salt

1¹/₂ teaspoons olive oil

4 lb (2 kg) lamb rib chops, trimmed of fat

¹/₄ cup (2 fl oz/60 ml) fresh lime juice

¹/₄ cup (1 oz/30 g) thinly sliced green (spring) onions, white and tender green parts

1 clove garlic, minced

¹/₂ teaspoon dried oregano

¹/₂ teaspoon ground cumin

Coarse sea salt and freshly ground pepper

16 fl oz (475 ml) light beer

Olive oil for brushing

MAKES 4–6 SERVINGS

To make the salsa, in a food processor, combine the mint, parsley, green onions, vinegar, lime juice, habanero, and 1 teaspoon salt and process until the mixture is minced. Transfer to a bowl and stir in the olive oil. Let stand at room temperature for at least 1 hour to allow the flavors to blend, or until ready to serve.

Place the lamb in a large bowl or baking dish. In a small bowl, stir together the lime juice, green onions, garlic, oregano, cumin, 1½ teaspoons salt, and ½ teaspoon pepper. Rub the mixture all over the chops. Let stand at room temperature for 10–15 minutes. Pour the beer over the chops, cover, and refrigerate for at least 20 minutes and up to overnight.

Build a fire in a charcoal grill for direct grilling over medium-high heat, or preheat a gas grill to medium-high (page 269). Generously oil the grill rack and position it 3–5 inches (7.5–13 cm) above the coals. Remove the lamb from the marinade and let it come to room temperature. Discard the marinade.

Arrange the ribs on the grill rack directly over the hot coals and grill for about 2 minutes per side for medium-rare or about 3 minutes per side for medium. Serve right away with the salsa.

Lamb is a celebratory food, cooked for large family gatherings on farms across South America. Lambs are usually cooked during the middle of the party so that everyone can enjoy the preparation—large cuts of lamb are roasted over a wood fire. Lamb chops are more manageable and are usually marinated in beer overnight and then seared until tender and juicy.

Feijoada

An ancient Portuguese recipe, the *feijoada* tradition was subsequently carried to Brazil, where it has come to be known as the country's national dish. In Brazil it is made with black beans and a panoply of smoked, dried, and sausage meats. In addition to lots of hot fluffy rice to soak up the stew juices and slices of orange to clean the palate and brighten the plate, the customary sides include fried pork belly; sautéed greens such as kale or collard; a dish of lightly pan-toasted manioc flour called *farofa*; and *molho*, a Brazilian rendition of *mojo* sauce. Serve with cold beer or Caipirinhas (page 43), the signature cocktail of Brazil.

Pick over the beans and discard any misshapen beans or stones. Rinse the beans under running cold water and drain. Place in a large bowl with cold water to cover generously. Rinse the salt pork, *carne seca*, linguiça, and pork ribs under running cold water. Drain and place in a large bowl or bowls with cold water to cover generously. Soak the beans and meats overnight, changing the water for the meats twice during the soaking time.

Drain the beans in a colander, rinse well, and set aside. Drain the meats in another colander. Transfer the linguiça to a stockpot or large saucepan and place over medium heat. Cook, stirring often, until the fat is rendered, 2–3 minutes. Remove from the heat. Transfer the linguiça to a plate and set aside. Pour off all but 3 tablespoons fat from the pot. If there is not enough rendered fat in the pot, add olive oil as needed to make 3 tablespoons. Place over medium-low heat and add the yellow and green onions and the garlic. Cook until the onions are translucent, about 5 minutes. Add the bay leaves, cumin, and ½ teaspoon pepper and cook until fragrant, about 2 minutes longer.

Add the beans, salt pork, *carne seca*, and pork ribs to the pot, and pour in 7 cups (56 fl oz/1.75 l) cold water. Bring to a boil over high heat. Reduce the heat to low, cover partially, and simmer, stirring occasionally, until the beans are tender but not cracked or mushy and the meats are fork-tender, 2–2½ hours. Stir in the linguiça during the last 20 minutes of cooking to warm through. If the meats are done before the beans, use tongs or a slotted spoon to remove each piece of meat as it reaches tenderness and transfer to a bowl while the beans finish cooking.

While the *feijoada* is cooking, place the pork belly in a frying pan over medium-low heat and cook until most of the fat is rendered and the pieces are lightly golden and crispy around the edges, 10–12 minutes. Transfer to paper towels to drain. Reserve the fat to make the sautéed kale or for another use.

When the beans are tender, remove any remaining meats from the pot and transfer to the bowl with the other meats. Remove the bay leaf from the beans, taste, and adjust the seasonings with salt and pepper.

Reheat the side dishes gently, if necessary, and transfer to serving bowls. Place wide, shallow bowls or plates at each place setting. Serve the *feijoada* right away, instructing diners to take some rice, beans, meat, orange slices, and some of each of the side dishes.

1 lb (500 g) dried black beans (about 2 cups/500 g)

½ lb (250 g) salt pork, cut into 1-inch (2.5-cm) pieces

½ lb (250 g) *carne seca* (page 278) or beef jerky, cut into 1-inch (2.5-cm) pieces

½ lb (250 g) linguiça or dry-cured chorizo, cut into slices ½ inch (13 mm) thick

½ lb (250 g) smoked pork ribs, cut into separate ribs

Olive oil

1 yellow onion, diced

3 tablespoons thinly sliced green (spring) onions

3 tablespoons minced garlic

3 bay leaves

½ teaspoon ground cumin

Salt and freshly ground pepper

½ lb (250 g) pork belly or pancetta, cut into pieces about 1 inch (2.5 cm) long and ½ inch (12 mm) thick

FOR SERVING

3 oranges, peeled, sliced, and seeded

Cooked white rice

Toasted Manioc (page 272)

Sautéed Kale (page 272)

Molho Sauce (page 275)

MAKES 10–12 SERVINGS

Pork Tamales with Red Chile Sauce

½ lb (250 g) boneless pork butt or shoulder, cut into ½-inch (12-mm) cubes

2 cloves garlic

2 peppercorns

Sea salt

2 tablespoons all-purpose (plain) flour

Canola oil

½ cup (4 fl oz/125 ml) Chicken Stock (page 270) or low-sodium broth

1 cup (8 fl oz/250 ml) Red Chile Sauce (page 273)

Sea salt

1½ cups (8¼ oz/255 g) masa harina

1 teaspoon pure chile powder

¾ teaspoon baking powder

Sea salt

⅔ cup (6 oz/188 g) fresh pork lard or solid vegetable shortening (vegetable lard), at room temperature

About 24 dried corn husks, soaked in hot water, drained, then dried, plus 2–3 husks cut lengthwise into 32 strips about ½ inch (12 cm) wide

MAKES 16 TAMALES

Put the pork, garlic, peppercorns, and ½ teaspoon salt in a heavy saucepan or small Dutch oven. Add 2 cups (16 fl oz/500 ml) water to cover. Bring to a low boil over medium-high heat, then reduce the heat to low, cover, and simmer until the pork is fork-tender, about 45 minutes. Remove from the heat and let cool in the broth, then transfer to a bowl.

In a large, dry frying pan over low heat, toast the flour, stirring constantly, for a few seconds, just until it starts to brown. Drizzle in enough oil to saturate the flour and continue to stir until the mixture is a rich brown. Stirring constantly, gradually add the stock and chile sauce, raise the heat to medium, and cook, stirring frequently, until the sauce thickens, about 3 minutes. Season to taste with salt. Pour half of the sauce into the bowl with the pork. Set aside the remaining sauce.

In a large bowl, stir together the masa harina, chile powder, baking powder, and 1 teaspoon salt. Stir in enough lukewarm water, about ¾ cup (6 fl oz/180 ml), to make a moist batter. In a small bowl using an electric mixer, beat the lard until creamy, about 5 minutes. Add to the masa harina mixture and continue beating until the mixture is light and spreadable, about 5 minutes longer, adding up to ¼ cup (2 fl oz/60 ml) more water if the mixture is too dry. Taste and adjust the seasoning with salt.

To wrap the tamales, using the 16 best corn husks, lay a husk in one palm, with the pointed end on your wrist. Spread a generous tablespoon of masa dough thinly down the center of the husk, leaving a margin on all sides. Place a few pieces of the meat and some sauce in the center of the dough, then fold the long edges of the husk over the filling, overlapping them and forming a narrow tamal. Tie both ends with a husk strip to secure.

To steam the tamales, fill a large pot with a steamer insert. Fill the bottom with 3 inches (7.5 cm) of water and place the steamer insert in the pot. Cover the bottom of the steamer insert with some of the corn husks, and place the tamales on top. Cover with more corn husks and a layer of plastic wrap, then with a tight-fitting lid. Bring to a low boil and steam without opening. After 45 minutes, test for doneness (see Note). When done, remove the tamales from the pot and let rest. Reheat the reserved sauce over low heat, adding more water if it is too thick.

To serve, place one or two tamales on individual plates and let diners untie their tamales at the table. Pass the chile sauce at the table.

Pork tamales are a classic Mexican treat, enjoyed for casual snacks as well as celebratory occasions. They are quite involved, so making them is typically a family affair. Because the ingredients are all tied up securely in a tight package, it is hard to test for doneness. To do so, after 45 minutes of cooking, remove a tamal from the pot, let sit for a few minutes, then carefully unwrap. The tamal is done when the dough easily pulls away from the husk.

Vegetables and Grains

About Vegetables and Grains

The indigenous people of Latin America rely on the sacred staples of their ancestors: corn, beans, squash, yuca (also called cassava), sweet potatoes, potatoes, quinoa, and amaranth. Delicious recipes based on these staples, both traditional and modern, are found in the following pages.

Traditional vegetable, grain, and legume dishes in Latin America cross both social and economic barriers. When enriched with butter, cream, or cheese, vegetable, grain, and legume dishes, such as rice and beans, are sometimes considered complete everyday meals. On other occasions, vegetables and grains are served as a separate course or side dish.

THE SACRED TRINITY

In Mexico, Central America, and temperate regions of South America, ears of tender young corn are grilled and served as a favorite snack. Mature corn is ground into fresh masa or flour for tortillas, tamales, or *arepas* (corn cakes), which appear at almost every meal. In the cornfields of the Americas, corn has traditionally been planted with beans and squash. These three plants form the sacred trinity of pre-Columbian foods, because they are the foundation of a well-balanced diet.

RICE AND PLANTAINS

Two foods introduced from the Old World, rice and plantains, have also become Latin American staples. Although the nutritional value of white rice is sometimes questioned, it is versatile, easy to digest, and has a mild and pleasant taste. It's no wonder that Latin America adopted it so willingly. The plantain on the other hand, is a nutritional powerhouse; rich in complex starches, high in fiber, extremely low in fat, and full of protein. It has even more potassium and

magnesium than its close cousin, the banana, and is a good source of vitamins A, B6, and C. Since plantains grow well in the tropics of the Caribbean and Central and South America, they are served in a variety of preparations, both as a savory side dish with yuca, rice, and beans, and glazed with sugar and transformed into sweet desserts.

POTATOES

Anthropologists tell us that the sweet potato has been cultivated along the coast of Peru since at least 2400 BC. By the time the Spanish arrived in the early fifteenth century, sweet potatoes had traveled north and were already well established among the Maya of the Yucatan Peninsula. Today, sweet potatoes appear in a wide range of recipes from Latin American kitchens. They are boiled and served alongside tangy ceviche or *escabeche,* or peeled, sliced, brushed with oil, and baked in the oven until crisp, as in Chile-Glazed Sweet Potatoes (page 205).

Potatoes are another versatile food from the Andes. The Inca cultivated an amazing four thousand varieties of potato, each suited to different altitudes, soils, and climate conditions. Many of these varieties are being carefully preserved at Potato Park, a botanical facility near Cuzco, Peru. Although some Andean varieties will probably remain regional, more shapes and colors of potatoes are now being sold at supermarkets around the world. The next time you prepare a classic potato

salad, try mixing antioxidant-rich purple potatoes with yellow- and white-fleshed varieties. It will give an old favorite a colorful, nutritious new twist.

GRAINS AND SEEDS

The ancient grains quinoa and amaranth are perhaps the least known but undoubtedly among the most nutritious New World crops. Quinoa, particularly, has caught the eye of both nutritionists and chefs. For culinary purposes, quinoa and amaranth are prepared like grains, but botanists classify them as "pseudo cereals" because they are not grasses, but actually tall, stalky annuals that develop colorful, plumelike seed heads. Quinoa and amaranth leaves also get excellent marks for nutrition, including lots of antioxidant vitamin A. When young and tender, they are cooked like spinach. The seeds of both plants are extremely nourishing, high in protein, minerals, and amino acids.

In Mexico, puffed amaranth seeds are sold as a dry breakfast cereal and used to make *alegrias*, a sweet similar to the rice–and-marshmallow bar cookies beloved of children in the United States. Since the seeds are so tiny and more or less dissolve and disappear with long cooking, they are often used as a thickener in soups.

Quinoa is more versatile, and may be used interchangeably with rice in most recipes. As a natural defense against insects, quinoa seeds are covered with a bitter coating that must be removed before cooking and eating the grain. While most packaged quinoa is marked "prewashed," it is a good idea to rinse it under cold running water several times and drain before use, to be sure that no trace of the coating remains.

Grilled Tomatoes with Chimichurri

Grilled tomatoes are a perennial side dish for the much-loved Argentinean *parrilla*, a mixture of grilled meats. They can be served warm in whole pieces, as in this recipe, or chopped to create a flavorful salsa. The juicy tomatoes and tangy *chimichurri* sauce freshen the palate and lighten any meal.

Build a fire in a charcoal grill for direct grilling over high heat, or preheat a gas grill to high (page 269). Generously oil the grill rack and position it 2–4 inches (5–10 cm) inches above the coals.

In a bowl, whisk together the 2 tablespoons olive oil, the lime juice, oregano, 1 teaspoon salt, and ½ teaspoon pepper and let stand at room temperature to let the flavors blend, about 10 minutes. Add the tomato halves to the bowl and turn to coat thoroughly with the olive-oil mixture.

Brush the cut sides of the tomatoes with the *chimichurri* and arrange on the grill rack directly over the hot coals, cut side down. Grill until nicely marked, about 5 minutes. Baste the tops with the *chimichurri*. Using tongs, turn the tomatoes and grill on the other side until warmed through and nicely grill marked but still holding together and not mushy, about 5 minutes longer. Serve right away.

2 tablespoons olive oil, plus more for brushing

1 tablespoon fresh lime juice

1 teaspoon dried oregano

Salt and freshly ground pepper

3 large ripe but firm tomatoes, halved

Traditional Chimichurri Sauce (page 274)

MAKES 4–6 SERVINGS

Grilled Corn with Crema and Chile

6 ears corn, unshucked

2 limes, quartered

**Crema (page 277)
or sour cream**

**Crumbled *queso añejo* or
grated Parmesan cheese**

**Ground pequín (page 23)
or other hot ground chile**

Sea salt

MAKES 6 SERVINGS

Grilled corn is one of Mexico's favorite street foods. Sometimes the juicy corn is lavished with thick cream, and other times with mayonnaise, but inevitably there are plenty of limes and a sprinkling of ground chiles. The field corn eaten in Mexico has a starchy texture and is not at all sweet. To better duplicate the flavor, look for corn that is not marketed as ultra or supersweet.

Carefully pull the husks back from the corn, remove the silk, and put the husks back in place. Soak the ears in cold water to cover for 30 minutes.

Build a fire in a charcoal grill for direct grilling over high heat, or preheat a gas grill to high (see page 269). Generously oil the grill rack and position it 4–5 inches (10–13 cm) above the coals.

Remove the corn from the water and place it directly on the grill rack over medium-hot coals. Grill, turning frequently, until the corn is tender, about 20 minutes. If the husk is burned but the corn is not yet tender, wrap in aluminum foil and continue roasting until done.

To serve, pull back the husks on the corn and tie them with strips of husk. Rub the corn with the lime quarters, drizzle with some of the *crema*, and sprinkle with the cheese, chile, and salt to taste. Transfer to a platter and serve right away.

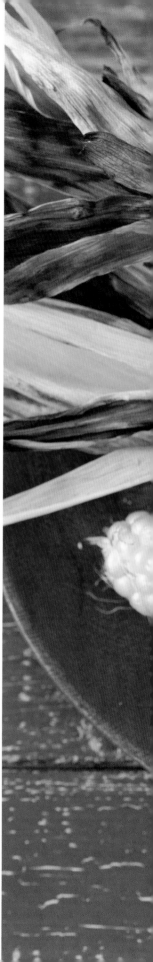

Beet and Potato Salad

This salad is perhaps the most popular way to serve beets in many South American countries such as Peru, Venezuela, and Argentina. You can also mound the salad in avocado halves and arrange the slices of egg on top. The secret to this *ensalada rusa,* which originated at the Hermitage restaurant in Moscow in the 1860s, is to let the vegetable mixture stand in the refrigerator for up to 2 hours before serving; this allows the flavors to develop.

Preheat the oven to 400°F (200°C). Wrap the beet halves in a piece of heavy-duty aluminum foil and place in a small baking dish. Bake until tender throughout when pierced with the tip of a sharp knife, about 45 minutes. Remove the dish from the oven and, when the beets are cool enough to handle, slip off the skins with your fingers. Cut the beets into ½-inch (12-mm) pieces.

Meanwhile, in a large saucepan fitted with a steamer basket, bring 1 inch (2.5 cm) water to a boil. Peel the potato and carrots and cut into ½-inch (12-mm) pieces. Place in the steamer basket, cover, and steam until tender but still firm, about 8 minutes. Remove from the heat and place under running cold water to stop the cooking. Drain thoroughly and let cool.

In a large bowl, combine the beet, potato, carrots, peas, pickle, 2 teaspoons salt, and ½ teaspoon pepper and toss to mix. Add the mayonnaise and stir gently with a fork until well combined. Cover and refrigerate for at least 10 minutes and up to 2 hours to allow the flavors to blend.

To serve, cut the hard-boiled eggs into slices ¼ inch (6 mm) thick. Place a lettuce leaf on each plate. Arrange 1–2 slices of hard-boiled egg on each lettuce leaf and mound the salad on top. Garnish with the parsley and serve right away.

1 large beet, about 8 oz (250 g), trimmed and halved

1 large white potato, about 8 oz (250 g)

2 medium carrots, about 6 oz (185 g) total weight

1 cup (5 oz/155 g) fresh or thawed frozen green peas

¼ cup (1½ oz/45 g) minced dill pickle

Salt and freshly ground pepper

1 cup (8 fl oz/250 ml) good-quality mayonnaise

FOR SERVING

2 hard-boiled eggs

4–6 lettuce leaves

2 tablespoons minced fresh flat-leaf (Italian) parsley

MAKES 4–6 SERVINGS

Red Beans and Rice

1 cup (7 oz/220 g) dried red beans

1 bay leaf

Sea salt and freshly ground pepper

2 teaspoons olive oil

3 strips thick-sliced bacon, diced

½ white onion, diced

½ green bell pepper (capsicum), seeded and diced

½ red bell pepper (capsicum), seeded and diced

2 cloves garlic, minced

2 teaspoons dried oregano

2 teaspoons ground cumin

1 can (8 fl oz/250 ml) tomato sauce

1½ cups (10½ oz/330 g) uncooked long-grain white rice

2½ cups (20 fl oz/625 ml) Chicken Stock (page 270), low-sodium broth, or water

MAKES 6 SERVINGS

Pick over the beans and discard any misshapen beans or stones. Rinse the beans under running cold water and drain. In a saucepan, combine the beans, bay leaf, and 8 cups (80 fl oz/2 l) water and bring to a boil over high heat. Reduce the heat to low and simmer for 1 hour. Add 1 teaspoon salt and simmer until the beans are very tender but not cracked, 2–3 hours. Remove from the heat and let the beans cool in their liquid.

When the beans are done, in a heavy frying pan with a lid over medium heat, warm the olive oil. Add the bacon and cook, stirring, until browned and crisp, about 8 minutes. Add the onion, bell peppers, and garlic and cook, stirring often, until the vegetables are softened, about 2 minutes. Add the oregano, cumin, and ½ teaspoon pepper and cook until fragrant, about 1 minute. Add the tomato sauce and cook until most of the liquid has evaporated, about 5 minutes longer.

Add the rice and stir to coat with the tomato mixture. Sauté until the rice has absorbed the tomato sauce. Add the stock, stir once, and bring to a boil. Reduce the heat to low, cover, and cook until the rice has absorbed all of the liquid, about 20 minutes.

Using a large spoon, transfer the beans, along with a few spoonfuls of the cooking liquid, to the pan with the rice and stir in. Cover and cook until the rice has absorbed all of the liquid from the beans, about 10 minutes. Remove from the heat and let stand, covered, for 5 minutes, then stir gently. Season to taste with salt. Divide among warmed bowls or plates and serve right away.

Beans and rice, or *congri*, is Cuban comfort food, the unofficial national dish of poor and rich alike. Two similar styles exist: *Moros y christianos,* made with black beans, is more popular in the eastern part of the island and is sometimes simply called "black rice." This recipe, made with creamy red beans, is equally authentic and very attractive. While there is little meat in *congri,* few dishes are as satisfying.

Potatoes with Creamy Onion Sauce

This delicious dish of tender creamed potatoes and onions is traditionally made with a variety of Andean potatoes called *papas rojas*. They are small, round potatoes with lightly pocked skins that are mostly red, but also spotted with yellow. Peeling just half of the skins in strips leaves some pleasing color.

Bring a saucepan three-fourths full of water to a boil over high heat. Using a vegetable peeler, peel off half of the potato skins in strips about ½ inch (12 mm) wide. Cut potatoes that are larger than 1½ inches (4 cm) in half.

Add 2 teaspoons salt to the boiling water and stir to dissolve. Reduce the heat to medium, add the potatoes, and cook until tender when pierced with the tip of a sharp knife, about 20 minutes. Drain in a colander and place under running cold water to stop the cooking. Drain again thoroughly and pat dry.

In a frying pan over medium-low heat, melt the butter with the olive oil. Add the yellow and green onions and sauté until softened, about 2 minutes. Add the tomato, garlic, achiote, cumin, ½ teaspoon salt, and ⅛ teaspoon pepper and cook until the onions are tender, 25–30 minutes longer. Add the milk, cream, and the 1 cup (4 oz/12 g) cheese and cook, stirring to melt the cheese, until the sauce is well blended and smooth.

To serve, arrange the potatoes in a serving bowl or on a platter, pour the sauce over, and garnish with the 2 tablespoons cheese. Serve warm.

2 lb (1 kg) small red or yellow potatoes, about 1½ inches (4 cm) in diameter

Salt and freshly ground pepper

1 tablespoon unsalted butter

1 tablespoon olive oil

½ cup (2 oz/60 g) thinly sliced yellow onion

4 green (spring) onions, white and tender green parts, cut finely lengthwise

1 large ripe tomato, peeled, seeded, and sliced

1 small clove garlic, minced

¼ teaspoon achiote paste (page 278)

¼ teaspoon ground cumin

½ cup (4 fl oz/125 ml) whole milk

½ cup (4 fl oz/125 ml) heavy (double) cream

1 cup (4 oz/12 g) shredded *queso blanco* or farmer cheese, plus 2 tablespoons cheese for serving

MAKES 6 SERVINGS

Black-Eyed Peas with Chorizo and Guiso

½ lb (250 g) dried black-eyed peas (about 1 cup/8 oz)

½ lb (250 g) dry-cured chorizo, cut into slices ¼ inch (6 mm) thick

FOR THE *GUISO*

3 tablespoons olive oil, as needed

1 large yellow onion, thinly sliced

¼ cup (1 oz/30 g) minced green (spring) onions, white and tender green parts

2 tomatoes, peeled and diced

¾ cup (4½ oz/140 g) seeded and finely diced *ají dulce* peppers (page 278) or sweet Italian peppers

2 cloves garlic, minced

½ teaspoon achiote paste (page 278)

½ teaspoon ground cumin

Salt and freshly ground pepper

5 sprigs fresh cilantro (fresh coriander), plus cilantro leaves for serving

MAKES 4–6 SERVINGS

Pick over the peas and discard any misshapen peas or stones. Rinse the peas under running cold water and drain. Place in a large bowl with cold water to cover generously and soak overnight.

Heat a frying pan over medium-high heat. Add the chorizo to the pan and sear, turning as needed, until browned on all sides, about 5 minutes total. Transfer the chorizo to a platter and set aside. Reserve the pan with the rendered fat.

To make the *guiso*, add olive oil as needed to the pan with the rendered fat to make 3 tablespoons total fat. (If you prefer, you can discard the rendered fat and use all olive oil.) Warm the fat over medium heat, then add the yellow and green onions and cook until translucent, about 5 minutes. Add the tomatoes, *ají dulce* peppers, garlic, achiote, cumin, ½ teaspoon salt, and ½ teaspoon pepper and stir to mix well. Reduce the heat to medium low, cover, and cook, stirring occasionally, until the vegetables are tender, about 20 minutes.

Meanwhile, in a wide pot three-fourths full of water and bring to a boil. Drain the peas in a colander and rinse well. Add the peas to the pot, reduce the heat, and simmer until very tender, about 30 minutes. Add 1 teaspoon salt and the cilantro sprigs and simmer to allow the flavors to blend, about 5 minutes. Drain the peas in a colander and remove the cilantro.

When ready to serve, spoon the peas onto a platter, top with the *guiso* and chorizo, and garnish with the cilantro leaves.

The most definitive preparation of black-eyed peas and beans throughout Latin America is to flavor them generously with pork. African slaves worked as cooks in many houses during the colonial era, and when the Spanish *conquistadores* departed, the food they left behind were only those they thought were of little value. The slaves mixed dried beans and peas with pig's legs, tail, and rib bones, giving the beans deep flavor and crisp, tasty bits of meat. The *guiso*, or seasoning sauce, is a traditional *criollo* accompaniment.

Chile-Glazed Sweet Potatoes

Sweet potatoes are believed to have originated in the Yucatan thousands of years ago, spreading through trade and migration throughout the Western Hemisphere. Called *camote* in Mexico, they are widely used in traditional Mexican cooking, in everything from soups and stews, such as *sopa azteca*, to *tortas*, drinks, and even desserts. This dish of roasted sweet potato balances the sweet, molasses character of *piloncillo* sugar with the smoky heat of chipotle chiles and the citrusy tang from the sour orange juice.

Preheat the oven to 400°F (200°C).

Peel the sweet potatoes and cut into 1½-inch (4-cm) chunks. In a bowl, combine the potatoes with the oil and 1 teaspoon salt and toss to coat well. Spread in a single layer on a rimmed baking sheet and bake, without turning, until tender-crisp and lightly browned, 35–40 minutes.

Remove the pan from the oven; leave the oven on. Using a thin-bladed spatula, carefully loosen the potatoes from the pan. Sprinkle with the sugar and chipotles and turn gently to coat. Spread into a single layer again on the baking sheet and bake for 5 minutes longer.

Transfer the potatoes to a serving dish and drizzle with the orange juice. Garnish with the cilantro and serve right away, with *crema* on the side.

2 lb (1 kg) orange-fleshed sweet potatoes

2 tablespoons vegetable oil

Kosher salt

1 tablespoon crushed *piloncillo* sugar (page 281) or dark brown sugar

1 tablespoon chipotle chiles in adobo, finely chopped

Juice of ½ small sour orange (page 280) or 1 teaspoon *each* orange juice and lemon juice

¼ cup (⅓ oz/10 g) chopped fresh cilantro (fresh coriander)

½ cup (4 oz/125 g) Crema (page 277) or sour cream

MAKES 4–6 SERVINGS

Zucchini and Corn Torta
with Cilantro-Lime Crema

Unsalted butter for greasing

2 large poblano or Anaheim chiles, roasted and peeled (page 268)

1 ear white sweet corn, husk and silk removed

3 tablespoons olive oil

1 white onion, chopped

Kosher salt and freshly ground pepper

1 lb (500 g) zucchini (courgette), thinly sliced

1/2 teaspoon dried oregano, preferably Mexican, crumbled

1 1/2 cups (6 oz/185 g) shredded Oaxacan or Monterey jack cheese

4 large eggs, beaten

1/4 cup (1 oz/30 g) crumbled *cotija* cheese

1/4 teaspoon ancho chile powder (optional)

FOR THE CILANTRO-LIME *CREMA*

1/3 cup (2 1/2 oz/75 g) Crema, (page 277) or sour cream

1 tablespoon fresh lime juice

1/4 cup (1/3 oz/10 g) minced fresh cilantro (fresh coriander)

1 tablespoon chipotle chiles in adobo, finely chopped

Kosher salt

MAKES 6–8 SERVINGS

Position a rack in the upper third of the oven and preheat to 325°F (165°C). Butter a 6-cup (48-fl oz/1.5-l) gratin dish or other shallow baking dish.

Cut the roasted chiles into 1-inch (2.5-cm) pieces. Set aside.

Holding the ear of corn upright on a cutting board, use a sharp knife to cut off the kernels, keeping the blade angled so you get the whole kernel but none of the tough cob. You should have about 3/4 cup (4 1/2 oz/14 g) kernels. Set aside.

In a frying pan over medium heat, warm 1 tablespoon of the olive oil. Add the chiles and onion and cook, stirring often, until the onion is tender, about 5 minutes. Stir in 1 teaspoon salt. Scrape into a colander and let cool.

Add the remaining 2 tablespoons olive oil to the pan and return the pan to medium heat. Add the corn and zucchini and cook, stirring often, until the zucchini are softened but not breaking up, about 5 minutes. Stir in the oregano, 1 teaspoon salt, and 1/4 teaspoon pepper and cook to blend the flavors, about 30 seconds. Add to the colander with the chiles. Let the cooked vegetables cool and drain for 15 minutes.

Spread 1 cup (8 oz/250 g) of the zucchini mixture in an even layer in the bottom of the prepared dish. Sprinkle half of the Oaxacan cheese on top. Repeat to make a second layer of the vegetables, top with the remaining Oaxacan cheese, and end with the remaining vegetables.

Season the eggs with 1 teaspoon salt and a pinch of pepper. Pour into the dish and use a spatula to spread evenly. Scatter the *cotija* cheese over the top and dust with the chile powder. Bake until puffed and lightly browned, about 30 minutes.

Meanwhile, in a small serving bowl, stir together the *crema*, lime juice, cilantro, chipotle, and 1/4 teaspoon salt. Taste and adjust the seasoning. Cover and refrigerate until ready to use.

Serve the *torta* warm or at room temperature with the *crema*.

Quick and easy to make, and infinitely adaptable, *tortas* are a favorite light supper dish in Mexico. This popular combination of zucchini, corn, and roasted poblano chile is the perfect thing to make in the summer, when fresh corn is at its peak. Dark green poblano chiles have a wonderful, rich flavor, but can be spicy. If heat is a concern, substitute mild Anaheim chiles for some or all of the chiles.

Yellow Potatoes with Pepper-Cheese Sauce

Papas a la huancaina transforms simple boiled potatoes with a blanket of delicious yellow Peruvian *ají amarillo* pepper sauce, a regional classic. The dish is most authentic when made with small, yellow Peruvian potatoes, a variety that is slightly sweet and very creamy when cooked, if you can find them. If you are using regular yellow potatoes, such as Yukon gold or Yellow Finn, be careful not to overcook them, as they can become grainy.

Bring a saucepan three-fourths full of water to a boil over high heat. Cut the potatoes into slices about ½ inch (13 mm) thick, or halve or quarter them to make equal-size chunks. Add 2 teaspoons salt to the boiling water and stir to dissolve. Reduce the heat to medium, add the potatoes, and cook until tender when pierced with the tip of a sharp knife, 20–25 minutes. Drain in a colander and place under running cold water to stop the cooking. Drain again and pat dry.

Cut 2 of the eggs in half and separate the yolks and whites. Reserve the whites for another use. Set the yolks aside. Cut the remaining 2 eggs into ¼-inch (6-mm) slices and refrigerate until ready to serve.

In a saucepan over medium heat, warm the olive oil. Add the onion and cook until translucent, about 5 minutes. Add the *ají* pastes and garlic and sauté until fragrant, about 2 minutes. Pour in the stock, raise the heat to medium-high, and bring to a boil. Reduce the heat to medium-low and simmer until the onion is tender, about 10 minutes longer. Remove from the heat and let cool slightly. Transfer the onion-stock mixture to a blender or food processor and add the reserved 2 egg yolks, the evaporated milk, the cheese, the crackers, and ½ teaspoon salt. Process until smooth. Set the sauce aside.

To serve, divide the potatoes evenly among individual plates and pour the sauce over the potatoes. Garnish with the egg slices and the olives, or serve alongside.

2 lb (1 kg) small yellow potatoes, preferably Peruvian, about 1½ inches (4 cm) in diameter, peeled

Salt

4 large eggs, hard-boiled

2 tablespoons olive oil

1 large red onion, thinly sliced

¼ cup (2 oz/60 g) *ají panca* paste (page 278)

1 tablespoon *ají amarillo* paste (page 278)

2 cloves garlic, minced

½ cup (4 fl oz/125 ml) Chicken Stock (page 270) or low-sodium broth

1 can (10 fl oz/310 ml) evaporated milk

1 cup (4 oz/125 g) shredded *queso blanco* or farmer's cheese

8 saltine crackers (savory biscuits) or 6–8 tablespoons fine dry bread crumbs

Cured black olives such as Botija or Kalamata, pitted

MAKES 4–6 SERVINGS

Lima Beans with Citrus-Herb Sauce

½ lb (250 g) dried lima beans (about 1 cup/8 oz)

Salt

¼ yellow onion

2 bay leaves

FOR THE SAUCE

2 tablespoons fresh lime juice

2 tablespoons minced fresh flat-leaf (Italian) parsley

1½ teaspoons sugar

1 teaspoon dried oregano

¼ teaspoon *aji amarillo* paste (page 278)

Salt and freshly ground pepper

½ cup (4 fl oz/125 ml) olive oil

FOR SERVING

2 large ripe tomatoes, thickly sliced

½ red onion, thinly sliced

MAKES 4–6 SERVINGS

Pick over the beans and discard any misshapen beans or stones, then rinse under running cold water. In a large bowl, combine 4 cups (32 fl oz/1 l) cold water and 1 teaspoon salt and stir to dissolve the salt. Add the beans and soak overnight.

Drain the beans in a colander and rinse well. In a large saucepan, combine the beans, onion, bay leaves, and 6 cups (48 fl oz/1.5 l) cold water and bring to a boil over medium heat. Reduce the heat to medium-low and simmer until the beans are tender but not cracked, about 20 minutes. Drain thoroughly and transfer to a bowl. Discard the bay leaves.

To make the sauce, in a bowl, whisk together the lime juice, parsley, sugar, oregano, *aji* paste, ½ teaspoon salt, and ½ teaspoon pepper. Add the olive oil in a thin stream, whisking constantly until smooth and emulsified.

Pour the sauce over the beans and stir gently to avoid breaking up the beans. Let stand at room temperature to allow the flavors to blend, at least 20 minutes or until ready to serve.

To serve, divide the beans evenly among individual plates. Arrange the tomato and onion slices alongside and serve right away.

Wild lima beans, named for Lima, the Peruvian capital, are of Andean ancestry and were exported to the rest of the Americas and Europe during the time of the Spanish Colonies. This salad is a simple mixture of tender lima beans tossed with a typical Peruvian flavors of lime, fresh and dried herbs, *aji amarillo* paste, and olive oil, and served with slices of ripe, juicy tomatoes and peppery red onions.

Poblano Chiles Stuffed with Greens and Cheese

In this hearty vegetarian recipe, poblano chiles are filled with a savory combination of cheese and *quelites*. *Quelites* are a type of wild green sometimes known as lamb's-quarters, pigweed, or goosefoot. The spinach-like leaves have a delightful flavor and are said to be even more nutritious than spinach and Swiss chard, to which they are related. Make sure to wash the greens well before using them in the stuffing.

Place the *quelites* in a saucepan with only the rinsing water clinging to the leaves and sprinkle with salt. Place over medium heat and cook, stirring, until wilted, about 5 minutes. Drain well, squeeze out any excess moisture, and chop coarsely.

Preheat the oven to 350°F (180°C). In a large frying pan over medium-high heat, warm the oil. Add the raisins, pine nuts, and greens and cook, stirring constantly, until totally dry, about 3 minutes. Pour in ½ cup (4 fl oz/125 ml) water. Continue to stir until the liquid has evaporated, about 5 minutes. Remove from the heat; let cool. Carefully peel the chiles. Leaving the stem end intact, make a lengthwise slit in each chile and remove the seeds and veins; do not cut through the chile.

Divide the greens and cheese among the chiles, stuffing them carefully so as not to tear them and allowing them to close completely with overlapping edges. Place in a shallow baking dish and cover with aluminum foil. Bake the chiles until they are heated through and the cheese is softened, 20–30 minutes.

To make the tomato sauce, line a heavy frying pan with heavy-duty aluminum foil and place over high heat. Arrange the tomatoes, onion, and garlic clove on the foil and roast until the flesh is soft and the skins are blackened on all sides. The garlic will be done after about 5 minutes, and the tomatoes and onion will take 10–15 minutes. Peel the garlic and put in a blender or food processor with the tomatoes and onion. Process until smooth, adding up to ½ cup (4 fl oz/ 125 ml) water if needed.

In a frying pan over medium-high heat, warm the oil until it is smoking. Pour the tomato mixture into the pan all at once—be careful, as it will splatter—and fry, stirring, for 1–2 minutes. Reduce the heat to medium-low and continue cooking until the sauce is quite thick, 15–20 minutes. Season with salt and keep warm.

Remove the chiles from the oven and transfer to a serving platter or individual plates. Pour the sauce around them, swirl on the *crema*, and serve right away.

2½ lb (1.25 kg) *quelites* (see Note) or spinach leaves, stems removed

Sea salt

¼ cup (2 fl oz/60 ml) olive oil

⅓ cup (2 oz/60 g) raisins

⅓ cup (2 oz/60 g) pine nuts

6 poblano chiles, roasted (page 268) and left whole

6 oz (185 g) *queso fresco*, thinly sliced

FOR THE TOMATO SAUCE

1½ lb (750 g) plum (Roma) tomatoes

1 small slice white onion

2 cloves garlic, unpeeled

1½ teaspoons olive oil

Sea salt

½ cup (4 fl oz/125 ml) Crema (page 277), or purchased, for serving

MAKES 6 SERVINGS

Mexican Red Rice

1 can (14½ oz/455 g) whole tomatoes, drained

3 tablespoons chopped white onion

2 small cloves garlic

¼ cup (2 fl oz/60 ml) canola oil

1 cup (7 oz/220 g) medium-grain white rice

⅓ cup (2 oz/60 g) *each* fresh or frozen peas, fresh or frozen corn kernels, and diced peeled carrot

3 serrano chiles, slit down one side

6 fresh cilantro (fresh coriander) sprigs, tied together, plus chopped cilantro leaves for serving

Sea salt

MAKES 4–6 SERVINGS

Put the tomatoes, onion, and garlic in a blender and process until smooth. Set aside. In a saucepan over medium-high heat, warm the oil. When hot, add the rice and stir until it just starts to change color, about 1 minute. Do not allow it to brown. Add the tomato mixture and stir gently to blend. Add 2 cups (16 fl oz/ 500 ml) hot water, the peas, corn, carrot, chiles, cilantro sprigs, and 1½ teaspoons salt. Bring to a boil, shaking the pan to mix the ingredients. Reduce the heat to low. Taste the broth and add more salt, if necessary, then cover and continue to cook, about 10 minutes.

Uncover and stir carefully so that all of the broth is mixed in (most will have been absorbed). Re-cover and cook until all the broth is absorbed, about 10 minutes longer. Remove from the heat and let stand, covered, for 10 minutes. Before serving, remove the cilantro sprigs and chiles and fluff the rice with a fork. Garnish with the chopped cilantro and serve right away.

In Mexico, rice is rarely served simply steamed without any seasonings. This red rice is a classic accompaniment to almost any meal, from fish and meat courses to tacos. You can make this rice spicy by adding 1–2 chipotle chiles in adobo to the blender with the tomatoes. Or, stir in 2–3 teaspoons achiote paste (page 278) to the blender with the tomatoes for an interesting spark of flavor.

Fried Green Plantains

These delicious green plantain fritters are enjoyed throughout Latin America. Some are thick and some are paper-thin, but *patacones* or *tostones* are among the most important foods to home cooks and restaurants alike. Although fried twice (once to cook and soften, and once to ensure they are golden and crisp), the fritters are very easy to prepare. They can also be made ahead of time (after being flattened) and frozen for up to 3 months.

To peel the green plantains, slice the ends off with a knife and make a lengthwise cut from one end to the other of the plantain skin. Remove the rest of the skin from the plantain. Slice the plantain into chunks 1–1½ inches (2.5–4 cm) wide.

To precook the plantains, heat the oil in a sauté pan over medium-high heat until it reaches 325°F (165°C) on an instant-read thermometer. Lower the heat to medium and add the plantain chunks to the oil. Deep-fry the chunks, 3–4 minutes. Remove the chunks with a slotted spoon and drain on paper towels.

You can use a wooden press to flatten the plantains or do it with a heavy pan. Place an opened plastic bag over your wooden press or on your counter, put each plantain chunk inside the bag, and smash it with the top of the wooden press or with a heavy frying pan; do this while the plantains are still warm.

To finish the plantains, warm the oil in the pan over medium-high heat until it reaches 350°F (180°C). Add the plantain chunks and deep-fry until lightly golden, about 2 minutes more. Sprinkle them with salt after removing them from the oil and place on paper towels to drain any excess oil. Serve right away.

2 green plantains

3 cups canola oil

Salt

MAKES 4–6 SERVINGS

Eggs

About Eggs

Throughout Latin America, eggs are served in similar ways, but with slight variations. Whether scrambled, fried, or poached, they are typically accompanied with tortillas or *arepas*, refried beans, and salsas or chile-spiced sauces.

Before the Spanish and Portuguese brought chickens to the Americas, the only bird's eggs available in the New World were a limited number of domesticated duck and turkey eggs, and wild bird eggs that had to be foraged for and were difficult to find. After the introduction of chickens to the Americas, eggs were no longer a rare treat. However, even after eggs were incorporated into the Latin diet, they were not often served at breakfast, as is customary in North America.

A typical Latin American breakfast might include coffee, fresh juice, sweet bread rolls with fruit jam, and a selection of fresh fruits, such as melons, papaya, mango, and strawberries. These days, eggs are offered for breakfast, but they are more likely to appear later in the day for a late breakfast or brunch, as a first course at the midday *comida*, or as a light entrée for the evening supper.

MEXICAN EGG DISHES

In Northern Mexico, cowboy-style eggs are scrambled with shredded dried beef *(machaca)* and served with refried pinto beans, a basket of warm flour tortillas, and a bowl of green chile salsa. Another Mexican egg dish which has gained an international following is *huevos rancheros*, fried eggs served on top of crisp corn tortillas and refried beans, then topped with salsa, Mexican *crema* (similar to sour cream and crème fraiche), crumbled cheese, diced avocados, and fresh cilantro. Riffs on *huevos rancheros* are popular in Cuba and

Central America, where peas, plantains, and ham are often added.

Since corn is a sacred staple, leftover tortillas are never wasted. The tradition of finding uses for day-old tortillas led to the development of many favorite dishes. Perhaps the most popular use of leftover tortillas is the Mexican dish called *chilaquiles*. Although the original version of the dish does not include eggs, heartier versions nowadays often do. To make *chilaquiles*, day-old tortillas are cut into strips, sautéed until crisp, then simmered in a casserole with either a red chile and tomato sauce or a green tomatillo sauce. When topped with eggs, sprinkled with crumbled *cotija* cheese, and served with a side of pinto or black beans, a meal of *chilaquiles* can fill you up for most of the day. Also popular in Mexico are scrambled eggs cooked with whatever fresh ingredients are on hand, such as cactus, roasted peppers, and onions.

CARIBBEAN EGG DISHES

In Cuba, the Dominican Republic, and Puerto Rico, egg dishes combine Spanish, New World, and African food influences. As in Spain, eggs are often prepared Andalucian style, simply fried in olive oil, topped with tomato sauce, sprinkled with peas, and served with rice. What makes the dish uniquely Caribbean is the addition of black or red beans and fried plantains. *Huevos habaneros*, another Caribbean recipe with a Spanish flavor, is an easy, delicious dish to serve when entertaining. Eggs are baked in a Spanish-style tomato

sauce, sprinkled with sherry, and garnished with chopped pimiento peppers. With a loaf of crusty Cuban bread and a fruit salad, the dish is an impressive brunch entrée.

CENTRAL AMERICAN AND SOUTH AMERICAN EGG DISHES

Central and South Americans are also creative with eggs. In Honduras, fresh corn tortillas hot off the *comal* (griddle) are topped with scrambled eggs, refried beans, stewed beef, shredded cheese, diced avocado, jalapeños, and *crema*. These *baleadas* are often folded in half and eaten like tacos.

In Venezuela and Colombia, land of the *arepa* (corn cake), street venders have an ingenious way of cooking eggs. *Arepas* are deep-fried until they puff up, a raw egg is slipped into the warm, hollow interior, and the whole package is re-fried in hot oil until the egg is softly cooked. Sometimes the *arepa* is opened again and shredded beef and tomato sauce are added to the pocket with the egg, or the sauce can be served on top. The resulting dish, *empanada de huevo* is an impressive show-stopper and well worth making at home.

Another popular egg dish in Venezuela is called *perico,* a simple preparation of scrambled eggs with diced onions, tomatoes, and minced hot chiles.

The recipes in this chapter highlight a sampling of classic Latin American egg dishes. Using the recipes as a guide, they can be varied by cooking the eggs differently and adding different salsas and toppings as desired. You can also omit the eggs and make a delicious pared-down version of many of the dishes in this chapter, such as *chilaquiles* or *baleadas.*

Huevos Rancheros

Huevos Rancheros is not only a popular breakfast dish in Mexico, but it has become a regular offering on breakfast and brunch menus throughout Latin America and the United States. Translated as "ranch eggs," the hearty dish was traditionally served as a mid-morning meal with beans and rice to satiate hungry farm workers.

To make the tomato sauce, in a food processor, combine the roasted tomatoes, chiles, onion, and garlic and process until blended but still chunky. In a large frying pan over medium-high heat, warm 1 tablespoon canola oil. Add the tomato mixture and cook, stirring constantly, until thickened, about 5 minutes. Stir in ½ teaspoon salt. Keep the sauce warm if making the *huevos rancheros* right away, or store in a tightly sealed container in the refrigerator for up to 2 days.

If the tortillas are still fresh, spread them in a single layer on a work surface and let them dry out for 5 minutes. Meanwhile, in a wide, shallow saucepan, warm the tomato sauce, if necessary.

In a large cast iron or nonstick frying pan over medium-high heat, warm the ¼ cup (2 fl oz/60 ml) oil. One at a time, fry the tortillas, turning over, to soften, about 5 seconds on each side. Using tongs, transfer to paper towels to drain. Put on a plate and place in a low 250°F (95°C) oven to keep warm.

Reduce the heat to medium-low and wait a couple of minutes for the frying pan to cool down. Break 4 eggs into the pan and fry them slowly until the whites are set and the yolks have begun to thicken but are not hard (cover the frying pan if you like firm yolks), about 3 minutes. Season to taste with salt and pepper. If serving 2 eggs per person, transfer the cooked eggs to a roasting pan and keep warm in the oven. Add a little more oil to the frying pan if necessary, and fry the remaining 4 eggs.

Remove the tortillas from the oven. Using tongs, dip each tortilla quickly in the warmed tomato sauce and place on warmed individual plates. Spread ¼ cup (2 oz/60 g) of the refried beans evenly on each tortilla and top each with 2 of the fried eggs. Spoon more of the tomato sauce generously over the edges of each tortilla. Spoon a little *crema* over the sauce, then sprinkle with the cheese and cilantro, and scatter the cubed avocado around the edges.

FOR THE TOMATO SAUCE

7 plum (Roma) tomatoes, roasted (page 268)

2–3 serrano chiles, stemmed, seeded, and minced

½ small white onion, chopped

1 large clove garlic

Sea salt

Canola oil

4 large, thick corn tortillas, preferably stale

¼ cup (2 fl oz/60 ml) canola oil, or as needed

4–8 large eggs

Fine sea salt and freshly ground pepper

1 cup (8 oz/250 g) refried pinto beans (page 276), or purchased

⅔ cup (5 fl oz/160 ml) Crema (page 277) or sour cream

⅓ cup (1½ oz/45 g) crumbled *queso añejo* or *panela* (pages 26, 278) or grated Monterey jack cheese

1 tablespoon coarsely chopped fresh cilantro (fresh coriander)

1 small avocado, pitted, peeled, and cut into ½-inch (12-mm) cubes

MAKES 4 SERVINGS

Chilaquiles with Poached Eggs and Tomatillo Sauce

FOR THE TOMATILLO SAUCE

12 tomatillos, husks removed, fruit washed

2 cloves garlic, chopped

1/2 small yellow onion, chopped

2 jalapeño chiles, seeded and coarsely chopped

1/4 cup (1/3 oz/10 g) chopped fresh cilantro (fresh coriander)

2 tablespoons canola, sunflower, or grapeseed oil

1 cup (8 fl oz/250 ml) Chicken Stock (page 270), or low-sodium broth

1/2 teaspoon salt

1/2 teaspoon freshly ground pepper

2 cups (16 fl oz/500 ml) canola oil

18 day-old corn tortillas, 6 inches (15 cm) in diameter, torn into strips

1/2 small yellow onion, chopped

1/4 lb (125 g) Monterey jack cheese, shredded

2 tablespoons chopped fresh oregano

1 teaspoon fresh lemon juice

4–6 large eggs

1/4 lb (125 g) *queso fresco*, crumbled

MAKES 4 SERVINGS

To make the tomatillo sauce, bring a large pot of water to boil over high heat. Reduce the heat to medium-high, add the tomatillos, and cook until they soften and become paler in color, 3–4 minutes. Using a slotted spoon, transfer the tomatillos to a cutting board and let cool. Chop and place in a blender or food processor. Add the garlic, onion, jalapeños, and cilantro and process until puréed.

In a large saucepan over medium heat, warm the oil. Add the tomatillo purée and cook, stirring, until the purée darkens, 4–5 minutes. Gradually add the stock and continue to cook, stirring occasionally, until a medium-thick sauce forms, about 10 minutes longer. Stir in the salt and pepper and set aside.

In a heavy frying pan over medium-high heat, warm the oil. Working in batches, add the tortilla strips and fry until golden on one side, about 30 seconds. Turn and fry until golden on the second side, 15–20 seconds. Transfer to paper towels.

Pour off all but 1–2 teaspoons of the oil from the pan and place over medium heat. Add the onion and cook, stirring, until translucent, about 1 minute. Add the tortilla strips and the tomatillo sauce and cook, stirring gently, until the chips are soft, 3–4 minutes. Stir in the cheese and half of the oregano. Continue to cook until the cheese has melted, 4–5 minutes longer. Remove from the heat and stir in the remaining oregano.

Pour water to a depth of 2 inches (5 cm) into a large saucepan and add the lemon juice. Place over medium heat and bring to a gentle simmer. Break an egg into a small bowl. Gently slide the egg into the simmering water and slide the egg into the water. Repeat with the remaining eggs, spacing them about 1 inch (2.5 cm) apart. Keep the water at a gentle simmer. Cook until the whites are set, 4–5 minutes.

Just before the eggs are done, divide the *chilaquiles* among 4 plates. Using a slotted spoon, lift each egg from the water, letting the excess water drain into the pan. Trim any ragged edges of egg white with kitchen scissors (shears). Top each serving with a poached egg and some of the *queso fresco*. Serve right away.

This traditional Mexican dish is a delicious way to transform day-old tortillas. The tortillas, torn into strips as they are here or cut into triangles like chips, are fried, covered with a zesty sauce, and cooked on the stove top or baked in the oven. The sauce for this version is made with fresh tomatillos and spiked with chiles. *Chilaquiles* are often served with poached, scrambled, or fried eggs and creamy black beans to make a colorful and hearty dish.

Arepas with Eggs and Tomato Sauce

Empanadas de huevo are also called *arepas de huevo,* and although purists say they are not *arepas,* local jargon will prove them wrong. They are usually made with yellow corn in cities like Cartagena in Colombia, but with white corn in others like Barranquilla or in Venezuela. Served in carts on streets, fried in front of your eyes, these are a delicacy that will keep you yearning for more.

To make the tomato sauce, in a saucepan over medium-low heat, warm the olive oil. Add the onion and cook, stirring often, until translucent, about 5 minutes. Add the tomatoes, *ají dulce* peppers, garlic, ¼ teaspoon salt, and pepper to taste. Cover and cook gently, stirring occasionally, until the tomatoes break down and the peppers are tender, about 20 minutes.

To make the *arepas,* in a bowl, stir together the cornmeal and 1 teaspoon salt. Add 1½ cups (12 fl oz/375 ml) water and stir until all of the cornmeal is moistened, adding up to 4 tablespoons (2 fl oz/60 ml) more water, 1–2 tablespoons at a time, as needed. Cover and let stand, about 2 minutes. Turn the dough out onto a work surface. Dampen your hands and knead until the dough is smooth, no longer sticky, and soft to the touch, about 5 minutes. (Do not cut the kneading time short or the *arepas* will not puff properly.) Shape the dough into a log about 8 inches (20 cm) long. Reserve 1 tablespoon of dough in case you need to patch any holes. Cut the log into 6 equal pieces and form each piece into a ball. Working with 1 ball of dough at a time, place between 2 sheets of plastic wrap and, using the palm of your hand, the bottom of a pot lid, or a wide spatula, flatten into a disk about 6 inches (15 cm) in diameter and ¼ inch (3 mm) thick. Patch any holes with pinches of the reserved dough, if necessary. Pour oil to a depth of 3 inches (7.5 cm) into a deep saucepan over medium-high heat and heat to 325°F (165°C) on a deep-frying thermometer. Line a large baking sheet with paper towels.

Slide 1 *arepa* into the hot oil and fry until lightly golden on the first side, about 1 minute. Using a slotted spoon, turn the *arepa* and fry until the second side is lightly golden and nicely puffed by about ½ inch (12 mm), 1–2 minutes longer. Transfer carefully to the prepared baking sheet to drain, placing it puffed side up. Let the oil return to 325°F (165°C). Repeat to fry the remaining *arepas.*

Using a small, sharp knife, cut a slit about 1½ inches (4 cm) long in the edge of each *arepa.* One at a time, break an egg into a small bowl and carefully pour the egg into an *arepa* through the slit. Place the *arepa* back into the hot oil, using the tongs to hold it upright in the oil so the egg doesn't ooze out. Fry for about 5 seconds to seal the hole and soft-cook the yolk. Fry for 1 minute for a hard-cooked yolk. Transfer to the paper towels to drain.

When all of the *arepas* are fried, divide them among individual serving plates and top each serving with a spoonful of the tomato sauce. Serve right away, passing more tomato sauce at the table.

FOR THE TOMATO SAUCE

3 tablespoons olive oil

1 small yellow onion, finely diced

2 large ripe tomatoes, peeled, seeded, and diced (about 2 cups/12 oz/375 g)

2 tablespoons seeded and minced *ají dulce* peppers (page 278) or sweet Italian peppers

1 garlic clove, minced

Salt and freshly ground pepper

1½ cups (7½ oz/235 g) precooked white cornmeal such as Harina P.A.N. or ArepArina (page 21)

Salt

Canola oil for frying

6 large eggs

MAKES 6 SERVINGS

Havana-Style Eggs

2 tablespoons vegetable oil

1 large white onion, diced

4 cloves garlic, minced

1 large green bell pepper
(capsicum), seeded and diced

2 plum (Roma) tomatoes,
diced, or 1 cup (6 oz/185 g)
drained, canned, and diced
tomatoes

½ cup (3 oz/90 g) jarred
diced red pimientos
(sweet peppers), drained

4 tablespoons (2 fl oz/60 ml)
dry sherry

Kosher salt and freshly
ground pepper

8 large eggs

2 tablespoons cold unsalted
butter, cut into 8 slices

MAKES 4 SERVINGS

In this simple Cuban classic, baked eggs are nestled in a thick, savory sauce of peppers and tomatoes, topped with butter and a heady drizzle of sherry. The dish can be made and served in one pan or in individual baking dishes. Perfect for brunch, this recipe is easily doubled or tripled for a large group and can be prepared in advance. *Huevos habaneros* can also be cooked on the stove top under a tight-fitting lid. Serve with Cuban bread and a bowl of fresh tropical fruit.

Position a rack in the upper third of the oven and preheat to 350°F (180°C).

In a shallow 10-inch (25-cm) cast iron pan or other flameproof pan over medium heat, warm the oil. Add the onion and garlic and cook, stirring, until translucent, 2–3 minutes. Add the bell pepper and cook, stirring, until beginning to soften, about 2 minutes. Stir in the tomatoes and cook until the mixture forms a thick, juicy sauce. Set aside 1 tablespoon of the pimientos and add the rest to the sauce. Add 3 tablespoons of the sherry, stir to mix well, and cook until heated through, about 2 minutes. Stir in 1 teaspoon salt and ½ teaspoon pepper.

To bake individually, transfer the tomato mixture to 4 shallow baking dishes, dividing evenly. Using the back of a large metal spoon, form 2 deep wells in the sauce. One at a time, break an egg into a small, shallow dish and then carefully slip into a well. Drizzle the eggs with the remaining 1 tablespoon sherry, sprinkle with a little more salt and pepper, and top each egg with a sliver of butter and some of the reserved pimiento. Alternatively, bake the eggs in the pan with the tomato mixture, forming 8 wells in the tomato mixture, using the same method as above to slip the eggs into each of the wells.

Bake, uncovered, until the eggs are done to your liking, about 10 minutes for a soft to runny yolk or 15 minutes for a hard-cooked yolk. Serve right away.

Chilaquiles with Scrambled Eggs and Red Chile Sauce

Chilaquiles are a favorite in many regions of Mexico for breakfast or a light supper, topped with scrambled eggs and beans, along with spoonfuls of hot sauce, *crema*, and *salsa fresca* or *pico de gallo*. *Chilaquiles* are simple and quick to make, and a great way to use up stale corn tortillas—fresh tortillas are likely to disintegrate when mixed with the other ingredients, so if you don't have stale tortillas, a brief frying (or a short time in the oven) will dry them out.

In a large frying pan over medium-high heat, pour oil to a depth of 1 inch (2.5 cm), and heat to 350°F (180°C) on a deep-frying thermometer. Line a large baking sheet with paper towels. Working in batches, fry the tortilla pieces until they soften and just stiffen again. Transfer to the paper towels to drain.

Pour off all but 2 tablespoons of the oil and place over medium heat. Add the onion and cook, stirring, until it begins to soften, about 1 minute. Add the garlic and tomatoes and cook, 1 minute longer. Return the tortillas to the pan and stir in the chile sauce, starting with 1/3 cup (3 fl oz/90 ml). (You want to add enough sauce to soften and generously coat the tortilla strips, but not so much that there is sauce left in the pan.) Cook, stirring often, until the tortillas are heated through and have absorbed the sauce, about 3 minutes. Stir in the cilantro.

Meanwhile, in another frying pan over medium heat, melt the butter. Add the eggs and cook, using a wooden spoon or silicone spatula to pull the cooked egg away from the sides and bottom of the pan as the curds form. Continue to cook until all the eggs are soft, moist scrambled curds.

Divide the *chilaquiles* among 4 warmed plates and top with a spoonful of hot beans and some scrambled eggs. Top with a dollop of salsa, and garnish with the jalapeño slices and cilantro. Serve right away with the hot sauce, *crema*, and cheese, if desired.

Canola oil for frying

12 day-old corn tortillas, 6 inches (15 cm) in diameter, torn into strips

1 white onion, diced

2 cloves garlic, finely chopped

2 plum (Roma) tomatoes, diced

1/3–1/2 cup (3–4 fl oz/ 90–125 ml) Red Chile Sauce (page 273)

1/4 cup (1/3 oz/10 g) coarsely chopped fresh cilantro (fresh coriander)

2 teaspoons unsalted butter

6 large eggs, beaten

1 1/2 cups cooked black beans (page 276), or canned beans, warmed in their juice

FOR SERVING

Salsa Fresca or Pico De Gallo (page 273)

Seeded and sliced jalapeño chiles

Fresh cilantro (fresh coriander) leaves

Hot pepper sauce

1/4 cup (2 oz/60 g) Crema (page 277) or sour cream

Crumbled *cotija* cheese (optional)

MAKES 4 SERVINGS

Baleadas with Scrambled Eggs and Shredded Beef

2 cups (10 oz/315 g) precooked white cornmeal such as Harina P.A.N. or ArepArina (page 21)

6–8 eggs

1 tablespoon unsalted butter

FOR THE TOPPINGS

Refried Beans (page 276), or purchased refried beans

Shredded Beef (page 276)

Shredded cheese such as *queso blanco* or Monterey jack

Diced avocado

Sliced jalapeño chiles

Crema (page 277) or sour cream

Hot pepper sauce

MAKES 4–6 SERVINGS

To make the tortillas, in a bowl, combine the cornmeal and 2 cups (8 fl oz/ 250 ml) water and stir until all of the cornmeal is moistened, adding more water, a tablespoon at a time, as needed. Cover and let stand, about 2 minutes. Turn the dough out onto a work surface. Dampen your hands and knead until the dough is smooth, and soft to the touch, about 5 minutes. Shape the dough into a log about 10 inches (25 cm) long. Cut the log into 16 equal pieces and form each piece into a ball. Follow the instructions on page 269 to flatten the dough balls into disks about 6 inches (15 cm) in diameter and ⅛ inch (3 mm) thick.

Heat a large nonstick frying pan over medium-high heat until very hot. Place a tortilla in the hot pan and cook, turning once, until it puffs up by about 1 inch, like a pita bread, 3–4 minutes per side. Using a wide spatula, flatten the tortilla, turn once more, and cook, about 1 minute longer. Transfer to a plate and repeat to cook the remaining tortillas. Keep in a warm oven until ready to serve.

When ready to serve, scramble the eggs. In a bowl, using a fork, beat together the eggs until blended. In a large frying pan over medium heat, melt the butter. Add the eggs and cook, stirring, until the curds have formed but are still soft, about 5 minutes.

Arrange the tortillas and toppings on a large platter and instruct guests to assemble their own *baleada*. Pass the hot pepper sauce at the table.

In Honduras, corn tortillas are made daily in homes. When eaten with eggs in the morning or with meat, cheese, and/or vegetable fillings during the rest of the day, the snack is called a *baleada*. Honduran tortillas may be made with corn flour, as in this recipe, or wheat flour. *Baleadas* are also a popular street food snack, sold from carts on the city streets day and night and offered with a variety of fillings. They are often folded in half over the fillings and eaten like a taco.

Desserts

About Desserts

Silky puddings, sweet chocolate cakes, fruit-flavored ice creams, and creamy pies were not typical dessert fare for the Mayas and Aztecs, who enjoyed simple sweets in the form of fresh fruits and confections sweetened with local honey and agave nectar.

The idea of a sweet finale to a meal came to the Americas from Europe, and it was well received. Many of the New World desserts and sweets were developed in convent kitchens. As they had in Europe, nuns in the convents of Mexico, the Caribbean, and Central and South America often used their culinary skills to produce sweets that were sold to raise money to support charitable works.

New World desserts also came from African cooks in the Caribbean and Brazil who worked in the kitchens of the "big houses" on sugar plantations. Their creativity, along with their skill at combining Old and New World ingredients, brought desserts like coconut rice pudding and coconut- and peanut-based cookies to the Latin American table.

FLANS AND PUDDINGS

Flan, the dessert most often associated with Latin American cooking, is a traditional Spanish and Portuguese sweet. In Spain and Portugal, custard desserts can be traced in part to the practice of using large quantities of egg whites to clarify wine during the production of sherry, Port, and Madeira—leaving a lot of egg yolks behind for cooking and baking. One extremely rich version, known as "heavenly bacon," or *tocino de cielo* in Spanish and *toucinho do céu* in Portuguese, calls for a full dozen egg yolks. Popular variations include chocolate, coffee, pumpkin, and coconut flans, which are topped with a dark caramel often flavored with rum.

Pudding is another favorite dessert throughout Latin America. A sweet and savory bread pudding with fresh and dried fruits, spices, and sharp cheese *(capirotada)* is traditionally served in Mexico during Lent, and rice pudding is a favorite at any time of year. Cubans also love rice pudding, often flavoring it with orange and lime zest and folding in crushed pineapple and rum. Brazilian cooks make a comforting coconut pudding with tapioca (small pearls of yuca starch), and in Peru, *mazamorra de quinoa* is a rich tasty pudding made with cooked quinoa.

CAKES, PIES, AND COOKIES

One of the most popular cakes in Latin America for fiestas is the *tres leches cake* (pronounced *ka-kay* in Cuba). While the recipe varies somewhat from country to country, the basic idea is the same: a white or yellow cake in a rich, sweet milk sauce made with evaporated milk, sweetened condensed milk, and heavy cream, and flavored with rum and vanilla. Some versions blanket the cake in sweetened whipped cream or with a fluffy meringue frosting. The cake is often decorated with fresh fruit or flowers.

While the Aztecs drank hot chocolate flavored with chiles and thickened with masa, they did not make chocolate cakes. Modern cooks in Mexico have reinvented the combination of chocolate and chiles to develop exciting new recipes like chocolate-ancho cake. Sweet innovations like this are exciting examples of the potential in contemporary cuisines to merge old traditions with new flavors and cooking applications.

In the elegant pastry shops of Buenos Aires, a luscious orange cake with passion fruit glaze *(Pastel de Naranja)* is a customer favorite, but it is also easy to make at home. Alfajores, crisp, delicate wafer cookies filled with *dulce de leche* (thick caramel sauce), are another specialty that Argentinians often purchase at the pastry shop. *Dulce de leche* is now quite easy to find in supermarkets in the United States and many other countries throughout the world, so the cookies are easy to make at home.

FRUITS AND ICES

Fruit compotes and poached fresh fruit have been popular Latin American desserts since the Spanish Conquest, but the sugary and rich fruit ice creams and sorbets that arrived in the nineteenth century took Latin America by storm. The first ice cream shops in Cuba were started by entrepreneurial Chinese immigrants from the United States, who arrived in Havana in the mid-1800s armed with a revolutionary new invention: the hand-crank ice-cream machine. Cubans immediately took to ice cream and the passion that spread throughout Latin America has not lessened today. Even today, although ice-cream making has become more commercialized, you can still find individually owned ice-cream shops or carts throughout Latin America turning out small batches of exotic ices and ice creams made with blackberries, coconut, banana, cherimoya, passion fruit, and açai berries, as well as the perhaps more expected but equally decadent flavors such as chocolate, strawberry, and vanilla.

Spiced Hot Chocolate with Churros

Hot chocolate has its roots in an ancient grain-based drink, or *atole*, once made exclusively for the pleasure of Aztec royalty. It was made with bitter cocoa beans, thickened with ground corn, and flavored with anise, vanilla, annatto seed, and other native spices. Today, sweet hot chocolate thickened with fine corn masa, called *champurrada*, is a favorite street food, served accompanied with a paper bag of piping-hot, crispy deep-fried *churros* for dunking.

To make the hot chocolate, in a small, dry frying pan over medium heat, stir the aniseed until lightly toasted, 1–2 minutes. Transfer to a mortar or a small bowl and, using a pestle or the end of a wooden spoon, crush the seeds. Set aside.

In a saucepan over medium-low heat, combine the masa harina and 2 cups (16 fl oz/ 500 ml) water and cook, whisking constantly, until the mixture thickens, about 3 minutes. Whisk in the milk. Add the chocolate and *piloncillo* sugar and stir until the chocolate melts and the sugar dissolves, about 3 minutes. Add the cinnamon, vanilla, and crushed aniseed and simmer, stirring constantly, for about 2 minutes. Reduce the heat to very low to keep the hot chocolate hot; do not let boil.

To make the *churros*, in another saucepan, combine 1 cup (8 fl oz/250 ml) water, 1 teaspoon salt, and 1 tablespoon of the granulated sugar. Bring to a boil over high heat, then remove from the heat and immediately add the flour, all at once. Beat with a wooden spoon until the dough is very smooth and pulls away from the sides of the pan, about 2 minutes. Let cool for 5 minutes, then beat in the eggs, about 1 tablespoon at a time. When all of the eggs are thoroughly incorporated, spoon the dough into a pastry bag fitted with a large star tip and twist the bag closed.

Pour oil to a depth of 1 inch (2.5 cm) into a heavy frying pan and place over medium heat. Add the lemon zest and cook until browned, about 5 minutes. Using a skimmer, a slotted spoon, or tongs, remove the zest and discard. Squeeze a ½-inch (12-mm) piece of dough through the piping tip of the pastry bag and cut it off with a knife or scissors (shears), dipping the dough piece into the hot oil. When bubbles form all around the dough piece, the temperature is correct. A deep-frying thermometer should read 350°F (180°C). Discard the test piece.

Pipe several strips of dough, each 3–4 inches (7.5–10 cm) long, directly into the hot oil, being careful not to crowd the pan. Cut the dough strips free from the piping tip with the knife or scissors and dip the tool in the oil before each cut. Fry the *churros*, turning as needed, until deep golden brown and very crisp, 3–5 minutes. Using the skimmer, slotted spoon, or tongs, transfer to paper towels to drain briefly, then place in a large bowl. Repeat to cook the remaining *churros*.

In a small bowl, stir together the cinnamon and the remaining 2 tablespoons granulated sugar. Add to the bowl with the warm *churros* and toss to coat evenly. Serve warm, with cups of the hot chocolate for sipping and dunking.

FOR THE HOT CHOCOLATE

¼ teaspoon aniseed

¼ cup (1¼ oz/37 g) masa harina

2 cups (16 fl oz/500 ml) whole milk

1 disk (3 oz/90 g) Mexican chocolate, coarsely chopped

3 tablespoons crushed *piloncillo* sugar (page 281) or brown sugar

½ teaspoon ground cinnamon

1 teaspoon pure vanilla extract

FOR THE *CHURROS*

Salt

3 tablespoons granulated sugar

1 cup (5 oz/155 g) all-purpose (plain) flour, sifted

2 large eggs, beaten

Canola oil for deep-frying

1 long strip lemon zest

1 tablespoon ground cinnamon

MAKES 4–6 SERVINGS

Tres Leches Cake

FOR THE CAKE

½ cup (4 oz/125 g) vegetable shortening (vegetable lard), plus shortening for greasing

1½ cups (12 oz/375 g) sugar

2 large eggs

2¼ cups (9 oz/280 g) sifted all-purpose (plain) flour, plus flour for dusting

2 teaspoons baking powder

Salt

1 cup (8 fl oz/250 ml) whole milk

1 teaspoon pure vanilla extract

FOR THE *TRES LECHES* SAUCE

1 can (14 fl oz/430 ml) sweetened condensed milk

1 can (12 fl oz/375 ml) evaporated milk

1 cup (8 fl oz/250 ml) heavy (double) cream

2 tablespoons dark rum

1 teaspoon pure vanilla extract

Meringue Frosting (page 277)

MAKES 12 SERVINGS

Preheat the oven to 350°F (180°C). Line a 9-by-12-inch (23-by-30-cm) baking pan with aluminum foil and lightly grease the foil. Dust the foil-lined pan with flour and tap to shake out the excess.

In a bowl, using an electric mixer set on high speed, beat the shortening until fluffy. Add the sugar a little at a time, beating until fluffy between each addition. Reduce the speed to low and add the eggs one at a time, beating until fully incorporated after each addition and scraping down the sides of the bowl as needed, about 2 minutes total.

Sift the flour again with the baking powder and ½ teaspoon salt into a large bowl. In a small bowl, whisk together the milk and vanilla. Add one-third of the milk mixture to the shortening and beat until well mixed, then add one-third of the flour mixture. Repeat twice more, beating well after each addition. Scrape the batter into the prepared pan and bake until a small wooden skewer or cake tester inserted into the center of the cake comes out clean, about 35 minutes. Transfer to a wire rack and let cool in the pan for 10 minutes, then invert the cake onto a platter large enough to hold it and let cool completely. (Alternatively, you can finish the cake and serve it from the pan.)

To make the *tres leches* sauce, in a bowl, whisk together the condensed milk, evaporated milk, cream, rum, and vanilla.

When the cake has cooled completely, poke it all over with the tines of a fork, and spoon the sauce over the surface, a little at a time, allowing the cake to absorb the sauce before adding more. By the end, a little sauce may have pooled on the platter, but the cake should absorb almost all of it. Cover the cake with plastic wrap and refrigerate for about 1 hour.

Spread the meringue frosting on the chilled cake, cover, and refrigerate until well chilled, at least 3 hours and up to 8 hours. Serve chilled, cut into squares.

Tres leches is made throughout the Spanish-speaking world, with many regional and national variations. In Cuba, a simple white cake is soaked in rich, luscious sauce made from three milks and a pungent hint of rum, and then spread with a fluffy, glossy meringue. It is as rich as pudding and definitely not for the calorie conscious. (Whipped cream is sometimes substituted for the meringue.) For a stunning presentation, serve on a colorful platter garnished with tropical fruits like papaya, mango, and pineapple.

Alfajores

Alfajores are arguably the most famous Argentinean dessert, sold worldwide and prepared in most countries in Latin America. The *dulce de leche* filling is also made throughout the continent, sometimes under different names, such as *arequipe* and *manjar blanco*, and varying in consistency from light to rich and heavy. *Alfajores* can be dipped in melted white or dark chocolate, or dusted with ground peanuts or flaked coconut. Another common variation is to dust the tops with a light layer of confectioners' (icing) sugar, but serving them plain allows the flavor of the *dulce de leche* to shine.

Preheat the oven to 325°F (165°C).

Line 2 baking sheets with aluminum foil or waxed paper. To make the dough, in a food processor, combine the flour and ¼ teaspoon salt. Pulse to blend, about 5 seconds. Add the butter, confectioners' sugar, and vanilla and pulse until the dough forms a ball and pulls away from the sides of the bowl. Turn the dough out onto a lightly floured work surface and pat into a disk.

Using a floured rolling pin, roll the dough out to a thickness of ⅛ inch (3 mm).

Using a 2½-inch (4-cm) cookie cutter, cut out 24 cookies. Briefly knead the dough scraps together just until smooth, roll out the dough, and cut out additional circles. (If the dough becomes too soft to handle, place it in the freezer for 2–3 minutes, then finish rolling and cutting.)

Transfer the cookies to the prepared baking sheets. Bake until dry to the touch (they should stay moist), 10–12 minutes. Transfer the cookies to wire racks and let cool completely.

Spread 1 tablespoon of the *dulce de leche* on the bottom, or flat side, of half the cookies. Place a second cookie, flat side down, on top of the filling.

Serve right away or embellish, if desired (see Note). Store in an airtight container at room temperature for up to 3 days.

2 cups (5 oz/155 g) all-purpose (plain) flour, sifted

Salt

¾ cup (6 oz/180 g) cold, unsalted butter, cut into tablespoons

4 tablespoons confectioners' (icing) sugar

2 teaspoons pure vanilla extract

¾ cup (6 fl oz/177 ml) purchased *dulce de leche*

MAKES 12 COOKIES

Blackberry Ice Cream

2 cups (8 oz/250 g)
blackberries, plus
blackberries for garnish

1¼ cups (10 fl oz/310 ml)
whole milk

1¼ cups (10 fl oz/310 ml)
heavy (double) cream

Salt

4 large egg yolks

¾ cup (6 oz/185 g) sugar

1 tablespoon cornstarch
(cornflour)

1 teaspoon pure vanilla
extract

MAKES ABOUT 1 QT (1 L)

In a blender or food processor, process the blackberries to a smooth purée. Strain the purée through a fine-mesh sieve set over a bowl, pushing on the solids with the back of a spoon to remove as much of the juice as possible. Cover and refrigerate until ready to use. Discard the seeds left in the sieve.

In a heavy-bottomed saucepan over medium-high heat, combine the milk, cream, and a pinch of salt. Bring to a simmer, then remove from the heat.

In a large bowl, whisk together the egg yolks and sugar until combined. In a small bowl, stir together the cornstarch and 1 tablespoon water.

Gradually pour the hot milk mixture into the yolk mixture, whisking constantly. Return the mixture to the same saucepan, place over medium-low heat, and whisk in the cornstarch mixture. Continue to cook, stirring slowly and constantly with a wooden spoon, until the custard thickens and leaves a path on the back of the spoon when a finger is drawn across it, about 5 minutes; do not allow to boil. Pour the custard through a medium-mesh sieve set over a clean bowl and stir in the vanilla. Refrigerate the custard until cold, at least 1 hour or up to overnight.

When ready to freeze, stir the purée into the custard. Pour the mixture into an ice cream maker and freeze according to the manufacturer's instructions. Transfer to a container, cover, and freeze until firm, at least 4 hours or up to 3 days.

Andean blackberries tend to be tart and even acidic, so taste them before using and increase the sugar to 1 cup (8 oz/250 g) if they seem especially tart. They come in two sizes, miniature and a size that resembles the varieties commonly found in the United States and Europe; either will work fine here, or substitute regular domestic blackberries. Crush a handful of extra berries with superfine (caster) sugar and lime juice to make a simple, fresh topping for the ice cream.

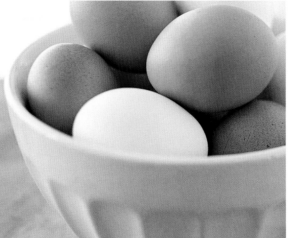

Coconut Meringue Cookies

Coconut cookies are beloved throughout South America. There are a few variations; some versions are more like meringues, others are denser cookies—but all renditions of this cookie classic are made with egg whites and coconut. Street vendors sell them in small plastic bags; markets display them packaged in their bakeries; and they are a perennial feature in pastry shops. This recipe yields cookies that are gorgeously soft and chewy on the inside and dry and crisp on the outside.

Preheat the oven to 325°F (165°C). Line 2 large baking sheets with parchment (baking) paper or waxed paper.

In a large bowl or the bowl of a stand mixer, combine the egg whites and ⅛ teaspoon salt. Using the stand mixer fitted with the whisk attachment or a handheld electric mixer set on medium speed, beat until the egg whites are very foamy, about 30 seconds. Increase the speed to high and beat until soft peaks form. With the mixer running, add the granulated sugar in a slow stream. Add the vanilla and continue beating until stiff, shiny peaks form.

In a separate bowl, whisk together the coconut and confectioners' sugar until the coconut is evenly coated with the sugar. Fold the coconut mixture gently into the egg whites just until blended.

Spoon heaping tablespoons of the batter onto the prepared baking sheets. Bake the cookies until dry on the bottom, about 20 minutes. To ensure these bake evenly, it is best to reverse the positions of the baking sheets halfway through the baking time. Let the cookies cool on the pans for 2–3 minutes, then transfer to wire racks and let cool completely. Store in an airtight container at room temperature for up to 3 days.

4 large egg whites

Salt

¾ cup (6 oz/185 g) granulated sugar

1 teaspoon pure vanilla extract

2⅓ cups (7 oz/220 g) sweetened flaked coconut

1⅓ cups (5½ oz/170 g) confectioners' (icing) sugar

MAKES 3–3½ DOZEN COOKIES

Kahlúa and Rum Flan

8 cups (64 fl oz/2 l) whole milk

1²/₃ cups (13 oz/405 g) sugar

2-inch (5-cm) piece true cinnamon bark or cinnamon stick

6 large eggs, plus 4 large egg yolks

2 tablespoons Kahlúa or other coffee liqueur

1 tablespoon dark rum

1 teaspoon pure vanilla extract

Ground cinnamon for serving (optional)

MAKES 6–8 SERVINGS

In a large saucepan over medium-low heat, bring the milk, 1 cup (8 oz/250 g) of the sugar, and the cinnamon to a boil, stirring to dissolve the sugar. Reduce the heat to low. Simmer uncovered, stirring frequently, until the milk is reduced to about 4 cups (32 oz/1 l), about 45 minutes. (In order to judge accurately when the milk has reduced sufficiently, pour half of the milk into the pan before you add the remainder, to see where the final level should be.) Set aside to cool.

Place the remaining ²/₃ cup (5 oz/155 g) sugar and ¼ cup (2 fl oz/60 ml) water in a small, heavy saucepan over medium-high heat and bring to a boil. Continue to boil without stirring until the syrup begins to color, about 15 minutes. Reduce the heat to a simmer, then swirl the pan until the syrup is a deep amber, about 1 minute. Immediately pour the caramel into individual custard cups or a 2½-qt (2½-l) soufflé dish, tilting to distribute the caramel evenly over the bottom. Some of the syrup may run up the sides of the dish, but try to keep most of it on the bottom. Set aside.

Preheat the oven to 350°F (180°C).

In a large bowl, beat the eggs, egg yolks, Kahlúa, rum, and vanilla until blended. Slowly beat in the milk mixture. Pour the mixture through a fine-mesh sieve into the prepared cups or dish. Place the cups or dish in a baking pan and pour in hot water to reach three-fourths up the side of the cups or dish. Cover loosely with aluminum foil.

Bake until just set and the tip of a knife inserted in the middle comes out clean, 30–40 minutes for individual cups and 40–50 minutes for the soufflé dish. Remove the baking pan from the oven and let the flan cool in the water. (The flan can be covered and refrigerated for up to 2 days.)

To unmold, run a knife around the edge of the mold(s) to loosen the custard. Invert a deep serving plate or individual plate over the top, and invert the flan and dish together. The flan should drop from the mold. If it resists unmolding, dip the mold(s) in hot water for just a few seconds, then invert. The flan should drop out easily. Sprinkle with ground cinnamon, if using, and serve at once.

Flan, one of Mexico's favorite desserts, traces its origins to the Spanish conquest, when the crucial ingredients—milk, eggs, and sugar—were brought to the new world. The traditional version is vanilla-scented, but this rendition is updated with the addition of Kahlúa and rum. It is a luxurious finale to an elegant Latin meal.

Tapioca Pudding with Mango

Tapioca balls are made from the tapioca plant, which is also called *manioca, mandioca, cassava,* or *yuca.* This starchy tuber is an important staple for all of South America. It is used for a dazzling array of delicious traditional foods, both sweet and savory, most famously, the longtime popular favorite from Brazil, tapioca pudding.

Preheat the oven to 350°F (180°C). Have ready an 8-inch (20-cm) or 10-inch (25-cm) ring mold (savarin mold).

In a small saucepan over medium-high heat, combine the sugar and ½ cup (4 fl oz/ 125 ml) water. Bring to a boil, stirring to dissolve the sugar. Reduce the heat to medium-low and simmer until the syrup turns golden, 10–15 minutes. Protecting your hand with a potholder, immediately pour the hot caramel into the cake pan and swirl to cover the bottom of the pan. Be careful, as the hot caramel may splatter. Set aside.

In a bowl, combine the tapioca, eggs, condensed milk, coconut milk, and whole milk and stir to mix well. Pour the mixture into the caramel-coated pan and cover the pan tightly with aluminum foil. Place the cake pan in a roasting pan and pour hot water into the roasting pan to come about 2 inches (5 cm) up the sides of the ring mold. Place the pudding in the oven and reduce the oven temperature to 300°F (150°C). Bake until the tapioca is set, 2–2½ hours for the 8-inch (20-cm) pan and 1½–2 hours for the 10-inch (25-cm) pan.

Remove the pan from the oven and transfer to a wire rack. Let cool completely. To unmold, run a small knife around the inside edge of the pan to loosen the pudding, then invert it onto a serving plate and remove the pan. Refrigerate until well chilled, at least 6 hours and up to 1 day. To serve, fill the hole in the middle of the pudding with the diced mango, or cut the pudding into wedges and serve on individual plates, with the mango on the side.

¾ cup (6 oz/185 g) sugar

1 cup (4 oz/125 g) instant tapioca, such as Minute Tapioca

3 large eggs

1 can (14 fl oz/430 ml) sweetened condensed milk

1 cup (8 fl oz/250 ml) well-shaken canned coconut milk

1 cup (8 fl oz/250 ml) whole milk

1 mango, peeled and cut into ½-inch (12-mm) pieces for serving

MAKES 6–8 SERVINGS

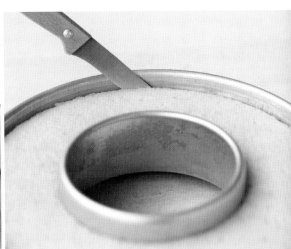

Quince Crescents

Unsalted butter for greasing

½ lb (8 oz/250 g) quince paste

¼ cup (2 fl oz/60 ml) apple juice

1 sheet frozen puff pastry, about 9 oz (280 g), thawed

¼ cup (2 oz/60 g) sugar

MAKES 32 COOKIES

Quince is a yellow pome fruit that is related to apples and pears and lies somewhere between them in shape. Most varieties are too hard and sour to eat raw, but are delicious when cooked in jams, jellies, and puddings. Very popular in Argentina, quince plays a role similar to that of guava in many other South American countries. Crescents, or *meidas lunas*, are small, curved cookies sold either plain or filled with all sorts of sweet and savory goodies.

Preheat the oven to 425°F (220°C). Lightly butter 2 baking sheets.

Cut the quince paste into ½-inch (12-mm) cubes and put in a saucepan. Add the apple juice and place over low heat. Cook, using a wooden spoon to stir and break up the quince, until the fruit is softened and the mixture is chunky but mostly blended. Remove from the heat and let cool completely before using.

On a lightly floured work surface, roll out the pastry into a 12-inch (30-cm) square. Cut into sixteen 3-inch (7.5-cm) squares, then cut each square in half on the diagonal to make 32 triangles. Spoon a heaping teaspoon of the softened quince paste into the center of a pastry triangle. Fold the long side of the pastry triangle over the filling and then roll up the pastry and pull the ends towards one another to make a crescent-moon shape. Repeat with the remaining pastry triangles and quince paste.

Arrange the cookies on the prepared baking sheets, seam side down and about 3 inches (7.5 cm) apart. Brush the tops with the leftover quince paste. Bake until the tops are lightly golden and the edges are crispy, about 20 minutes. Transfer the cookies to wire racks and let cool completely. Store in an airtight container at room temperature for up to 3 days.

Coconut Ice Cream

For a double coconut treat, stir ½ cup (1½ oz/45 g) toasted shredded coconut into the ice cream during the final minute of processing. To make a colorful sundae, garnish the ice cream with sliced or diced tropical fruit, such as papaya or mango. For a more savory variation, serve with sliced avocados and drizzle the ice cream with extra virgin olive oil and coarse sea salt.

Place the coconut in a large, heavy saucepan over medium-high heat. Stir the coconut until it begins to brown, about 7 minutes. Add the half-and-half and bring to a simmer. Remove from the heat. Cover and let stand for 30 minutes.

Pour the coconut mixture through a medium-mesh sieve set over a bowl, pressing on the coconut with a silicone spatula to extract as much liquid as possible; discard the coconut. Return the coconut milk to the same saucepan and place over medium-high heat. Add the cream of coconut and bring to a simmer. Remove from the heat.

In a large bowl, whisk together the egg yolks and sugar until combined. Form a kitchen towel into a ring and place the bowl on top to prevent it from moving. Gradually pour the hot coconut-milk mixture into the yolk mixture, whisking constantly. Return the mixture to the same saucepan and place over medium-low heat. Cook, stirring slowly and continuously with the silicone spatula, until the custard thickens and leaves a path on the back of a spatula when a finger is drawn across it, about 5 minutes; do not allow it to boil.

Pour the custard through the medium-mesh sieve set over a clean bowl. Add the cream and stir well. Refrigerate the custard until cold, about 1 hour.

Pour the custard into an ice cream maker and freeze according to the manufacturer's instructions. Transfer to a container; cover and freeze until firm, at least 4 hours or for up to 3 days.

¼ cup (5 oz/155 g) firmly packed sweetened flaked coconut

1½ cups (12 fl oz/375 ml) half-and-half (half cream)

¾ cup (6 fl oz/180 ml) canned sweetened cream of coconut

6 large egg yolks

⅓ cup (3 oz/90 g) sugar

1½ cups (12 fl oz/375 ml) heavy (double) cream

MAKES ABOUT 1 QT (1 L)

Chocolate–Ancho Chile Cake

Nonstick vegetable oil cooking spray

2 ancho chiles, seeded, toasted, and ground (page 268), or 2 tablespoons ancho chile powder

1 tablet (3 oz/90 g) Mexican chocolate, coarsely chopped

1 cup (5½ oz/170 g) blanched almonds, toasted (page 268)

⅓ cup (1½ oz/45 g) all-purpose (plain) flour, sifted

¼ cup (¾ oz/20 g) Dutch-process cocoa powder, sifted

½ cup (4 oz/125 g) unsalted butter, at room temperature

1 cup (8 oz/250 g) granulated sugar

6 large eggs, separated, at room temperature

1 tablespoon Kahlúa or crème de cacao liqueur

¼ teaspoon pure almond extract

Sea salt

FOR THE ANCHO WHIPPED CREAM

1⅔ cup (13 fl oz/410 ml) heavy (double) cream

1 tablespoon pure vanilla extract

3 tablespoons confectioners' (icing) sugar

Finely grated bittersweet chocolate or chocolate curls

MAKES 10–12 SERVINGS

Preheat the oven to 350°F (180°C). Line the bottom of a round springform pan 9 inches (23 cm) in diameter and 2½ inches (6 cm) deep with parchment (baking) paper. Lightly coat the sides of the pan with the cooking spray.

Reserve 1 teaspoon of the ground chile for the whipped cream. In a food processor, combine the chocolate and almonds and pulse to grind finely. Transfer to a medium bowl; add the flour, cocoa, and the remaining ground chile and whisk to mix. In a large bowl, using an electric mixer on medium speed, beat the butter until pale, about 2 minutes. Reduce the speed to low and gradually add ½ cup (4 oz/125 g) of the granulated sugar, stopping the mixer at times to scrape down the sides of the bowl. Increase the speed to medium and beat until the mixture is light and fluffy, 3–5 minutes. Add the egg yolks one at a time, beating until the mixture is smooth, stopping to scrape down the sides of the bowl. With the mixer on low speed, add the chocolate mixture, Kahlúa, and almond extract and beat just until blended.

In a large bowl, combine the egg whites and a pinch of sea salt. Using clean beaters, beat on medium speed for 30 seconds. Increase the speed to high and beat until soft peaks form. With the mixer running, add the remaining granulated sugar in a slow stream. Beat until stiff, shiny peaks form. Using a large rubber spatula, gently fold one-third of the whites into the batter. Fold in the remaining whites in 2 batches just until combined.

Transfer the batter to the prepared pan and smooth the surface. Place the pan on a baking sheet to catch any drips. Bake the cake until a toothpick comes out clean, 40–45 minutes. Transfer to a wire rack and let cool for 15 minutes, then release the sides of the pan and lift off. Let the cake cool completely.

To make the ancho whipped cream, in a small bowl, whisk together ⅓ cup (3 fl oz/ 80 ml) of the cream and the reserved 1 teaspoon ground chile. Let stand for up to 5 minutes. Whisk again and pour into a chilled large bowl. Add the remaining 1⅓ cups (10 fl oz/310 ml) cream and the vanilla extract and, using an electric mixer on low speed, beat until the cream thickens. Increase the speed to medium-high and beat until soft peaks form. Reduce the speed to medium and gradually add the confectioners' sugar, beating until soft mounds form and the cream is thick enough to hold its shape. Slice the cake and place each slice on a plate. Add a dollop of the whipped cream, top with grated chocolate, and serve right away.

This rich, chile-spiked chocolate cake is a Latin twist on the always crowd-pleasing dense chocolate cake. The accompanying whipped cream also gets a hit of chile powder to complement the flavor of the cake. If you prefer a fudgier consistency, reduce the baking time to 35–40 minutes, or until a toothpick inserted into the center of the cake comes out almost clean.

Creamy Coconut Tart

Mexican cooks work wonders with fresh coconut, as in this subtle and delicious dessert from the Yucatan. And although this recipe uses canned coconut water and shredded dried coconut for ease, for a more authentic dish you can extract the meat and water from a fresh coconut (see page 268). Delicious by itself, it's even better served with chocolate sauce, fresh whipped cream, or diced tropical fruit such as papaya, pineapple, or banana.

Preheat the oven to 350°F (180°C).

Put the cookies in a blender or food processor and pulse just until fine crumbs form. Alternatively, put the cookies in a large zippered plastic bag, close tightly, and pound with a rolling pin or small, heavy frying pan until fine crumbs form. You should have about 1½ cups (6 oz/185 g) crumbs.

In a bowl, combine the cookie crumbs and sugar and stir to mix well. Add the melted butter and stir until the crumbs are well coated with the butter and hold together when pinched. Transfer the crumbs to an 11-inch (28-cm) tart pan with removable sides. Press the crumbs evenly in the bottom and up the sides of the pan, using your fingers and the bottom of a glass to pack the crumbs firmly. Transfer the pan to a rimmed baking sheet and bake until the crust is golden and lightly puffed on the bottom, about 7 minutes. Remove from the oven and press firmly on the crumbs again with the bottom of the glass while the crust is still hot.

Pour the coconut water into a small saucepan. Add the dried coconut to the saucepan and stir to mix well. Bring the coconut mixture to a boil over medium-high heat. Reduce the heat to medium-low and simmer for 10 minutes. Remove from the heat and let cool completely. In a large bowl, whisk together the condensed milk and eggs until thoroughly blended. Stir in the vanilla and the cooled coconut mixture.

Pour the filling into the crust and bake until the top is slightly puffed, the center is set, and a small wooden skewer inserted into the center of the tart comes out clean, about 35 minutes. Transfer to a wire rack and let cool.

If using fresh coconut to make the garnish, using a vegetable peeler, peel off strips of coconut from the whole piece. Place the strips in a pie tin and toast in the oven, stirring once or twice, until golden brown, 5–10 minutes. Scatter the toasted coconut over the tart. Remove the sides from the tart pan, cut the tart into wedges, and serve right away.

24 shortbread cookies, or vanilla or chocolate wafer cookies

¼ cup (2 oz/60 g) sugar

6 tablespoons (3 oz/90 g) unsalted butter, melted

1 cup (8 fl oz/250 ml) canned or thawed frozen coconut water

1½ cups (3½ oz/99 g) sweetened shredded dried coconut

1 cup (8 fl oz/250 ml) sweetened condensed milk

3 large eggs plus 1 large egg yolk, beaten

2 teaspoons pure vanilla extract

1 small piece (about 3 oz/ 85 g) fresh coconut, or ½ cup (1½ oz/45 g) toasted flaked coconut, for garnish

MAKES 8–10 SERVINGS

Sopaipillas

FOR THE DOUGH

1 teaspoon active dry yeast

1 teaspoon granulated sugar

2½ cups (12½ oz/390 g) all-purpose (plain) flour, or as needed, plus more for dusting

Salt

¾ cup (6 fl oz/180 ml) whole milk

2 tablespoons unsalted butter

Canola for frying

FOR SERVING

Confectioners' (icing) sugar

Honey

MAKES 24 *SOPAIPILLAS*

In a small bowl, dissolve the yeast and sugar in ¼ cup (2 fl oz/60 ml) warm water (105°–115°F/40°–46°C) and let stand until foamy, about 5 minutes.

In a food processor, combine 2 cups (10 oz/315 g) of the flour and ½ teaspoon salt and pulse to mix, about 5 seconds. Add the yeast mixture, the milk, and the butter and pulse to mix, about 20 seconds. Add the remaining ½ cup (2½ oz/75 g) flour and process just until a moist dough forms and pulls away from the sides of the bowl, about 10 seconds. If the dough seems too sticky, add 2 tablespoons flour and pulse until soft but not sticky, about 10 seconds.

Lightly oil a large bowl. Place the dough in the bowl and turn to coat with the oil. Cover with a clean kitchen towel and let stand in a warm, dark place until doubled in bulk, about 1 hour.

When the dough has risen, pour oil to a depth of 3 inches (7.5 cm) into a deep saucepan over medium-high heat and heat to 375°F (190°C) on a deep-frying thermometer. Line 1 large baking sheet with parchment (baking) paper or waxed paper and 1 baking sheet with paper towels.

Turn the dough out onto a lightly floured work surface and roll out to a thickness of about ¼ inch (6 mm). Using a small, sharp knife or a round cookie cutter, cut out 24 squares or rounds. Place on the parchment-lined baking sheet.

Slip a few *sopaipillas* into the hot oil and fry, using tongs to turn as needed, until lightly golden on all sides, 2–3 minutes total. Transfer to the paper towel–lined baking sheet to drain. Repeat to fry the remaining *sopaipillas*. Divide the *sopaipillas* among individual plates and dust with confectioners' sugar. Serve right away, with honey on the side for drizzling.

Sopaipillas appear in many forms throughout Central and South America, and under almost as many names, including *hojaldras* or *hojuelas*. Some quick-bread versions, albeit with less airy results, are made with baking powder or baking soda (bicarbonate of soda) in place of yeast, and some use richer batters with cooked *zapallo* (pumpkin) folded in. This basic recipe is perfect with black coffee any time of day.

Coconut Rice Pudding

Here, *arroz con leche*, the soothing and probably most traditional Mexican dessert, is glorified with the addition of coconut milk, shredded coconut, and a voluptuous chocolate sauce. The pudding can be made 1–2 days ahead, covered, and refrigerated. Before serving, warm with a few tablespoons of milk.

To make the pudding, in a heavy saucepan over medium heat, combine the milk, coconut milk, the 1 cup (4 oz/125 g) dried coconut, and the rice. Bring to a slow boil, reduce the heat to very low, and simmer, uncovered, stirring frequently, until the rice is very tender and all of the liquid is absorbed, about 1 hour.

In a small bowl, whisk together the egg yolks, sugar, and vanilla. Whisk in ½ cup (4 fl oz/125 ml) of the cooked rice, and then stir the mixture back into the rice. The pudding can be served warm, at room temperature, or cold, but wait to make the sauce until just before serving.

To make the chocolate sauce, stir the cream and sugar together in a heavy saucepan. Scrape the seeds from the vanilla bean into the cream. Bring to a rolling boil over medium heat, remove from the heat, and stir in the coffee granules and chocolate. Stir until melted, about 1 minute. Whisk until shiny and smooth, then whisk in the butter.

Spoon the pudding into individual serving glasses or bowls and top with the sauce and remaining 2 tablespoons toasted coconut. Serve right away.

FOR THE PUDDING

3 cups (24 fl oz/750 ml) whole milk

1 cup (8 fl oz/250 ml) canned coconut milk

1 cup (4 oz/125 g) sweetened shredded dried coconut, plus 2 tablespoons toasted coconut for garnish

½ cup (3½ oz/105 g) medium-grain white rice

2 egg yolks

1 tablespoon sugar

1 teaspoon pure vanilla extract

FOR THE CHOCOLATE SAUCE

½ cup (4 fl oz/125 ml) heavy (double) cream

2 tablespoons sugar

½ vanilla bean, split lengthwise

1½ teaspoons instant espresso coffee granules

3 oz (90 g) high-quality bittersweet chocolate, finely chopped

1 tablespoon unsalted butter

MAKES 4 SERVINGS

Orange–Passion Fruit Cake

FOR THE CAKE

Unsalted butter for greasing

3 cups (15 oz/470 g) all-purpose (plain) flour, plus more for dusting

2½ teaspoons baking soda (bicarbonate of soda)

½ teaspoon baking powder

Salt

1½ cups (12 oz/375 g) unsalted butter, at room temperature

2 cups (1 lb/500 g) granulated sugar

3 large eggs

½ cup (4 fl oz/125 ml) buttermilk

¼ cup (2 oz/60 g) fresh or thawed frozen passion fruit pulp (page 281)

1 tablespoon grated orange zest

¼ cup (2 fl oz/60 ml) fresh orange juice

FOR THE GLAZE

2 heavy passion fruits or ¼ cup (2 oz/60 g) thawed frozen passion fruit pulp

1⅓ cups (5½ oz/170 g) confectioners' (icing) sugar

2 tablespoons unsalted butter, at room temperature

MAKES 12–14 SERVINGS

Preheat the oven to 350°F (180°C). Butter a 10-inch (25-cm) Bundt pan or tube pan. Dust with flour and tap to shake out the excess.

In a bowl, whisk together the 3 cups (15 oz/475 g) flour, the baking soda, baking powder, and ½ teaspoon salt.

In a large bowl, combine the butter and granulated sugar. Using an electric mixer on high speed, beat until very smooth, 5–7 minutes. Beat in ¼ cup (1½ oz/45 g) of the flour mixture. Reduce the speed to low and add the eggs one at a time, beating until fully incorporated after each addition and scraping down the sides of the bowl as needed, about 2 minutes total. Turn the mixer off. Add the remaining flour mixture, the buttermilk, passion fruit pulp, and orange zest and juice and beat on low speed for 30 seconds. Raise the speed to medium and mix just until combined, about 1 minute longer. Scrape the batter into the prepared pan.

Bake the cake until it is golden brown and springs back when pressed in the center, 50–60 minutes. Transfer to a wire rack and let cool for 10 minutes.

While the cake is cooling, make the glaze. If working with fresh passion fruit, cut the fruit open, scoop the pulp and seeds into a fine-mesh sieve, and press it through the mesh, using the back of the spoon to extract as much of the juice and pulp as possible. Discard the solids left in the sieve. Measure ¼ cup (2 oz/60 g) pulp and reserve the rest for another use.

In a bowl, using a wooden spoon or silicone spatula, stir together the passion fruit pulp, confectioners' sugar, and butter until smooth.

To unmold the cake, run a small knife around the inside edge of the pan to loosen the cake, then invert it onto a serving plate and remove the pan. Drizzle with the glaze, cut into wedges, and serve.

This traditional cake is eaten in many Argentinean homes, often as an accompaniment to afternoon tea. It is usually purchased in pastry shops, but this straightforward recipe is well worth the effort. Passion fruit is used in many ways in Latin America: juice for drinking; as flavoring for ice creams, glazes, toppings, and other desserts; and for adding sweetness and complexity to salsas, sauces, and savory dishes. You can find frozen passion fruit pulp in most Latin markets.

Mexican Wedding Cookies

Although quick and easy to make, these cookies are considered special-occasion treats because they use what were once the most prized and expensive ingredients in Mexico: nuts, sugar, and butter. These hard-to-come-by ingredients were brought to Mexico from the Spanish by way of the Arabs during the 16th century conquest. Often served at Christmastime, these cookies are sometimes known as "snowball cookies."

In a bowl, using an electric mixer on medium speed, beat together the butter and shortening until creamy. Add 1½ cups (6 oz/190 g) of the confectioners' sugar, the orange zest, and orange juice and beat until blended.

In another bowl, stir together the flour, walnuts, and ¼ teaspoon salt. Add the flour mixture 1 tablespoon at a time to the butter mixture, beating until thoroughly incorporated. The dough will be crumbly. Transfer the dough to a large sheet of plastic wrap and press the dough into a ball. Wrap and refrigerate for at least 1 hour.

Position a rack in the upper third of the oven and preheat to 325°F (165°C). Line a baking sheet with parchment (baking) paper or with a silicone baking mat.

Using your hands, roll small pieces of the dough into ¾-inch (2-cm) balls. Place the balls on the prepared baking sheet, spacing them about 1 inch (2.5 cm) apart and gently pressing them to flatten slightly.

Bake the cookies until the edges turn pale gold, 10–15 minutes.

Meanwhile, place the remaining 1 cup (4 oz/125 g) confectioners' sugar in a shallow bowl. When the cookies are ready, remove the baking sheet from the oven. While they are still hot, using a spatula, remove the cookies one at a time and carefully roll them in the sugar. Set aside on a rack and let cool completely, then roll them again in the sugar, shaking off any excess.

Serve the cookies at once, or layer between sheets of parchment paper in an airtight container and store at room temperature for up to 3 days.

½ cup (4 oz/125 g) unsalted butter, at room temperature

½ cup (4 oz/125 g) solid vegetable shortening (vegetable lard)

2½ cups (8 oz/250 g) sifted confectioners' (icing) sugar

1 teaspoon finely grated orange zest

1 tablespoon fresh orange juice

2 cups (10 oz/315 g) all-purpose (plain) flour

⅔ cup (2½ oz/75 g) ground walnuts

Sea salt

MAKES ABOUT 3 DOZEN COOKIES

Basic Techniques

The rich, layered flavors in Latin cuisine are mostly gleaned from just a handful of ingredients that are either roasted, toasted, ground, or blended in different ways to create uniquely flavored dishes. To help you succeed with the recipes, here are some of the techniques used in this book.

Toasting Nuts and Seeds

Position a rack in the middle of the oven and preheat to 325°F (165°C). To toast nuts, spread them in a single layer in a shallow pan. Toast, stirring occasionally, until the nuts are fragrant and their color deepens by a shade or two, about 5 minutes. Remove from the oven and let cool. To toast seeds, such as sesame seeds, place them in a small nonstick pan over medium heat. Toast, stirring, until the seeds are a shade or two darker, 3–5 minutes.

TO GRIND: If toasting the nuts or seeds, first allow them to cool. Transfer to a spice grinder or a clean coffee grinder and pulse until coarsely or finely ground, as the recipe specifies. If grinding a large quantity of nuts or seeds, use a food processor.

Working with Dried Chiles

Capsaicin, the chemical responsible for the degree of heat in chiles, can cause pain if it comes into contact with eyes or other parts of the body. If possible, wear disposable gloves when handling chiles.

TO SEED: Clean the chiles with a damp cloth. Split them lengthwise, then use a small, sharp knife to remove the seeds.

TO TOAST: Clean the chiles with a damp cloth. Heat a heavy frying pan over medium heat. Add the whole or seeded chiles to the pan. Press down firmly for several seconds with a spatula, then turn the chiles and press down for a few seconds more before removing.

The chiles should change color only slightly and start to give off their aroma.

TO CRUSH OR GRIND: Stem the chiles, and seed, if desired. Tear the chiles into small pieces. To crush, add the pieces to a mortar and use a pestle to break up into smaller pieces. To grind, add the chile pieces to a spice grinder or a clean coffee grinder. Grind until the chiles form a fine powder.

Working with Fresh Peppers and Chiles

TO ROAST: If using a gas stove, using tongs, hold the peppers or chiles over a high flame and roast, turning often, until the skin is charred and blistered, 2–3 minutes. If using a charcoal or gas grill, place the peppers or chiles on the grill over a very hot fire for 3–5 minutes, turning often with tongs. If using a broiler (griller), set an oven rack 6 inches (15 cm) from the heat source. Place the peppers or chiles on an aluminum foil–lined pan and broil (grill), turning often, until blackened, 5–10 minutes. (Broiled peppers and chiles will be too soft to stuff but can be used for other recipes.)

TO REMOVE THE SKIN: After roasting, place the peppers or chiles in a paper bag or heatproof bowl covered with plastic wrap and let sweat for about 8 minutes to loosen the skin. This will also soften the flesh, so do not leave them too long. Pick and peel away as much skin as possible. Don't worry if some charred bits remain.

TO SEED: If stuffing the pepper or chile, using a small knife, cut a lengthwise slit in each chile

from the stem end to the bottom, leaving ½ inch (12 mm) uncut on top and at least ¼ inch (6 mm) on the bottom. Leaving the stem intact, remove the seeds and membranes with your fingers. Wipe the inside with a damp towel and dry well. For slicing or chopping, cut a lengthwise slit and spread it flat on a cutting surface. Cut out the stem, then remove the seeds and membranes.

Pan-Roasting Vegetables

To pan-roast vegetables and aromatics such as tomatoes, husked tomatillos, onions, and garlic, place an aluminum foil–lined heavy frying pan over medium-high heat. Place the vegetables on the foil and roast until the flesh is soft and the skins are blackened on all sides. Let the vegetables sit undisturbed as they blacken, turning just a few times to roast all sides. The garlic and chiles will be done first, in about 5 minutes; the tomatoes and tomatillos will take 10–15 minutes. The blackened skin of the tomatoes and tomatillos and the skin of the garlic and onions, if remaining, is often removed before using.

Working with Coconuts

IF USING A GREEN (YOUNG) COCONUT: Place the coconut on its side and, using a cleaver or the wide part of the blade of a large knife, shave off the top portion of the white husk around the tip to expose a "lid" of shell. Using the cleaver or knife, whack the exposed coconut shell to cut it along the seam, rotating the fruit in a circle and continuing to make cuts until the lid is scored completely around the perimeter. Pry the lid open and pour the coconut water through a fine-mesh sieve placed over a glass measuring pitcher. Using a metal spoon or ice-cream scoop, scrape the inside of the coconut to remove the meat. Chop or shred the coconut meat, as directed in the recipe.

IF USING A BROWN COCONUT: Pierce one of the eyes with a screwdriver. Pour the coconut water through a fine-mesh sieve into a glass measuring pitcher. Break apart the coconut with a hammer and use the screwdriver to pry the meat away from the shell. Using a vegetable peeler, remove any brown skin clinging to the meat, and chop or shred the coconut meat, as directed in the recipe.

TO MAKE FRESH COCONUT MILK: Extract the water from the coconut, as directed above, and set aside. Chop the coconut meat and add it to a food processor or blender along with the coconut water. Process or blend the mixture, adding hot water as necessary to thin it, until it is smooth. Strain over a cheesecloth-lined strainer.

Pitting Olives

To pit olives, use a cherry/olive pitter to punch the pit through the end of the olive. Or, put the olives in a sealable plastic bag, force out the excess air, and seal the bag. Using a meat pounder or a rolling pin, gently pound the olives to loosen the pits. Remove the crushed olives from the bag and separate the pits from the flesh. Use a paring knife to cut the flesh from the pits of any stubborn olives. Chop or slice the olives as directed in the recipe.

Preparing Banana Leaves

If frozen, thaw the leaves in a large bowl or pot of warm water. If fresh, rinse the leaves in water. Wipe the leaves clean with a damp kitchen towel. Using tongs, hold a leaf 2 inches (5 cm) above the flame of a gas burner on the stove top, passing each side over the flame a few times until it turns a uniform brighter green; this softens the leaves and helps prevent cracking.

Repeat with the rest of the leaves. Stack the leaves on a clean work surface and use as directed in the recipe.

Hard-Boiling Eggs

Fill a saucepan with water and add the eggs. Bring to a full boil over high heat, then reduce the heat to low and simmer for 6 minutes for medium-firm yolks and 8 minutes for firm yolks. Transfer the eggs to a bowl of ice water to stop the cooking. When cool, remove the eggs from the water and hit them against a counter to crack them all over, then peel.

Using a Tortilla Press

Line a tortilla press with 2 sheets of plastic wrap. Or, cut a quart-sized plastic storage bag along the sides, leaving the bottom seam of the bag intact. Place the opened up storage bag in the tortilla press.

Place a dough ball between the plastic and gently push down the top plate of the press. You might need to rotate the dough once or twice and press again to produce the desired shape. Open the press and peel off the top sheet of plastic. Invert the tortilla onto one hand and remove the remaining plastic.

Charcoal Grilling

Ignite the coals using a chimney starter. When fully lit, dump the coals in the fire bed. If needed, pour in more coals; they will ignite from the heat of the already-lit coals.

For direct-heat grilling, spread the coals two or three layers deep in one-third of the fire bed, one or two layers deep in another one-third of the fire bed, and leave one-third of the fire bed free of coals. Position the grill rack in its

slots over the coals. Be sure the grill rack is well oiled before placing food on it, to prevent the food from sticking.

For indirect-heat grilling, arrange the coals into 2 equal piles on either side of the fire bed and place a foil drip pan in the center, leaving the middle of the grill without heat. Pour water into the pan and replace the rack with its handles over the coals. For even cooking, tie or truss the food into a compact shape. Put the food on the center of the grill rack directly over the drip pan and cover the grill.

Gas Grilling

For direct-heat grilling, turn on all heat elements to high. It will take 10–15 minutes for the grill rack to preheat. Adjust the heat level to the temperature that is specified in the recipe and place the food directly over the heat elements to cook.

For indirect-heat grilling, first preheat the grill using all of the burners, then turn off the burner directly below where the food will sit. Gas grills come with a drip pan to collect the grease. Put the food over the no-heat zone and adjust the burners on either side of the food if using a two-burner grill.

Basic Recipes

Latin meals rely on stocks, pastes, and rubs to build flavor; freshly made tortillas, beans, and rice to accompany the main dish; and a wide variety of salsas and sauces to add zest and spice. These basic recipes will help you create meals with layers of flavors.

Vegetable Stock

4–5 peppercorns

4 fresh flat-leaf (Italian) parsley sprigs

1 fresh thyme sprig

1 bay leaf

¼ cup (2 fl oz/60 ml) olive oil

1 yellow onion, coarsely chopped

1 carrot, peeled and coarsely chopped

2 celery stalks, coarsely chopped

½ cup (4 fl oz/125 ml) dry white wine

Wrap the peppercorns, parsley, thyme, and bay leaf in a piece of cheesecloth (muslin) and secure with kitchen string.

In a stockpot over medium heat, warm the oil until shimmering. Add the onion, carrot, and celery and sauté until lightly browned, 5–8 minutes. Add the wine and deglaze the pot, stirring to scrape up the browned bits from the pan bottom. Raise the heat to medium-high and cook until the wine is almost completely evaporated. Add 4 qt (4 l) water and the herb bundle and bring to a boil. Reduce the heat to low and let simmer, uncovered, for about 45 minutes.

Strain the stock through a sieve into a heatproof container and discard the solids. Let the stock cool completely, stirring it occasionally to help the heat dissipate. Cover and refrigerate for up to 2 days or freeze in airtight containers for up to 3 months.

Makes about 3 qt (3 l)

Chicken Stock

5 lb (2.5 kg) chicken backs and necks

1 leek, including tender green parts, coarsely chopped

2 carrots, coarsely chopped

1 celery stalk, coarsely chopped

12 fresh flat-leaf (Italian) parsley sprigs

1 fresh thyme sprig

8–10 black peppercorns

In a stockpot, combine the chicken parts, leek, carrots, celery, parsley, thyme, and peppercorns. Add cold water to cover by 1 inch (2.5 cm). Place the pot over medium-high heat and slowly bring almost to a boil. Using a large spoon, skim off any scum and froth from the surface. Reduce the heat to low and simmer uncovered, skimming the surface as needed and adding more water if necessary to keep the ingredients immersed, until the meat has fallen off the bones and the stock is fragrant and flavorful, about 3 hours.

Remove from the heat and let stand until the liquid is almost room temperature, about 1 hour. Line a fine-mesh sieve with cheesecloth, set over a heatproof container, and pour the stock through the sieve. Discard the solids. Use a large metal spoon to skim the clear yellow fat from the surface of the stock and use right away. Alternatively, let the stock cool to room temperature, then cover and refrigerate until fully chilled. Using a spoon, lift off the congealed layer of fat on top and discard. Cover and refrigerate for up to 5 days or freeze in airtight containers for up to 2 months.

Makes about 3½ qt (3½ l)

Shellfish Stock

4–5 peppercorns

4 fresh flat-leaf (Italian) parsley sprigs

1 fresh thyme sprig

1 bay leaf

¼ cup (2 fl oz/60 ml) olive oil

1 yellow onion, coarsely chopped

1 carrot, peeled and coarsely chopped

2 celery stalks, coarsely chopped

1 tablespoon tomato paste

½ cup (4 fl oz/125 ml) dry white wine

6 cups (6 oz/185 g) shrimp (prawn) shells

Wrap the peppercorns, parsley, thyme, and bay leaf in a piece of cheesecloth (muslin) and tie with a kitchen string.

In a large stockpot over medium heat, heat the oil until shimmering. Add the onion, carrot, and celery and sauté until softened but not browned, 4–5 minutes. Add the tomato paste and stir for another 2 minutes.

Add the wine and deglaze the pot, stirring to scrape up the browned bits from the pan bottom. Raise the heat to medium-high and cook until the wine is almost completely evaporated. Add 4 qt (4 l) cold water, the shrimp shells, and herb bundle and bring to a boil. Reduce the heat to low and simmer, uncovered, for about 30 minutes, using a spoon or skimmer to regularly skim the foam that rises to the surface of the stock. Taste and adjust the seasonings.

Strain the stock through a fine-mesh sieve lined with cheesecloth (muslin) into a heatproof container. Discard the solids. Let the stock cool completely, stirring it occasionally to help the heat dissipate. Cover and refrigerate for up to 2 days, or freeze in airtight containers for up to 3 months.

Makes about 3¾ qt (3¾ l)

Beef Stock

6 lb (3 kg) meaty beef and veal shanks

2 yellow onions, coarsely chopped

1 leek, including tender green parts, coarsely chopped

2 carrots, coarsely chopped

1 celery stalk, coarsely chopped

6 cloves garlic

4 fresh flat-leaf (Italian) parsley sprigs

3 fresh thyme sprigs

2 small bay leaves

10–12 black peppercorns

In a stockpot, combine the beef and veal shanks and add cold water to cover. Place the pot over medium-high heat and slowly bring almost to a boil. Using a large spoon, skim off any scum and froth from the surface. Reduce the heat to low and simmer uncovered, skimming the surface as needed and adding more water if necessary to keep the shanks immersed, for 2 hours.

Add the onions, leek, carrots, celery, garlic, parsley, thyme, bay leaves, and peppercorns and continue to simmer over low heat, uncovered, until the meat begins to fall from the bones and the stock is very flavorful, about 2 hours longer.

Remove from the heat and let stand until the liquid is almost room temperature, about 1 hour. Line a fine-mesh sieve with cheesecloth, set over a heatproof container, and pour the stock through the sieve. Discard the solids. Use a large metal spoon to skim the clear yellow fat from the surface of the stock and use right away. Alternatively, let the stock cool to room temperature, then cover and refrigerate until fully chilled. Using a spoon, lift off the congealed layer of fat on top and discard. Cover and refrigerate for up to 5 days or freeze in airtight containers for up to 2 months.

Makes about 5 qt (5 l)

Fish Stock

2½ lb (1¼ kg) fish bones, heads, and skin, well rinsed

1 large yellow onion, coarsely chopped

½ fennel bulb, trimmed and coarsely chopped

3 celery stalks, coarsely chopped

1 carrot, peeled and diced

1 leek, including tender green parts, chopped

2 cups (16 fl oz/500 ml) dry white wine

In a large saucepan, combine the fish parts, onion, fennel, celery, carrot, leek, 6 cups (48 fl oz/1.5 l) water, and the wine. Place over medium heat and bring gradually to a boil, skimming off foam as needed. Cover partially, reduce the heat to low, and simmer until the flesh starts to fall off the bones, about 25 minutes. Line a sieve with cheesecloth (muslin) and place over a clean container. Strain the stock through the sieve. Cover and refrigerate for up to 3 days or freeze in airtight containers for up to 3 months.

Makes about 2 qt (2l)

Seasoned White Rice

2 cups (14 oz/440 g) medium- or long-grain white rice

½ white onion, coarsely chopped

2 cloves garlic

5 tablespoons (2½ fl oz/75 ml) canola oil

½ teaspoon fresh lime juice

3 fresh flat-leaf (Italian) parsley sprigs

Sea salt

Rinse the rice in water, swishing the grains, and then drain. Repeat 2 or 3 times, draining well. Spread the rice out on a kitchen towel and let stand to air-dry for about 10 minutes.

Put the onion, garlic, and 3 tablespoons cold water in a blender and process until smooth.

In a Dutch oven or other heavy pot with a tight-fitting lid, warm the oil over medium-high heat until it is smoking. Add the rice and cook, stirring, until the rice has absorbed the oil and the grains turn a toasty golden color, have a nutty aroma, and begin to crackle, 7–10 minutes. Stir the onion purée into the rice and cook, stirring constantly, for 1 minute. Pour in 4 cups (32 fl oz/1 l) hot water and add the lime juice, parsley, and 1 teaspoon salt. Bring to a simmer, then reduce the heat to medium-low, cover, and cook for 15 minutes without lifting the lid. Remove from the heat and let stand, covered, for 10 minutes. Transfer the rice to individual plates or a serving bowl and discard the parsley sprigs. Fluff the grains gently with a fork and serve hot.

Makes 6 servings

Cilantro Rice

½ cup (½ oz/15 g) firmly packed fresh cilantro (fresh coriander) leaves, plus 1 tablespoon chopped

¼ white onion

1 poblano chile, roasted, peeled, and seeded (page 268)

½ jalapeño chile, seeded

1 large clove garlic

Sea salt

¼ cup (2 fl oz/60 ml) vegetable oil

1 cup (7 oz/220 g) medium- or long-grain white rice

In a blender or food processor, combine the ½ cup (½ oz/15 g) cilantro, the onion, poblano, jalapeño, garlic, 1 teaspoon salt, and ¼ cup (2 fl oz/60 ml) water. Process until a smooth, bright green purée forms, stopping the machine and scraping down the sides often.

In a saucepan with a tight-fitting lid, warm the oil over medium heat. Add the rice and cook, stirring, until the rice has absorbed the oil and the grains turn a light golden color, about 5 minutes. Add the cilantro purée and cook, stirring, until the purée is fragrant and thickens slightly, about 1 minute. Add 1¾ cups (14 fl oz/ 430 ml) water, stir once, and bring to a gentle boil. Cover, reduce the heat to low, and cook until all the liquid has been absorbed, 15–20 minutes. Do not stir.

Remove from the heat and let stand, covered, for 5 minutes. Transfer the rice to individual plates or a serving bowl and fluff the grains gently with a fork. Scatter the chopped cilantro on top and serve hot.

Makes 4–6 servings

Coconut Rice

1–3 large green (young) coconut(s)

Canned or frozen fresh coconut water as needed (optional)

1 cup (7 oz/220 g) medium- or long-grain white rice

⅓ cup (2 oz/60 g) raisins

1 teaspoon unsalted butter

Sea salt

Extract the water and meat from the coconut(s) following the directions on page 268. Measure out 2½ cups (20 fl oz/625 ml) coconut water. Depending on the size and number of coconuts you are using, add canned or frozen fresh coconut water as needed to equal 2½ cups. Finely chop the coconut meat and measure out ½ cup (2 oz/60 g). (Reserve the remaining coconut meat and water for another use.)

In a saucepan with a tight-fitting lid, combine the coconut water, rice, raisins, butter, and 1 teaspoon salt. Stir once to settle and bring to a gentle boil over medium heat. Cover and reduce the heat to low. Cook until all of the liquid has been absorbed, 15–20 minutes. Do not stir.

Remove from the heat and let stand, covered, for 5 minutes. Transfer the rice to individual plates or a serving bowl and fluff the grains gently with a fork. Gently stir in the coconut meat and serve hot.

Makes 4–6 servings

Toasted Manioc

3 tablespoons unsalted butter

2 tablespoons thinly sliced green (spring) onions

½ cube chicken bouillon

Sea salt and freshly ground black pepper

2 cups (10 oz/315 g) manioc flour (farinha di mesa fina or torrada)

In a saucepan over medium-low heat, melt the butter. Add the green onion, bouillon, and salt and pepper to taste and cook until the onion is softened, about 1 minute. Add the manioc flour and stir until the manioc absorbs the butter to form a grainy mixture. Cover to keep warm until ready to serve.

Makes 10–12 servings

Sautéed Kale

3 tablespoons rendered pork fat or olive oil

1½ tablespoons minced garlic

1½ lb (750 g) kale, tough center ribs removed, thinly sliced crosswise

Sea salt and freshly ground black pepper

In a saucepan over medium heat, warm the pork fat. Add the garlic and cook until fragrant, about 1 minute. Add the kale and stir to coat with the oil. Cover and cook, stirring occasionally, until the kale is tender-crisp, 3–4 minutes. Season to taste with salt and pepper. Cover to keep warm until ready to serve.

Makes 10–12 servings

Tomato-Avocado Salsa

¼ cup (2 fl oz/60 ml) olive oil

¼ cup (1 oz/30 g) minced green (spring) onions, white and tender green parts

¼ cup (⅓ oz/10 g) minced fresh cilantro (fresh coriander)

¼ cup (2 fl oz/60 ml) fresh lime juice

1 teaspoon dried oregano

Sea salt and freshly ground black pepper

2 large ripe tomatoes, seeded and diced (about 2 cups/14 oz/440 g)

1 ripe avocado, pitted, peeled, and diced

In a nonreactive bowl, whisk together the olive oil, green onion, cilantro, lime juice, oregano, 2 teaspoons salt, and ½ teaspoon pepper and stir to mix well. Add the tomatoes and avocado and stir gently to coat with the dressing. Refrigerate until ready to serve.

Makes 4–6 servings

Basic Guacamole

6 tablespoons (2 oz/60 g) finely chopped white onion

2 serrano chiles, seeded and finely chopped

1 clove garlic, minced (optional)

2 ripe Hass avocados, halved, pitted, and peeled

1 large ripe tomato, finely chopped

¼ cup (¼ oz/7 g) lightly packed fresh cilantro (fresh coriander) leaves, finely chopped

1 tablespoon fresh lime juice

Sea salt

In a mortar or bowl, combine 4 tablespoons (1½ oz/45 g) of the onion, the chiles, and the garlic, if using. Using a pestle or a fork, mash to form a coarse paste. Add the avocado and mash until well incorporated. Stir in all but

2 tablespoons of the tomato and all of the cilantro and lime juice. Season to taste with salt. Let stand for a few minutes before serving to allow the flavors to blend. Sprinkle the guacamole with the remaining onion and tomato before serving.

Makes about 2½ cups (20 oz/625 g)

Roasted Tomato Salsa

2 tomatillos

4 plum (Roma) or large pear tomatoes

1 or 2 whole serrano or jalapeño chiles

2 cloves garlic, unpeeled

1 white onion, diced

½ cup (¾ oz/20 g) coarsely chopped fresh cilantro (fresh coriander)

Sea salt

Remove the papery husks from the tomatillos and rinse under warm running water to remove the sticky residue on the skins. Pat dry.

Pan-roast the tomatillos, tomatoes, chile, and garlic according to the instructions on page 268. When cool enough to handle, peel the garlic and stem the chile.

In a blender or food processor, combine the chile, garlic, and onion and pulse several times. Add the tomatoes and tomatillos and process until the salsa is fairly smooth but still has some texture. Add the cilantro and 1 teaspoon salt and pulse several times just to combine.

Taste and add more salt, if needed. Serve right away, or store in an airtight container in the refrigerator for up to 3 days. Let come to room temperature and taste and adjust the seasoning before serving.

Makes about 2 cups (16 oz/500 g)

Red Chile Sauce

10 large guajillo chiles

1 plum (Roma) tomato, chopped

4 cloves garlic

Sea salt

2 teaspoons vegetable oil

3 tablespoons finely minced white onion

Heat a large, heavy frying pan or griddle over medium-high heat. Wipe the chiles clean with a dry paper towel. Working in batches, place the chiles in the hot pan and press with a spatula, holding them flat for about 10 seconds each. Turn the chiles and press flat on the other side for 20–30 seconds longer, being careful not to let them burn. Transfer the chiles to a plate and let cool. When cool enough to handle, remove the stems, seeds, and ribs and tear the chiles into pieces. Transfer to a bowl, pour in 2 cups (16 fl oz/500 ml) water, and stir well. Let soak at room temperature, stirring several times, until well softened, about 1 hour.

Transfer the chiles and their soaking liquid to a blender. Add the tomato, garlic, and 1 teaspoon salt and process to a thick, smooth purée.

In a frying pan over medium heat, warm the oil. Add the onion and cook, stirring often, until just softened, 3–5 minutes. Pour the chile purée into the frying pan. Add ¼ cup (2 fl oz/60 ml) water to the blender, swirl to wash down the residue of the purée from the sides, and add to the pan. Fry the sauce, stirring constantly, until fragrant and slightly thickened, 3–5 minutes.

Add enough water to make 4 cups (32 fl oz/ 1 l) sauce, or thin to the desired consistency. (The sauce will thicken when fried with tortillas for Chilaquiles, page 231.) Taste and add more salt, if needed. Serve right away, or store in an airtight container in the refrigerator for up to 5 days.

Makes about 4 cups (32 fl oz/1 l)

Salsa Fresca

2 plum (Roma) tomatoes, seeded and finely diced

¼ white onion, seeded and finely diced

2 tablespoons finely chopped fresh cilantro (fresh coriander)

Sea salt

In a bowl, combine the tomatoes, onion, cilantro, and ½ teaspoon salt and stir to mix well. Taste and add more salt, if needed. Serve right away, or store in an airtight container in the refrigerator for up to 3 days. Let come to room temperature and taste and adjust the seasoning before using.

PICO DE GALLO SALSA VARIATION: Add 1 serrano or jalapeño chile, minced with its seeds, and fresh lime juice to taste to the salsa fresca.

Makes about ¾ cup (4½ oz/140 g)

Avocado-Tomatillo Salsa

12 tomatillos, about ½ lb (250 g) total weight

3 serrano chiles, seeded and coarsely chopped

½ white onion, cut into small chunks

¾ cup (1½ oz/45 g) chopped fresh cilantro (fresh coriander), plus whole leaves for garnish

1 teaspoon dark brown sugar

2 avocados, halved and pitted

Sea salt

Remove the papery husks from the tomatillos and rinse under warm running water to remove the sticky residue on the skins. Chop coarsely and set aside.

In a blender or food processor, combine the chiles, onion, and ½ cup (4 fl oz/125 ml) water. Process until partially smooth. Add the tomatillos, cilantro, and brown sugar and blend until the mixture is roughly textured.

Scoop the avocado into a bowl and mash coarsely with a fork. It should be chunky. Stir in the chile sauce and season to taste with salt. Garnish with the cilantro leaves and serve right away, or store in an airtight container in the refrigerator for up to 3 hours. Let come to room temperature and taste and adjust the seasoning before serving.

Makes about 3 cups (24 fl oz/750 ml)

Pasilla and Árbol Chile Salsa

4 árbol chiles

2 pasilla chiles

2 cloves garlic, unpeeled

6 ripe plum (Roma) tomatoes, coarsely chopped

Juice of ¹⁄₂ lime

Sea salt

Pan-roast the chiles, garlic, and tomatoes according to the instructions on page 268. When cool enough to handle, stem and seed the chiles and peel the garlic.

In a saucepan over medium heat, combine the chiles with water to cover and bring to a simmer. Cook for 5 minutes, remove from the heat, and set aside to soak for about 10 minutes.

In a blender or food processor, combine the garlic, tomatoes, and lime juice and process just until broken up. Drain the chiles, tear them into small pieces, and add to the tomato mixture. Add ¹⁄₂ teaspoon salt and process until the salsa is fairly smooth but still has some texture. If the mixture is too thick, add a few tablespoons of water.

Pour into a bowl and serve right away, or store in an airtight container in the refrigerator for up to 1 day. Let come to room temperature and taste and adjust the seasoning before serving.

Makes about 2 cups (16 fl oz/500 ml)

Tomatillo Salsa

1 lb (500 g) tomatillos

3 tablespoons coarsely chopped white onion

3 serrano chiles, seeded and coarsely chopped

2 cloves garlic, coarsely chopped

Sea salt

¹⁄₄ cup (¹⁄₃ oz/10 g) finely chopped fresh cilantro (fresh coriander)

Remove the papery husks from the tomatillos and rinse under warm running water to remove the sticky residue on the skins. In a saucepan over medium heat, combine the tomatillos with water to cover and bring to a gentle boil. Cook, uncovered, until soft but not soggy, 8–10 minutes. Drain, then transfer to a blender or food processor. Add the onion, chiles, garlic, and ¹⁄₂ teaspoon salt and process until the salsa is fairly smooth but still has some texture.

Pour into a bowl, stir in the cilantro, and serve right away, or store in an airtight container in the refrigerator for up to 3 days. Let come to room temperature and taste and adjust the seasoning before serving.

Makes about 2 cups (16 fl oz/500 ml)

Chipotle Chile Salsa

2 cloves garlic, unpeeled

2 ripe tomatoes, about 1 lb (500 g)

3 dried chipotle chiles or canned chipotles in adobo

Sea salt

Pan-roast the garlic and tomatoes according to the instructions on page 268. When cool enough to handle, peel the garlic.

If using dried chiles, place in a saucepan with salted water to cover. Bring to a boil over medium-high heat and simmer until softened, 10–15 minutes. Drain, reserving the cooking liquid, and place the chiles in a blender or food processor along with about ¹⁄₄ cup (2 fl oz/60 ml) of the cooking liquid. If using canned chiles, scrape off some of the adobo sauce, and place the chiles in a blender or food processor.

Add the garlic and tomatoes to the blender and process very briefly. The mixture should be thick and slightly chunky. Pour into a bowl, season to taste with salt, cover, and let stand at room temperature for 20–30 minutes to allow the flavors to blend. Taste and add more salt, if needed.

Serve right away, or store in an airtight container in the refrigerator for up to 3 days. Let the salsa come to room temperature and taste and adjust the seasoning before serving.

Makes about 1 cup (8 fl oz/250 ml)

Traditional Chimichurri Sauce

Salt and freshly ground pepper

4 cloves garlic, minced

1 tablespoon dried oregano

1 tablespoon dried rosemary, minced

1 tablespoon dried thyme

2 bay leaves, finely crumbled

1 teaspoon chile powder

¹⁄₂ cup (4 fl oz/125 ml) white vinegar

2 tablespoons olive oil

To make the chimichurri sauce, in a saucepan, bring 1 cup (8 fl oz/250 ml) water to a boil over high heat. Add 1½ teaspoons salt and stir to dissolve. Meanwhile, in a heatproof glass jar with a tight-fitting lid, combine the garlic, oregano, rosemary, thyme, bay leaves, chile powder, and ¼ teaspoon pepper. Pour the hot salted water into the jar. Add the vinegar and olive oil, cover tightly, and store in a dark place for at least 4 hours, but ideally 1 week.

Makes about 1 cup (8 fl oz/250 ml)

Red Chile-Cilantro Chimichurri Sauce

½ cup (½ oz/15 g) firmly packed fresh cilantro (fresh coriander) leaves, coarsely chopped

½ cup (½ oz/15 g) firmly packed fresh flat-leaf (Italian) parsley leaves, coarsely chopped

2 tablespoons coarsely chopped green (spring) onion

2 teaspoons fresh lime juice

2 teaspoons white vinegar

2 bay leaves, finely crumbled

1 teaspoon seeded and coarsely chopped red or green chile, such as jalapeño or serrano

Sea salt and freshly ground black pepper

½ cup (4 fl oz/125 ml) olive oil

In a food processor, combine the cilantro, parsley, green onion, lime juice, vinegar, bay leaves, chile, ½ teaspoon salt, and ¼ teaspoon pepper and process until the mixture is minced, about 10 seconds. Transfer to a bowl and stir in the olive oil. Let stand at room temperature for at least 1 hour to allow the flavors to blend, or until ready to serve.

Makes about 1 cup (8 fl oz/250 ml)

Parsley-Garlic Chimichurri Sauce

1 cup (1 oz/30 g) firmly packed fresh flat-leaf (Italian) parsley

½ cup (4 fl oz/125 ml) red wine vinegar

4 cloves garlic, minced

1 teaspoon dried oregano

1 teaspoon paprika

Sea salt and freshly ground pepper

½ cup (4 fl oz/125 ml) olive oil

In a food processor, combine the parsley, vinegar, garlic, oregano, paprika, ½ teaspoon salt, and ¼ teaspoon pepper and process until the parsley and garlic are uniformly minced, about 10 seconds. Transfer to a bowl and stir in the olive oil. Let stand at room temperature for at least 1 hour to allow the flavors to blend, or until ready to serve.

Makes about 1 cup (8 fl oz/250 ml)

Pickled Red Onions

1 habanero chile

2 small red onions, thinly sliced

Boiling water as needed

⅓ cup (3 fl oz/80 ml) fresh lime juice

2 cloves garlic, slightly smashed

Sea salt and freshly ground pepper

⅛ teaspoon dried oregano, preferably Mexican

Pan-roast the chile according to the instructions on page 268. Set aside to cool.

Place the onion slices in a heatproof bowl and add boiling water to cover. Let soak for 2–3 minutes. Drain well, transfer to a small bowl, and toss with the lime juice, garlic, 1 teaspoon salt, ¼ teaspoon pepper, and the

oregano. Tuck the chile under the onions and marinate at room temperature for 1 hour, stirring occasionally.

Before serving, retrieve the chile and place it on top of the onion slices. Serve right away, or store in an airtight container in the refrigerator for up to 2 weeks.

Makes about 2 cups (7 oz/220 g)

Molho Sauce

½ cup (4 fl oz/125 ml) Beef Stock (page 271), or purchased beef broth

1 tablespoon white vinegar

2 tablespoons thinly sliced green (spring) onions

2 tablespoons seeded and finely diced green bell pepper (capsicum)

2 tablespoons seeded and diced tomato

2 tablespoons minced fresh cilantro (fresh coriander)

1 habanero chile, seeded and minced

Sea salt

1 tablespoon olive oil

In a bowl, combine the beef stock, vinegar, green onion, bell pepper, tomato, cilantro, habanero, ½ teaspoon salt, and the olive oil and stir to mix well. Set aside at room temperature.

Makes about ¾ cup (6 fl oz/177 ml)

Shredded Beef

2 lb (1 kg) skirt steak, cut into strips about 2 inches (5 cm) wide

1 yellow onion, quartered

¼ red bell pepper (capsicum), seeded or 2 ancho chiles (see Note)

½ teaspoon achiote paste

¼ teaspoon ground cumin

In a large soup pot, combine the beef, onion, bell pepper, achiote, cumin, and 6 cups (48 fl oz/1.5 l) water. Bring to a boil over high heat. Reduce the heat to medium-low, cover, and simmer until the meat is falling-apart tender, about 1½ hours. When the beef is done, drain in a colander set over a saucepan and reserve the cooking liquid. When it is cool enough to handle, use your fingers or 2 forks to shred the beef finely. Discard the onion and bell pepper. NOTE: If making sopes (page 79), replace the red bell pepper with 2 crumbled ancho chiles.

Makes 6–10 servings

Seasoned Beef Filling

2 large ripe tomatoes, diced

2 large yellow onions, cut into 1-inch (2.5-cm) chunks

¾ cup (4½ oz/140 g) seeded and chopped *ají dulce* peppers (page 278) or sweet Italian peppers

8 cloves garlic

3 tablespoons fresh cilantro (fresh coriander) leaves

½ teaspoon achiote paste (page 278)

¼ teaspoon ground cumin

Salt and freshly ground pepper

5 tablespoons (3 fl oz/80 ml) canola oil

Shredded Beef (above), cooking liquid reserved

In a food processor, combine the tomatoes, onions, peppers, garlic, cilantro, achiote, cumin, 1 teaspoon salt, and ½ teaspoon pepper and process to a chunky sauce. In a large saucepan over medium-low heat, warm the oil. Add the sauce and cook, stirring constantly, until fragrant, about 2 minutes. Reduce the heat to low, cover, and cook, stirring occasionally, until the ingredients are tender and the sauce has

thickened, about 25 minutes. Taste and adjust the seasoning. Remove from the heat. (If making Beef Tamales, set aside half of the sauce. See page 162.)

Add the shredded beef, ½ teaspoon salt, and ½ cup (4 fl oz/125 ml) of the reserved beef cooking liquid to the saucepan with the remaining sauce. Cook over medium heat until the beef soaks up some of the sauce and the flavors have blended, about 5 minutes. Remove from the heat and let cool completely.

Makes 4–6 servings

Cooked Beans

1 lb (500 g) dried black or pinto beans

2 tablespoons fresh pork lard, rendered bacon fat, or canola oil

½ white onion, coarsely chopped

2 fresh epazote sprigs (page 279), if cooking black beans, or 2 fresh cilantro (fresh coriander) sprigs

Sea salt

3 oz (90 g) *queso fresco* (page 278), crumbled, for serving (optional)

Pick over the beans and discard any misshapen beans or stones. Rinse the beans under cold running water and drain. Transfer to a pot and add water to cover by 3–4 inches (7.5–10 cm). Bring to a gentle boil over medium-high heat, reduce the heat to medium-low, and maintain a gentle simmer.

Meanwhile, in a small frying pan over medium heat, melt the lard or fat or warm the oil. Add the onion and sauté until browned, about 8 minutes. Add to the beans, scraping in all of the melted fat. Cover partially and cook until the beans are just tender, 2–3 hours, stirring occasionally and adding water if necessary to maintain the level of water well above the beans. Add the epazote if using black beans, or

add cilantro and 1½ teaspoons salt and continue to cook until the beans are very soft, 40–60 minutes longer. Taste and adjust the seasoning with more salt, if needed.

The beans will keep, covered, in the refrigerator for up to 4 days. If serving the beans as they are, ladle the broth and beans into bowls and garnish with the cheese, if using, or drain the beans and use as directed in the recipe.

Makes 6–8 servings

Refried Beans

½ cup (4 oz/125 g) fresh pork lard or canola oil

½ white onion, finely chopped

4 cups (28 oz/875 g) Cooked Beans (left) with 2 cups (16 fl oz/500 ml) cooking liquid, or 4 cups (28 oz/875 g) canned beans, drained, with 2 cups (16 fl oz/500 ml) water

Sea salt

In a large, heavy frying pan over medium heat, melt the lard or warm the oil. Add the onion and sauté, stirring often, until golden and soft, about 5 minutes.

Pour in 1 cup (7 oz/220 g) of the beans with some of the cooking liquid, smashing them down with a potato masher or the back of a large spoon. Continue until all of the beans and their broth have been added and mashed. Raise the heat to medium-high and cook until the beans begin to dry out, about 10 minutes. Taste and season with salt, if needed.

Makes 4–6 servings

Corn Tortillas

1 pound (500 g) freshly prepared tortilla masa or 1¾ cups (9 oz/280 g) masa harina for tortillas (see page 21)

Sea salt

1 cup (8 fl oz/250 ml) plus 2 tablespoons warm water, if using masa harina

If using fresh masa, put in a bowl and knead with 1 teaspoon salt, adding a little warm water, if needed, to make a soft dough. If using masa harina, put in a bowl, add the warm water, and mix with your hands. Allow the dough to rest 5 minutes, then add 1 teaspoon salt and knead for 1 minute. Shape into golf ball–sized balls, then cover with a damp kitchen towel or plastic wrap. Use a tortilla press to flatten the masa into thin disks (see page 269).

Heat a large griddle, cast-iron frying pan, or *comal* over medium heat. Slide the tortilla off your hand—do not flip it—onto the hot griddle. Cook until the underside is freckled, about 30 seconds. Flip over and cook for another 20–30 seconds, then flip back to the first side for just a second. Transfer to a plate. As the tortillas are cooked, stack them on a plate and cover with a kitchen towel to keep warm.

NOTE: To reheat tortillas, wrap stacks of 5 tortillas each in aluminum foil and warm in a 275°F (135°C) oven for 5–10 minutes. To reheat fewer, put them back on the pan and reheat for several seconds on each side.

Makes about 10 tortillas

Tortilla Chips

8 purchased thin corn tortillas, 4–6 inches (10–15 cm) in diameter

Corn or peanut oil for frying

Sea salt (optional)

Stack the tortillas in 2 equal piles. Cut each pile into 4–6 triangular wedges, strips ¼ inch (6 mm) wide by 1 inch (2.5 cm) long, or small squares. Spread in a single layer, cover with a heavy kitchen towel or wire rack to prevent curling, and let dry for at least several hours.

Pour oil to a depth of 1 inch (2.5 cm) into a heavy frying pan and heat to 375°F (190°C) on a deep-frying thermometer. Add the tortilla wedges or strips a few at a time and fry, tossing them, until light gold. Do not let them darken, or they will be bitter. Lift out and drain on paper towels. Salt the cooked chips, if desired, while still hot.

Cover with a dry kitchen towel and keep warm for up to 30 minutes in a 200°F (95°C) oven. Store for up to 1 day in an airtight plastic bag. Recrisp, if necessary, for a few minutes in a 200°F (95°C) oven.

Makes 3 cups (3 oz/90 g) chips

Crema

1 cup (8 fl oz/250 ml) heavy cream

1 tablespoon buttermilk or good-quality plain yogurt with active cultures

In a small nonaluminum bowl, stir together the cream and buttermilk. Cover with plastic wrap, poke a few holes in the plastic, and leave at warm room temperature (about 85°F/30°C) until well thickened, 8–24 hours. Stir, cover with fresh plastic wrap, and refrigerate until firm and well chilled, about 6 hours. If the *crema* becomes too thick, thin with a little whole milk or half-and-half (half cream).

Makes about 1 cup (8 fl oz/250 ml)

Meringue Frosting

1 cup (8 oz/250 g) sugar

4 large egg whites, at room temperature

¼ teaspoon cream of tartar

In a small, heavy saucepan, combine the sugar and ½ cup (4 fl oz/125 ml) water and bring to a boil over medium-high heat, stirring to dissolve

the sugar. Reduce the heat to medium-low and simmer, washing down the sides of the pan as crystals form with a pastry brush dipped in cold water. When the syrup comes to a boil, in a clean metal bowl, combine the egg whites and cream of tartar and, using an electric mixer set on high speed, beat until stiff peaks form. Meanwhile, cook the sugar syrup until a candy thermometer registers 230°F (110°C), 10–12 minutes.

Slowly add the boiling syrup in a thin stream to the beating egg whites until all the syrup is incorporated. Continue beating until the meringue frosting is cooled and glossy. Cover and refrigerate until ready to use.

Makes enough frosting for one 9-by-12-inch (23-by-30-cm) cake

Simple Syrup

1 cup (8 fl oz/250 ml) sugar

In a saucepan over medium-high heat, bring 1 cup (8 fl oz/250 ml) water to a simmer in a saucepan set over medium-high heat. Add the sugar and stir until it completely dissolves. Remove the pan from the heat and set aside to cool to room temperature. Pour the syrup into a 2-cup (16–fl oz/500-ml) airtight container and refrigerate until needed.

Makes 1½ cups (12 fl oz/355 ml)

Glossary

ACAI BERRIES The fruit of a palm tree, açai berries look like grapes but have a berry flavor.

ACHIOTE PASTE This seasoning paste is made from the hard, brick-red seeds of the tropical annatto tree. The seeds are ground with spices and mixed with garlic and vinegar or the juice of bitter oranges. The paste is popular in the Yucatán peninsula, where it lends a mild flowery flavor and deep yellow-orange color to dishes.

ADOBO In Mexico, adobo is a seasoning made from dried chiles, herbs, salt, and spices, ground together with vinegar to the consistency of a thick paste. It is similar to the Spanish mixture of same name, which calls for vinegar, olive oil, and spices. Because vinegar and salt are natural preservatives, the use of adobo was originally a technique for pickling and preserving meats.

AJÍ In many Latin American countries, the word *ají* refers to any chile or chile sauce. *Ají* peppers themselves, however, hail from Peru. There are many varieties of *ají* peppers: *amarillo* or yellow, *verde* or green, *dulce* or sweet, *picante* or hot, and the popular *ají panca*. Fresh *ají* peppers are hard to come by, but dried *ajíes* and *ají* pastes can be found at specialty Latin markets or online (www.latinmerchant.com).

Ají amarillo The fresh *ají amarillo* pepper is long, narrow, and yellow to orange in color. It is hot with notes of sweet fruit. To make your own paste: In a pot, boil 2–3 halved and seeded habanero or Scotch bonnet chiles for 1 minute. Discard the water and repeat 2 more times. In a frying pan over medium-low heat, warm 2 tablespoons *each* butter and canola oil. Add 1 chopped red onion and 2 seeded and chopped yellow bell peppers to the pan and sauté until the onions are translucent, 5–6 minutes. Add the habaneros and cook for 2 more minutes. Purée in a blender to form a smooth paste.

Ají panca The fresh *ají panca* pepper is dark brown, mildly hot, and sweet. To make your own paste, follow the method for making the *ají amarillo paste*, using 1–2 habanero or scotch bonnet chiles and 2 seeded and chopped red bell peppers instead of the yellow bell peppers.

Ají verde The fresh *ají verde* pepper is actually a small orange-colored pepper. To make your own paste, follow the method for making the *ají amarillo* paste, replacing the habaneros with 6 halved and seeded jalapeños, and omitting the bell peppers.

AREPAS *Arepas* are white or yellow cornmeal patties, which may be grilled, baked, or fried. In Venezuela, *arepas* are stuffed with meats, cheeses, or other delicious fillings, whereas in Colombia these fillings are stacked on top of thinner and wider cakes. Today, *arepas* are made with a specialty precooked cornmeal (see Masa, Masarepa, page 21) for convenience.

AVOCADO LEAVES The leathery leaves of the avocado tree are used as a seasoning in south-central Mexico. They may be used fresh or dried and added whole or crumbled to contribute an aniselike taste to savory dishes.

BANANA LEAVES The large, pliable leaves of the banana tree are used to wrap tamales for steaming and seafood, poultry, or meat for steaming, grilling, or roasting. They protect the food while contributing a mild grassy flavor. Frozen banana leaves can be found in the frozen section of specialty Latin and Asian markets. Before using the leaves, soften them by steaming them or passing over a flame; see page 269.

BEANS Beans are a staple of Latin American cuisine. Varieties come in a virtual kaleidoscope of earthy colors. Most are sold dried, and may require soaking; buy dried beans from a store with high turnover so that they are as fresh as possible and require less cooking time.

Black Also called turtle, Mexican, or Spanish black beans, these small and shiny black beans are used widely for pot beans, soups and dips.

Black-Eyed Pea Also called cow pea or black-eyed beans, these cream-colored, kidney-shaped beans have a characteristic black dot with a yellow center and a mild flavor. These legumes require less soaking than most dried beans.

Lima Also called butter beans, these large, flat, white to pale green beans are sweet-tasting and are sold frozen, dried, or occasionally fresh. They grow in wide, flat inedible green pods.

Pinto A pale brown bean with an earthy flavor and darker, sometimes pinkish streaks, which disappear during cooking. This bean is a staple in Mexican refried beans (see page 276).

BREADFRUIT This tropical staple from a tall flowering tree has a flavor like potatoes or, as its name suggests, fresh-baked bread when cooked.

CARNE SECA This Mexican beef jerky is made from thin slices of meat that are salted and marinated with lemon, dried, and then grilled. You can use other soft, high-quality beef jerky.

CHAYOTE A pear-shaped member of the squash family, the chayote has a mild, cucumber-like flavor. Indigenous to Mexico, it comes in a varieties with skin ranging from a smooth-textured ivory to prickly dark green.

CHEESE Latin American cuisine is known best for its fresh cheeses, but there are some aged varieties as well.

Cotija This hard, salty, strongly flavored cheese is named after a town in Mexico where it comes from. Its flavor is similar to Parmesan or feta; it is also called *queso blanco*.

Farmer's cheese This is a mild form of cottage cheese drained of most liquid. It is sold in a fairly solid loaf shape, and is mild and slightly tangy.

Queso añejo Queso fresco is pressed in a mold to increase density and aged to create *queso añejo.* The aging process gives the cheese a saltier flavor and a medium sharpness. Like *queso fresco, queso añejo* is a fine melting cheese; longer aging produces a firmness suitable for grating, so *añejo* cheese is often used to make an even cheese layer in dishes like enchiladas.

Queso fresco This fresh, moist, lightly salted cheese is somewhere between ricotta and mild feta in taste and consistency.

Queso menonita This mild, Cheddar-like cheese with an excellent melting quality is made by Menonite communities in Mexico and Central America.

Queso Oaxaca The state of Oaxaca, Mexico, is famous for its white, string-like cheese, rolled up like giant balls of yarn and stacked in the markets. Like mozzarella, it is the product of a stretching process. It is delicious melted.

Queso panela Fresh curds are drained through a basket-shaped mold, giving a textured surface to this cheese. *Panela* is best eaten fresh.

CHERIMOYA This evergreen fruit has sweet, white flesh that becomes soft and creamy like custard when fully rip.

CHILES For information on most chiles, see pages 22–23.

CHIMICHURRI In Argentina, the condiment *chimichurri* is ubiquitous, accompanying nearly anything that is fried, grilled, or roasted. It is a must with the mixed-meat grill known as *asado,* and may also be used as a marinade. The texture ranges from smooth to chunky, and the ingredients vary, but the constants are olive oil, vinegar or lemon juice, garlic, and herbs.

CHOCOLATE Cocoa beans are native to the tropics and were a major culinary contribution of the New World. Today, so-called Mexican chocolate is sold in large tablets, and contains ground cacao, sugar, cinnamon, and sometimes almonds. Blended with milk it makes *champurrada*, or Mexican hot chocolate. Chocolate also marries with spices in traditional, iconic *mole poblano* (page 154).

CHORIZO Well-seasoned links of fresh pork sausage from both Mexico and Spain; Mexican chorizo is the spicier and more fragrant of the two. It is delicious grilled or sautéed, but is also an important element in a number of preparations, infusing potent spicy, smoky flavor in any dish it joins. (Also see Linguiça, page 280.)

COCONUT Growing on palm trees in tropical climates, the coconut is the world's largest nut. Its nutmeat is firm, creamy, and snowy white, and is a favorite ingredient for sweet baked goods. When selecting a fresh coconut, shake it to be sure it's full of coconut water, and pass up any with signs of mold around the "eyes." For more on working with fresh coconut, see page 268.

Coconut milk Coconut milk differs from coconut water. The milk is extracted from grated coconut meat, and may be made at home (see page 268). Canned unsweetened coconut milk is a fine convenience product. It is available in full-fat and reduced-fat forms. Don't confuse this with sweetened coconut mixes for mixed drinks, or products labeled coconut cream.

Shredded coconut Bags of shredded dried coconut are available in the baking supply aisles of most supermarkets. Shredded dried coconut is almost always sweetened, but it is possible to buy it unsweetened. Check the bag and your recipe to make sure you have the correct type.

CRÈME DE CACAO Crème de cacao is a chocolate liqueur that frequents Latin American desserts. Its flavor comes from a combination of the cacao (chocolate) bean and vanilla bean. It comes in dark and white varieties; the latter is clear. (Also see Kahlúa, page 280.)

DULCE DE LECHE This popular dessert syrup is similar to caramel in appearance and flavor and is the product of heavily sugared milk that has been slowly simmered for several hours. *Dulce de leche* can be found in a multitude of dessert preparations, topping ice cream, spread on crêpes, or drizzled over fruit.

EGGS, RAW Uncooked eggs carry a risk of being infected with salmonella or other bacteria, which can lead to food poisoning. This risk is of most concern to young chidren, older people, pregnant women, and anyone with a compromised immune system. If you have health and safety concerns, do not consume raw egg; rather, seek out a pasteurized egg product to replace it. Eggs can be made safe by heating them to 160°F (71°C).

EMPANADAS Half-moon-shaped empanadas and empanaditas, their miniature look-alikes, are similar to the pielike pastries and turnovers of Spain, and were baked in Latin America as soon as the Spanish settlers began to grow wheat. The tender flour crusts may hold savory or sweet fillings. They are ideal party fare.

EPAZOTE Considered a tenacious weed by many gardeners, pungent epazote (also called wormseed) is looked on as a culinary treasure by Mexican cooks. Ideally, epazote is used fresh, but dried epazote, stocked in Mexican markets, can be used in beans and soups. Enclose about 1 teaspoon in a tea ball for easy removal of the woody stems.

FLAN Originally introduced to the New World by Spain, this popular dessert has been embraced throughout Latin America. Rich with eggs and cream or sweetened condensed milk, flan is baked in caramel-lined ramekins, which are chilled then inverted before serving, creating an irresistible caramel topping for the custard.

GUAVA Delicious and sweet-smelling guava is popular in tropical climes around the world. Vaguely pear shaped, guavas can be as small as a walnut or as large as an apple, with pale yellow-green skin, and flesh that can be white, pink, yellow, or red. The flavor recalls strawberries, bananas, or pineapple. Some are seedless, but others have small edible seeds towards the center. The best have a creamy texture and edible rind. Select specimens that yield to gentle pressure, and have a floral fragrance. In Latin America, sugary guava paste is served with cheese as a dessert, or is sometimes eaten alone, much like a candy bar.

HEART OF PALM The tender, edible core of a young cabbage palm tree is a delicacy in tropical countries. Hearts of palm are slender and white, with many thin, concentric layers, like a leek. They resemble white asparagus, and taste similar to artichokes. They may be served as part of a salad, or included in lightly cooked dishes. Fresh hearts of palm are rare, but they are commonly available canned in water.

HORCHATA Among Mexico's many *aguas frescas*, *horchata* is a fresh, cooling drink. *Horchata*'s opaque white color distinguishes it from the other fruit-based beverages; it is made with a base of ground rice or melon seeds and is often flavored with cinnamon and almonds. The best *horchata* is milky, lightly sweet, lightly spiced, and immensely refreshing.

JAMAICA (hibiscus) See page 40.

JICAMA A member of the large legume family, the crunchy, ivory-fleshed, brown-skinned jicama is a tuber used throughout Mexico, its country of origin. Jicama has a bland taste that benefits from being marinated raw in lime juice or from

being combined with fruits or vegetables. Before using, peel away the skin and the fibrous layer beneath it with a sharp knife.

KAHLÚA This brandname coffee liqueur is similar to *crème de cacao* (see page 279) and is also a frequent ingredient in desserts. Other good quality coffee liqueurs may be substituted. It pairs particularly well with milk or cream, as in the popular White Russian cocktail.

LEMONGRASS An Asian import, lemongrass is a long, fibrous, grayish-green grass with a paler bulblike base and a mild lemon fragrance. Its fragrance and bright flavor are enjoyed in many Latin dishes. To use it, peel away any dry leaves from the base and trim off the grassy top section. Remove large pieces before serving.

LINGUIÇA This pork sausage native to Portugal is strongly flavored with heady amounts of garlic and red pepper. Like chorizo (see page 279), linguiça is frequently used as an ingredient in other dishes, especially traditional Brazilian fare. It may also be grilled.

MALANGA a starchy tuber similar to taro root, malanga is typically eaten boiled and mashed.

MANGO Native to India, but grown in tropical climates worldwide, this fragrant, oval-shaped fruit has skin that ranges from green to pale yellow or orange. The flesh is sweet, juicy, and aromatic. Ripe mangoes give slightly when pressed and are highly fragrant at their stem end.

MASA See page 21.

MOJO SAUCE *Mojo* (pronounced *mo-ho*) is a Cuban sauce that may be served hot or cold. It typically contains olive oil, fresh citrus juice, garlic, chopped fresh herbs, and aromatic seasonings, often cumin. It is used as a marinade, a table sauce, and a dip, and is a traditional accompaniment to suckling pig

and roasted or grilled vegetables.

MOLE These traditional complex sauce preparations are often reserved for special celebrations in Mexico. There are many types of moles that span a full spectrum of colors and flavors: *amarillo* (yellow), *verde* (green), *manchamanteles* ("stains tablecloths"). The iconic *mole poblano* is nearly black in color, infused spices and chocolate.

MUDDLER A bat or pestle, usually made from wood and about 6 inches (15 cm) long, that is used to crush and blend ingredients—such as mint leaves, sugar cubes, or pieces of fruit—in a serving glass.

NOPALES See page 105.

OCTOPUS A diet of clams and scallops gives the octopus a rich flavor, but its meat can be quite tough and rubbery if not properly tenderized and cooked. Like squid, octopus is best cooked quickly over high heat or very slowly over low heat. It can be eaten raw, lightly pickled, sautéed, grilled, fried, boiled, or stewed. Look for fresh or frozen octopus, already-cleaned, or peeled and portioned tentacles. Pound or quickly blanch octopus to tenderize it before cooking.

ORANGE, SOUR Also known as the Seville orange or bitter orange and native to southeast Asia, the sour orange was the first orange to arrive in the New World by way of Spain. It has a thick peel and bitter juice. It is often used to make marmalades and acidic sauce, such as the Cuban *mojo* sauce.

OREGANO, MEXICAN A member of the mint family, oregano is an aromatic, pungent, and spicy herb, it is used as a seasoning for all kinds of savory dishes. It is common in the Mediterranean, but the Mexican variety is much stronger and spicier in flavor. Both varieties of oregano are widely available.

PAPAYA With its distinctive earthy aroma and flavor, papaya is the quintessential tropical fruit. Native to Central America, the fruit looks like a large pear, with thin, pale green skin with blotches of yellow and orange. It's hollow center holds a mass of small, slick black seeds, which are edible and have a slightly peppery flavor.

PASSION FRUIT This fruit's yellow-orange pulp, at once sweet and tart, is delicious spooned straight from its skin, or in salads, sauces, dressings, desserts, and beverages. The glossy black seeds may be eaten, although they are often discarded. Select specimens with skin that is uniformly wrinkled. Frozen passion fruit pulp can be found at Latin markets.

PEPITAS Pumpkin seeds have been used by Mexican cooks since pre-Columbian times. Whether fat or skinny, raw or roasted, hulled or not, tasty *pepitas* are an essential ingredient in many sweets, snacks, and savory dishes. Raw green pumpkin seeds can be found in natural-foods stores and in many supermarkets. Toasting makes the hulls crisp and edible (see page 268).

PILONCILLO This unrefined sugar is an everyday sweetener, mainly produced in Colombia. Dark brown boiled sugarcane syrup is hardened in cone-, bar-, or disk-shaped molds. The molds can be quite hard and often need to be chopped into pieces, though they will dissolve easily in liquid. Dark brown sugar can be substituted.

PISCO See page 32.

PLANTAINS Closely related to the banana, the plantain is larger, starchier, and firmer. When ripe, fresh plantains have almost uniformly black skins and will yield to gentle pressure. It must always be cooked before eating, but unlike the banana, the sturdy plantain won't fall apart or become mushy when baked, stewed, panfried, or deep-fried, as it is to make popular *tostones* and *patacones* (see page 217).

QUINCE PASTE Made from the fruit of the quince tree, this sweet paste is deep reddish-orange in color. It is a popular ingredient in South American pastries, and can be found at specialty food stores.

QUINOA Originally cultivated by the Incas, quinoa is a hearty Peruvian grain that has won the hearts of health-conscious cooks worldwide. Similar to a brown rice, quinoa boasts a tremendous protein and amino acid content. It is also convenient, cooking up fluffy and tender in a matter of minutes. Rinse to remove its natural residue, which is bitter.

RUM A spirit that originated in the Caribbean, rum is distilled from sugarcane juice or molasses. This slightly sweet liquor is especially suited for mixed drinks and desserts. Generally, the darker the rum, the stronger its flavor; lighter rums tends to be preferred for cocktails versus darker rums for cooking.

SAFFRON The orange-red stamens of a crocus flower, saffron is among the most treasured spices in the world. The distinctive earthy flavor and rich gold color make it worth its high price. Threads are sold in small quantities; store them in a cool, dark place, and crush before using. Saffron lends its characteristic vibrant yellow tint to both paella and *arroz con pollo*.

SALSA Literally translated, salsa means "sauce," and may refer to any sauce made with a wide range of ingredients, from chiles to chocolate. Non-Spanish speakers, however, think of the quintessential chile-fruit-cilantro combinations, either cooked or raw.

Pico de gallo Also known as *salsa mexicana* or *salsa crudo*, *pico de gallo* is a chunky fresh Mexican salsa. The salsa is made with a combination of ripe tomatoes, finely chopped white onion, chopped fresh cilantro (fresh coriander), and chiles such as serrano or jalapeño are simply tossed with a little lime juice and salt.

Roja This salsa is the "red" of the ubiquitous red-and-green salsa combination that graces nearly every Latin table. Tomatillo salsa is its green counterpart. *Salsa roja* has a tomato and chile base.

SQUID Caught off coasts from Mexico to Argentina, this soft-bodied shellfish has a mild, sweet flavor and a slightly chewy texture that is at its best when quickly cooked or slowly simmered. Fresh squid will have a mild, delicate taste and a light gray color. *Chipirones* are baby squid; they are especially tender and sweet.

TAMARIND A podlike fruit from an evergreen tree, the fruit is used mainly for its acidic pulp in jams, syrups, and juices.

TEQUILA A liquor made from the distilled juice of the blue agave plant. *Blanco* (silver or white) tequila may go directly from the still to the bottle, but is often left to settle first for a few weeks in steel vats. Caramel coloring is added to *blanco* to create gold tequila. *Reposado* tequila must spend 2 to 12 weeks in wooden casks, while the more refined *añejo* spends at least a year in wood and often longer.

TOMATILLO Like the tomato, the tomatillo is a member of the nightshade family. It is covered with a parchment-like husk, which is removed. The fruits, which have a unique texture and tart flavor, are the basis for many cooked sauces, pipianes, and moles, and are occasionally used raw in salsas. Carefully rinse off the sticky residue that covers the skin before using.

Index

PHOTOGRAPHS
SHERI GIBLIN All photography except for the following:
JEFF TUCKER & KEVIN HOSSLER Pages 63, 71 (middle), 157 (middle), 197 (left), 244 (right)
BILL BETTENCOURT Pages 71, 97 (left), 115 (middle, right), 193, 197 (middle, right), 244 (middle)
IGNACIO URQUIZA Pages 8, 9, 20 (middle), 21, 26

ACKNOWLEDGMENTS
Weldon Owen would like to thank the following people for their generous support in producing this book: Ken DellaPenta, Melanie Duerkopp, Judith Dunham, Peggy Fallon, Amanda Haas, Shay Harrington, Lesli J. Neilson, Carrie Bradley Neves, Fanny Pan, Jason Wheeler

Some content adapted from original recipes by Brigit Binns, Dana Jacobi, Susana Palazuelos, and Marilyn Townsend.

Oxmoor
House®

OXMOOR HOUSE
Oxmoor House books are distributed by Time Inc. Home Entertainment
135 West 50th Street, New York, NY 10020
VP and Associate Publisher Jim Childs
Director of Marketing Sydney Webber
Brand Manager Victoria Alfonso

WILLIAMS-SONOMA, INC.
Founder & Vice-Chairman Chuck Williams

WELDON OWEN INC.
CEO and President Terry Newell
VP, Sales and New Business Development Amy Kaneko
Senior VP, International Sales Stuart Laurence
Director of Finance Mark Perrigo
VP and Publisher Hannah Rahill
Executive Editors Kim Laidlaw, Jennifer Newens
Associate Editor Julia Humes
Editorial Assistant Becky Duffett
Associate Creative Director Emma Boys
Senior Designer Diana Heom
Designer Rachel Lopez Metzger
Production Director Chris Hemesath
Production Manager Michelle Duggan
Color Manager Teri Bell
Food Stylist Karen Shinto
Prop Stylist Christine Wolheim

Group Publisher, Bonnier Publishing Group John Owen

THE ESSENTIALS SERIES
Conceived and produced by
WELDON OWEN INC.
415 Jackson Street, Suite 200, San Francisco, CA 94111
Telephone: 415-291-0100 Fax: 415-291-8841
www.weldonowen.com

In Collaboration with Williams-Sonoma, Inc.
3250 Van Ness Avenue, San Francisco, CA 94109

A WELDON OWEN PRODUCTION
Copyright © 2010 Weldon Owen Inc.
and Williams-Sonoma, Inc.

First printed in 2010
10 9 8 7 6 5 4 3 2 1

ISBN 13: 978-0-8487-3328-5
ISBN 10: 0-8487-3328-2

Printed by Toppan-Leefung
Printed in China